SPARK

How Fanfiction and Fandom Can Set Your Creativity on Fire

Edited by

Atlin Merrick

Improbable
PRESS

First published by Improbable Press in 2023

Improbable Press is an imprint of:
Clan Destine Press
www.clandestinepress.net
PO Box 121, Bittern Victoria 3918 Australia

National Library of Australia Cataloguing-In-Publication data:

Atlin Merrick
Spark: How Fanfiction and Fandom Can Set Your Creativity on Fire

ISBN: 978-1-922904-11-9 (hb)
ISBN: 978-1-922904-01-0 (pb)
ISBN: 978-1-922904-02-7 (eb)

Cover artwork by © Willsin Rowe
Layout & Typesetting by Dimitra Stathopoulos

Improbable Press
improbablepress.com

For
FANDOM
which changed my life in
the most wondrous ways

for
MARY JO WATTS
who said "Why don't you make it a book?"

and for
JOSEPH CAREY MERRICK
always

TABLE OF CONTENTS

LIST OF ARTWORKS

WE DON'T NEED NO ELEPHANTS IN FANDOM (AN EMPHATIC INTRODUCTION)
Wendy C Fries

Elephants are great. They're beautiful, big, cultured, cool. Who on earth doesn't like elephants?

Well, me. Me when they show up uninvited, like they very often do when anyone says the word fanfiction.

So, because some folks are going to look at this book and unload a pachyderm of prejudice onto it, I'd like to have a quick look at this elephant ill-informed people keep bringing into the fanfic room, figure out why it's here, then wave it buh-bye.

Fanfiction...

Fanart...

Fan works of every kind – video edits, podfics, comics, novels, paintings, badges, dolls, and dozens of other things – these are absolutely-not-times-infinity-*ever* bad, they're not about selling someone else's creations, they are about finding community, learning a craft, developing your creative voice, and bringing *your* face to a media world that may too often exclude you.

We've all gone to a gallery and seen an artist standing left of the Frida Kahlo or right of the Vincent van Gogh, copying those paintings or just as often veering wildly in style. We've all plucked up fat anthologies full of stories by authors writing in the style of Jane Austen or Arthur Conan Doyle, just as we've watched TV shows and films labeled reboots, re-imaginings, or re-tellings.

Every one of these is a fan work.

If you're Neil Gaiman writing award-winning Conan Doyle/Lovecraft fic some will laud it as pastiche. If you're Shakespeare writing real person fic about Richard III, or Herman Melville writing of the Essex Tragedy in *Moby-Dick*, they'll call it historical fiction. If you're Anne Rice, Bram Stoker, or Stephenie Meyer, you're 'reclaiming' vampire folklore, but no matter how expensive your production values, no matter where you are on the bestseller list, if you're writing stories based on other people's tales or legends, it's fanfiction and it's probably old as storytelling itself.

Oscar-winning filmmaker Chloé Zhao, award-winning novelists Kerry Greenwood, Mary Robinette Kowal, and Gaiman have said *yes, I've written fic* (Zhao and Kowal still do). So has David Shore, the creator of the long-running American TV show *House, M.D.,* whose House and Wilson were inspired by Holmes and Watson. Bryan Fuller, creator of the TV show *Hannibal,* says the show is a long and lavish mash note to Thomas Harris' Red Dragon book series. Peter Tonkin's Trojan Murders series is *marketed* as Homer-meets-Holmes in stories that retell the Iliad. John Updike has a series of novels with the characters from *The Scarlet Letter,* while Mark Twain ficced Arthur Conan Doyle in *A Double Barrelled Detective Story.* Hell, ACD himself wrote that Edgar Allan Poe's fictional detective C. Auguste Dupin birthed his own legendary boffin.

The list goes on. The film *Shaun of the Dead* is a fan love letter to *Dawn of the Dead* and every zombie story there ever was. America's 'Weird Al' Yankovic has for decades crafted parody songs from other people's hits. The Brothers Grimm retold already-ancient tales, written centuries before they were born, while Vijayendra Prasad and S.S. Rajamouli wrote real person fic about freedon fighters Alluri Sitarama Raju and Komaram Bheem in *RRR.* And there's an entire thesis or three on how much of George Lucas's Star Wars series is fanfic of Frank Herbert's *Dune,* with the Jedi, the Force, Tatooine, droids, Anakin Skywalker, midi-chlorians, and Darth Vader+Jabba absolutely being Lucas' fan versions of the Bene Gesserit, the Voice, Arrakis, Mentats, Paul Atreides, spice, and Baron Harkonnen.

If anyone explains these as 'not fanfiction,' they do not know what fanfiction is and can be safely ignored. And if that someone thinks fic is bad, but these TV programs, songs, books, and films are fine, what they're saying is it's okay to use someone else's characters only if you're famous or make big money on it.

This is a foolish, laughable *lie*. It's also called punching down.

All the works above are art made by people paying homage to what's gone before. That's what creation is, that's what creators do. That's fanfiction, too.

That's not all fanfic is though.

Fanfic is about finding our place, our voice, our *face* in current media. It's about finding a way to exist in a world that may not see us at all if we're disabled, neurodivergent, LGBTQIA+, a person of color, or female. Fanfiction is a way to create our own power, strength, and community.

As nice as elephants are, we never need let them into our sweet, safe places. They don't belong here, we need never hold our breath hoping they go away, no. When someone says "fanfiction is bad and here's why" we absolutely have the right to ignore them and walk away, because they're wrong now, tomorrow, and forever. Fanfiction is power and people who have it want to deny it to people who don't.

Do not let them.

The essays in this book sing the praises of what fic is, and what its writers – pro and amateur – get from writing it; these essays talk about why fic is *fine*, and how, how, how it truly sets creativity on fire.

So step right up for shouty words on speaking for yourself; calm ones on fandom safe spaces; and words which wax lyrical about how there's nothing new under the sun. Enjoy Sebastian Jack's "Boldly Going Where No Amputee Has Gone Before," Jamie Ashbird's words on how fic can help us find (and accept) our sexuality, and editor Anne Jamison's words (she of the seminal work *Fic: Why Fanfiction is Taking Over the World*) on what fic means to the status quo. George Ivanoff, author of over one hundred books, talks about how fanfic helped him go pro, emerging writer Kameo Llyn Douglas discusses why the well-outfitted writer needs kneepads, and chart-topping authors Claire O'Dell, Diane Duane, KJ

Charles, Lyndsay Faye, and others share why, absolutely why *the garbage will do* when we sit down to write.

There are more than four dozen writers and artists here as well as many vignettes, quotes, snippets, and revelations, every one of them a fuel for *your* fire. In *Spark* you'll find inspiration, support, and perspective, words to give you words when you want them, words to help you understand what fic is, why so many of us love it, and how to write it, share it, and grow from it.

Now if you'd be so kind, please take a seat and know this:

You are among friends.

Wendy C Fries is an editor, writer, publisher and has been in fandoms big and small. Fandom inspired her to get her first degree at age fifty, her second at fifty-six, and it inspired the publication of her first book. And it's because of fandom she's traveled to meet so many of those who share her love of writing and reading fanfiction for Star Wars, Sherlock Holmes, and more. Wendy continues to find fandom an endless fiery inspiration.

1

FIC AND FICTION
It's All Fine

SPEAK FOR YOURSELF (AND TAKE UP SPACE)
Atlin Merrick

Do me a favor? Look at the photo on this page. It's of the Long Room at Trinity College Dublin.

Imagine being in this room which contains 200,000 volumes, a single example of every book published in Ireland and Britain between 1801 and about 1880.

While Jane Austen is there in that room, while the Brontës are there too, you know, *you know* that most of the voices in that beautiful room, bound inside covers of gold-stamped leather, are the voices of men, as are fifty-one of the busts lining the room's long length.

In that library and libraries the world over men of means – they are traditionally the ones with the resources and free time – are the voices that have spoken for everyone else. For you.

About you.

About who you are, what you want, need, and *deserve*.

If you are gay, disabled, Black, if you are neurodivergent, poor, female, it doesn't matter, upper class men have historically *spoken for you.*

They continue to do so today.

While the world is changing – hosanna! – it's safe to say the lion's share of popular media is still made by the same voices as those which fill the Long Room to its lovely, lofty rafters.

Fandom, fanfiction, fanworks of all kinds? They have become vital, precious spaces for raising the voices of everyone else.

Fandom is so important because fandom, and what we create in it, is about you and me – and everyone else who's been spoken over or spoken *for* – speaking for ourselves instead.

Fandom, fanfic, fan art, is even more: it's about *taking up space*.

In a world where we don't yet hear enough from women, disabled, autistic, minority, ethnic, or LGBTQIA+ people, fandom has become a place where people who identify as any or all of these can come together, share their voice, their needs and wants, their perspectives and (this is very important) their *desires*.

The world needs the voices of women and Black people, disabled people and asexual people. The world needs your voice, your viewpoint, your *stories*.

The world needs your stories.

One more time…the libraries of the world, the ones full to their lofty rafters of mostly one kind of voice speaking for all the others? Those rooms need you, and you are good enough to be there.

Saying that one again too…you. are. good. enough.

And for some, that journey begins in fandom.

You've read long-winded work after privileged work by people who are not your gender or color or sexuality telling others *what we're like*. Fandom is a delicious, delectable, wonderful way to shut those voices up the very best way there is – by shouting loud and long and proud and clear about what it's really like to be your color or sexuality or disability.

Do you know how you do that? You do because you're reading this book, but I'll tell you anyway.

You do it by sharing your story or artwork with the fandom you love. You consume and comment on fic and art and songs and podfics voraciously, too. These both embolden you if boldness you wish, and when you feel bold maybe you speak up outside fandom. Maybe you send your work out to a press, a magazine, a newspaper. It doesn't matter if you're ace or autistic and your work has nothing to do with being ace or autistic. What matters is that you have raised your voice.

"You should be represented and taking part in fandom is a brilliant, incredible, ever-effervescent place for you to do that, with every creative bone in your beautiful body"

A couple hundred years ago a beautiful room was literally filled to the ceiling with mostly one voice. While we can revere that beautiful room, while we can honor the creations in it, we absolutely do not ever have to be okay with the fact that they spoke for us. We do not have to let the future be represented by those same voices.

You should be represented and taking part in fandom is a brilliant, incredible, ever-effervescent place for you to do that, with every creative bone in your beautiful body. And when you do, when you raise your voice with fic or art or comments, you do something else:

Take up space.

Taking up space is about finding your place in the world, and insisting that you deserve to be there.

When you're a woman, ethnic, gay, neurodivergent, disabled, short, wide, whatever, to most media you can be invisible. Sure, yes, yep, there's Captain Marvel, Nanisca, and Furiosa, but there are still media execs saying female-led movies are just, you know, not something they want to keep making. If fifty-one percent of the human population isn't considered worthy of stories, what are the chances that we'll see trans or genderqueer heroes, that we'll see characters who look, act, dream, and want just like *people you and I know?*

Fandom, fic, fanart...they help us take up space as we tell better stories. They help us visualize a place – Tatooine, Gallifrey, London – and then give us the freedom to put faces like ours in it.

Fic and fandom set creativity on fire because it helps us imagine more.

Fanfiction isn't about turning us into 'real' writers, fanart isn't about making us 'real' artists. We already are. If we write or draw or paint we're *real*, end of.

Fic and fandom are catalysts, places for fuel, community, respite, and joy. They help us soar higher if higher we want to be – and *we* decide what the heck higher is.

Higher might mean going pro and making money on our writing or art. Higher might mean meeting some of the people whose work we admire. Higher has hundreds of meanings and we get to decide the definition of ours.

Fandom has helped me have courage and joy, it's set me on fire in all the ways that helped me dream and then do. I published my first book at fifty. Got my first degree at fifty-three, a second book and a second degree not long after. And it was fandom that sparked me, focused me, and supported me through it all.

That is what the simple act of writing fanfiction and sharing it online one day helped me do.

No one, not anyone, not a single person has to understand our love of fandom or fic or fanworks, any more than they asked us to come to grips with their fantasy football team. Love isn't a committee decision. Neither is changing the world so it represents more of us than it does now.

Fandom at its best is was and ever shall be about expanding the conventional narratives at last and figuring out how to put *our* faces into familiar worlds.

It's about finding joy in a world too often short of it.

So along with delight, fandom is about taking up space by expressing our dreams and desires. It's about believing your voice matters and it should be heard because "you're never really a whole person if you remain silent, because there's always that one little piece inside you that wants to be spoken out, and if you keep ignoring it, it gets madder and madder and hotter and hotter, and if you don't speak it out one day it will just up and punch you in the mouth from the inside."

Audre Lorde's famous essay *The Transformation of Silence into*

Language and Action includes the above quote from her daughter Elizabeth Lorde-Rollins, and isn't it a glory? Those words are direct, she said what she said damn it, and those words are like Lorde's essay – perfect, potent, and about *shouting*.

No, wait, that's wrong.

For me they're about shouting. Because how I communicate best includes arm waving, wide eyes, and volume. So hotter and hotter and punching and *maaaad?* They resonate with me and like every one of the words in Lorde's brief essay I hope, hope, hope they resonate with you.

There's a reason for that.

Women and minorities are socialized to silence.

Told that her cancer was almost certainly malignant, Audre Lorde – writer, activist, feminist, and librarian – lived through three weeks before learning it was benign and those hell weeks "put fear into a perspective...I was going to die, if not sooner then later, whether or not I had ever spoken myself. My silences had not protected me."

Queer, BIPOC, female, disabled, autistic, LGBTQIA+, people speak for us all the time. Sometimes they shout louder, they're literally larger, they dominate the conversation, they take over.

We can take back, with our words, our fic, poems, songs, essays, drawings, dissertations...we can find our way to speak for ourselves *about* ourselves.

Lorde said that we have been socialized to respect fear more than our own needs for language, and in the wait for the courage to speak, our silence chokes us.

Lorde was gay, Black, and female and so thrice damned in almost any country you care to name, including America, where she was born. She, like so many women, so many minority people, have been taught with meticulous care the value of their own silence, of remaining civil even while being abused, while others do neither, then speak in our name.

Maybe you don't write. Maybe you do, but you decline to

shout. That's great too. I can't sing opera, or fix a roof, or knit. Nor do I want to do any of those things.

So if you can't break the silence, if you feel like your fear is justified and silence brings comfort? Please, stay silent. Find comfort. There are enough mountains to climb as it is.

Maybe instead you can stand behind someone who *does* speak for you. Raise their voices with reblogs or retweets. They're already out there talking or shouting, *help them reach more people.*

And for the love of all that's holy if you can find it in you to speak for yourself, for others, *speak.* Write fanfiction, novels, poems, songs. Share them online, or send them to an editor, agent, publisher. You're reading this book so you're probably a creator or want to be...if it helps you to know that someone else will talk about you if you remain silent, if it helps motivate you to courage, please let it do that.

"There are so many silences to be broken."

This is the final sentence in Lorde's essay and I hear it as a rallying cry to speak, to take up space, to relish in who we are. To make a difference in our own lives, whether we're gay or disabled, whether we're someone so often silenced because others have spoken over us, breaking silences is encouragement to define, delight, and represent ourselves without apology.

There are hundreds of ways to speak for ourselves, fanfiction is just one. It's an important one though, because with the aid of fic and fandom we can find our fuel and fire. Creating and consuming fanfiction and fanart, encourages us to grow *from* it.

Hundreds of years ago a beautiful, long room was built to house thousands of books and fifty-one busts and most of them represent one kind of voice.

We all want to and deserve to see our faces, our desires, our *stories* told, and if the powers that be won't tell those stories *we'll take it from here.*

Your book, your art, your short story should be represented. Please stop believing, "No one would read me," as you write thousands of words of fanfic or pen entire unpublished books of poetry or graphic novels or art. Send those stories out, those poems, those drawings. Stop *stopping* yourself.

Stop letting one kind of person be your voice.

Be your own.

Atlin Merrick (she/they) is commissioning editor at Improbable Press, has been in fandoms for a long time, but really *been involved for the last dozen years, writing over a million words of fanfiction. Fandom has been an endless inspiration and if* you *ever need inspiration, drop Atlin an email over at ImprobablePress.com and she'll shout gleeful encouragement at you. Seriously.*

Fanfiction is real writing.

— Mary Robinette Kowal
  Hugo award-winning writer of *The Calculating Stars*

BUILDING ON THE BONES
OF WHAT'S COME BEFORE
Merinda Brayfield

Too often people hear the words fanfiction and react with derision. Fanfiction is seen as something for teenagers or people who aren't *real* writers. It's treated like something lesser, something that shouldn't be talked about in polite company.

This is bullshit.

Fanfiction *is* real writing. And fanfiction isn't cheating.

People have been making transformative works for as long as there have been stories. It can easily be said that Dante's Inferno is biblical fanfiction. In fact, biblical fan art and fanfiction are the classic works of much of Western civilization. Going back further, one could argue that Roman mythology is fanfiction of the Greeks. They took the parts and pieces they liked and turned them into something for themselves.

For more modern examples, look no farther than a book like *Wicked*, which is based on the works of L. Frank Baum. *The Wind Done Gone* is an alternative retelling of *Gone with the Wind*. While *Oh Brother, Where Art Thou* is a more modern version of *The Odyssey*.

All of these and more are, at the end of the day, fanfiction. After all, the very definition is: "fiction written by fans of a TV series, movie, etc., using existing characters and situations to develop new plots."

All stories are built on what's come before; there is nothing new under the sun. Any fantasy book you pick up is influenced by folk tales and J.R.R. Tolkien. Any romance is touched by Jane Austen or perhaps Danielle Steele. The bones of every story were created deep in antiquity and it's only the arrangement and covering of those bones that has changed.

All creations have bones, but it's the arrangement and size that determines if it's to be an elephant or a weasel. In the same way, humans take arrangements of the bones of story and create their own compositions; two people can begin from the same general idea and come to vastly different conclusions. A quest to retrieve an item can result in tragedy, or comedy, or something in between. *The Hobbit* and *Guardians of the Galaxy* are both about quests for an item of power, but are quite different in execution.

There are so many pieces a creator can work with. If someone is working with elves and magic, they're probably writing a fantasy story. If they're dealing with two characters reluctantly falling in love, it's probably romance. All stories use the bones of what's come before. It's why there are tropes and archetypes. If there's a gun on the mantel in the first act, we expect it to be used by the third, to borrow another trope. We recognize certain motifs and shortcuts because they've been used over and over again. That said, humans also like a good plot twist, where expectations are subverted.

Which leads us back to fanfiction.

Plenty of people have read Tolkien, or Anne McCaffrey, or the Brothers Grimm, and thought, 'well I can write a fantasy story' and then they've done so. Some of it is good, some of it's bad, and a great deal of it has been professionally published. Scratch the surface of so many stories and you'll find those older bones underneath, like a sketch under a painting. Fanfiction simply makes those bones more visible. If we're going with Tolkien, then it's writing Legolas and Gimli having further adventures beyond where the book ends. Or perhaps having a family. Or it could be taking the Fellowship of the Ring and transferring the story to high school.

This is where too often people roll their eyes and dismiss it out of hand. "Why are you writing *that*? Why not write your own worlds?" But you see, we are. Yes, the characters may have come from a book or a movie, but the hard work of writing, the story itself? That's us. That's our talent and skill and time. Lots of things fall under the banner of fanfiction. Maybe it's a story where everyone survives the Battle of Five Armies. Maybe Bilbo and Thorin are openly in love.

Maybe it's Bilbo and Thorin but they've got nothing to do with Middle Earth and are instead running a coffee shop in Cleveland.

See, that's the key. Sure the characters may be the same, but it's what you do with them that creates a story. You can create the most interesting character in the world, but without something happening to them, there is no story. Yes, even in a tale that's pure unadulterated smut there's still story, still motivation and give and take, there still needs to be a reason for these characters to be in that moment.

"The art and craft of a writer is storytelling. And that's it. Fanfiction is writing. Fanfiction is storytelling"

Fanfiction also allows writers to explore corners of a story that aren't in the original text, or are only alluded to. For instance, *Wicked* is the story from the point of view of the Wicked Witch of the West. *The Wind Done Gone* is from the point of view of Scarlett's slave half-sister. Another example would be *Rosencrantz and Guildenstern are Dead,* which is Hamlet from the point of view of two minor characters.

Quite a bit of fanfiction is written by and about characters that are not often represented in popular media, or not represented positively. Writers can make a favorite character explicitly transgender, gay, asexual, or queer. They can change a character's gender. In a world where many people feel underrepresented, they can use a familiar world and make it better reflect the real world they themselves see and experience.

Even in fanfiction that hews close to the original, say, a story about Sherlock Holmes on a case, it's disingenuous to say that it isn't real writing. People act like anyone can write, and in a way that's true. Anyone can put words on a page. But to create *story,* that's different.

Fanfiction takes the bones of an existing story and transforms it into something else. That's why it's a transformative work. If you take a box of Legos that is supposed to be a fire engine and decide to make a plane instead, it doesn't mean you did something wrong. It simply means you saw the building blocks and used your imagination to create something different than intended.

The bones underpinning all of our popular media use pieces from the millions of stories that have come before. Even in an original work the author carries unconscious biases and half-remembered slivers of all the stories they've ever read. Fanfiction explicitly acknowledges its source material. It says "Yes, I used the bones of this fox." Even though the fox is now purple, it's still recognizably the fox.

Storytelling is one of our oldest gifts. Before we had writing, we had stories. There are myths and folklore that appear in different forms all over the world. For example, The Hero's Journey is a story we humans tell over and over again. Each telling is slightly different, some of the specifics may change, but the hero's journey is the hero's journey whether you're talking about Jane Eyre, Huckleberry Finn, Rey, or Simba.

Humans take comfort in the familiar. There's nothing wrong with writing the 4,834th version of two people falling in love. People have been falling in love since time immemorial and will continue to do so into eternity. Simply because someone uses fanfiction to tell those stories doesn't make it lesser.

Fanfiction is story. There is professional fanfiction that is sanctioned by authors and estates and corporations, and there is free fanfiction written by people who enjoy transforming works that they love. Some amateurs want to become professionals, others simply enjoy the act of creating. There's nothing wrong with creating fanfiction for free. Plenty of free fanfiction is better than many published works. If one chooses to branch out into something professional, that's fine, but a paycheck is not required to call oneself a writer.

The art and craft of a writer is storytelling. And that's it. Fanfiction is writing. Fanfiction is storytelling. You are a writer and that is true whether we can see the bones or not. Fanfiction isn't cheating. Have no shame about it, and know you're carrying on one of our oldest traditions.

Merinda has told stories all her life. Her day job is tech support, but her passion is writing. She's a prolific writer of fanfiction and has recently published a novel. She's a creative dreamer that loves encouraging those around her. She has a degree in film and media studies with a focus on screenwriting.

Fire and Water by Camille Happert

IN DEFENSE OF FANFICTION
L.S.

So, you think famous wordsmiths like Homer, Shakespeare, and Chaucer were 'original' or merely 'inspired' by other works? Think again.

I am a professional writer and editor. I have a double degree in English and writing, and I studied patterns in literature from the beginning of the written word to our modern day.

Academia uses the word *intertextuality* to describe how works of literature connect with other works. But this intertextuality often doesn't end with just minor references. Many of the world's most celebrated stories intentionally lift core elements from previous texts, including setting, plot, syntax, format, and characters.

Here's how several famous historical works function as proto-fanfiction – an intentionally derivative work published before the word *fanfiction* existed as a label:

ANCIENT / OLD LITERATURE
~1300-1000 BCE: A Mesopotamian priest named Sîn-lēqi-unninni is credited with gathering some local legends into a connected story. The result, the *Epic of Gilgamesh*, functions as a prototype of real person fiction because the main character was probably a real historical king of Uruk, but legend had updated Gilgamesh into a demigod interacting with Mesopotamian mythology.[1]

The epic also involves Gilgamesh meeting the character of Utnapishtim. This character had survived a massive flood by building a ship per the instructions of a god, and ultimately landing on a mountain in the Middle East. Utnapishtim's story is like Noah's from the Bible, and there's too many startling overlaps to classify Utnapishtim and Noah as only a coincidence. This leaves the possibility that one is a derivative, or that both are based on earlier source content – again, a sort of real person fic.

SPARK

~800-700 BCE: An anonymous Greek poet – or a group of poets – under the name of Homer, finally wrote down a couple of important oral epic poems, including *The Iliad* and *The Odyssey*. Writing down oral poems meant that Homer's work represented entire generations of poets tweaking and elaborating on scenes in their own derivative way for hundreds of years prior. "Homer" didn't just invent or develop the stories himself but became the definitive version.[2]

~650 BCE: Characters from both epics got a major encore in the *Little Iliad* by Lesches of Mitylene, who expanded on Homer's work.

~440 BCE: In his play, *Ajax*, Greek playwright Sophocles expanded on Ajax from Homer's *The Iliad* and *The Little Iliad*, showing the warrior in a tragedy. Sophocles also explores other Homerian characters too, like Odysseus.

~260 BCE: Greek poet Theocritus, in his poem *Idyll XI*, rejected the war-like themes of Homer and rewrote the evil cyclops (Polyphemus) of Homer's *The Odyssey* into a sympathetic character who is love-sick for a sea nymph.[3]

~20 BCE: The Roman author Virgil wrote *The Aeneid* as a direct sequel to the previously written epic *The Iliad*, with a previous background character, Aeneas, now in focus as the protagonist. Ultimately, Virgil lifted setting, descriptions, syntax, character attributes, and plot episodes from Homer's work to apply them to his own culture's mythology.

MEDIEVAL ERA (500-1500ish CE)

~700-1000 CE: *The Alphabet of ben Sirach* was an anonymous collection of Hebrew satires and legends, which included a parody of the biblical story of Adam and Eve. The story gave Adam a totally different wife by the name of Lilith, the character of which was inspired by Babylonian mythology. The whole of the collection is additionally wrapped in a fictional account of telling the stories to the historical figure of the Babylonian king Nebuchadnezzar – resulting in another real person fiction.

22

~**1000-1012 CE:** The world's first novel, *The Tale of Genji* by Lady Murasaki Shikibu, involved characters based off real people in the Japanese royal court.[4] This inspired Japanese Noh theater plays involving characters from the novel, such as the play *Aoi no Ue* (*Lady Aoi*), which is attributed to Zeami Motokiyo. This play appropriates the Lady Aoi from Shikibu's novel to explore the character's death.

1308-1320 CE: Dante Alighieri's *The Divine Comedy* (known most famously for *Inferno*) is a self-insertion epic poem expanding on biblical/Catholic texts with extensive creative detail. In addition, the poem functions as a quasi-sequel to *The Iliad* by showing the afterlife fates of various characters and even the author, Homer. Dante also appropriated Virgil, who copied *The Iliad* to write *The Aeneid*, to be his ghostly guide through the afterlife. And if that wasn't enough, the work also included insertions of real peers that Dante didn't like, suffering in hell.[5] *The Divine Comedy* is one of the most self-indulgent proto-fanfictions ever created, while also being named one of the greatest poems in literature.

1392: Geoffrey Chaucer – known as the father of English literature – wrote a famous collection called *The Canterbury Tales*. The collection's basic format mimics Italian author Giovanni Boccaccio's *The Decameron*, written in 1351. They share some similar stories and characters too, but the authors have their own unique takes.

> "If you're writing fanfiction, know that fic is the legacy of literature. It's a tradition spanning millennia, and resulted in some of humanity's most beloved stories"

RENAISSANCE ERA (1550-1660ish CE)

1590: English poet Edmund Spenser riffed off legends of King Arthur made popular in Geoffrey of Monmouth's work, *Historia Regum Britanniae*. In Spenser's epic poem, *The Faerie Queen*, Arthur is pretty love-sick over the fairy queen.

1597: English playwright Shakespeare often mixed mythology, previously written texts like Geoffrey Monmouth's work, and historical figures together to create his plays. Not even his most popular play, *Romeo and Juliet*, was original. He took the idea from a poem written by Arthur Brooke in 1562 called "The Tragicall Hystorye of Romeus and Iuliet." But the borrowing didn't end there. Brooke had taken his idea from the 1554 *Giulietta e Romeo* by Italian author Matteo Bandello, who had taken the idea from Luigi da Porto's *Historia Novellamente Ritrovata di due Nobili Amant* in 1530, whose idea is reflected in Masuccio Salernitano's story of Mariotto and Ganozza published in 1476 as part of *Il Novellino*.[6] It's probably worth mentioning that the Capulets and Montagues appear in the Purgatory section, Canto 6, of Dante Alighieri's *The Divine Comedy* from the early 1300s.

ENLIGHTENMENT ERA (1660-1789)

1667: English poet John Milton wrote *Paradise Lost*, an epic poem based on the biblical book of Genesis, about the fall of creation. The poem massively expands on biblical characters and setting in creative ways.

1712: English poet Alexander Pope wrote a mock-heroic epic poem called *The Rape of the Lock* to make fun of all the serious epic writers before him, borrowing such images as how epic warriors put on armor and connecting it to the way rich people put on ornate clothing and jewelry. He used other standard epic elements as repeated throughout *The Iliad*, *The Aeneid*, and so forth.

ROMANTIC ERA (1789-1850)

1819: In *Don Juan*, English poet Lord Byron remixed the pre-dated legend of Don Juan (which has several written spinoffs beginning with Spanish playwright Tirso de Molina in his 1630 work, *The Trickster of Seville and the Stone Guest*). The play was about a man who seduced a lot of women, but Lord Byron reversed the original plot so that Don Juan ended up seduced by a lot of women. Several other versions of the story have since been published, including Menotti Lerro's 2015 play, *Donna Giovanna, The Trickster of Salerno*, featuring a genderbent Don Juan.

1820: English poet John Keats borrowed heavily from Greek mythology and literature for his poems, as well as English Renaissance poet Edmund Spenser. His idolization was such that his first work was called, "Imitation of Spenser" (1814), borrowing from Spenser's epic, *The Faerie Queene*.

1844: French writer Alexander Dumas borrowed characters for *The Three Musketeers* from such works as *The Memoirs of Monsieur d'Artagnan*, written in 1700 by French author Gatien de Courtilz de Sandras.[7]

1845: American author Edgar Allan Poe wrote *The Thousand and Second Tale of Scheherazade*, in which the character of Scheherazade from *The Arabian Nights* tells another story about the sailor, Sinbad.

1861: Hungarian author Imre Madach wrote *The Tragedy of Man*, which reverses the biblical moral principles of God and Satan. In this story, God is the violent and evil ruler, and Satan is the jaded trickster-victim trying to open humanity's eyes to the truth.

1905: Hungarian-British author and playwright Baroness Orczy wrote *The Scarlet Pimpernel*, a novel about a wealthy, vain nobleman, Sir Percy Blakeney, who also had a secret identity as a masked, helpful vigilante, the Scarlet Pimpernel. The novel is set during the French Revolution. This story later inspired a variety of other masked superheroes with very similar alter egos but in alternate universes – including Don Diego de le Vega/Zorro and Bruce Wayne/Batman.[8]

MODERN ERA (1900ish–1950S)

1922: Irish novelist James Joyce wrote his stream-of-consciousness novel *Ulysses*, which was based on Homer's *The Odyssey*, to a point where he took the characters and simply renamed them, as well as aligned the structure of his book to the various episodes in Homer's work.

1937: English writer J.R.R Tolkien wrote *The Hobbit* and then *The Lord of the Rings* later in the 1950s. You can find similar names of characters, character descriptions, and places in the Icelandic sagas *Poetic Edda* and *Prose Edda* written by Snorri Sturluson, including stories of powerful and destructive rings.[9] English adaptations of Sturluson's descriptions, like that of the dark, magical forest "Mirkwood," appeared before Tolkien as well – including in William Morris' 1888 *A Tale of the House of Wolfings*, and Sir Walter Scott's 1814 *Waverley*.[10]

1930s-present: DC and Marvel comics updated mythological gods and goddesses for a modern era, appropriating their names, special relics, and abilities for their heroes, and then mixing them with some modern-day cover identities in the vein of Sir Percy Blakeney from *The Scarlet Pimpernel*. As an example, Wonder Woman's origins are based on Greek mythology and tales of the Amazonian women. As another example, the Flash is a reproduction of the Greek god Hermes, down to his winged helmet as a nod to the winged sandals of Hermes. Sometimes the appropriation from mythology is obvious, as in the case of Thor and Loki from Norse mythology first written down by Snorri Sturluson.

1949: British author George Orwell published his famous book *1984* in this year. But prior to that, he reviewed a book called *We* by Russian author Yevgeny Zamyatin, published in 1924. Orwell wrote a rave review on it and declared someone should write something similar, which ultimately became *1984*. His book shares many similar plot points and concepts while bringing the story of *We* into a more realistic environment.[11] The novel *We* also appears to have heavy influence on characterization, worldbuilding, and naming conventions in Ayn Rand's dystopian *Anthem*, down to how Zamyatin named his characters with numbers and dashes.

1950s: British author C.S. Lewis noted in a letter that his series, *The Chronicles of Narnia*, was designed as an alternate universe retelling of the biblical story of Jesus Christ.[12]

POSTMODERN ERA (1950S-PRESENT, DEBATABLY)

1987: British playwright Andrew Lloyd Webber didn't come up with *The Phantom of the Opera* as a concept, because a French writer named Gaston Leroux wrote *Le Fantôme de l'Opéra* in 1909-1910. Interestingly, Webber's Phantom also writes a play about the legend of Don Juan, *Don Juan Triumphant*, hearkening back to the works of Lord Byron, Tirso de Molina, and others in a very meta way.

1990: British novelist Susan Kay published a sequel to Gaston Leroux's novel, which she called *Phantom*.

1997-2007: The *Harry Potter* series by British author J. K. Rowling takes a good portion of its magical worldbuilding and character naming conventions from the 1652 book *Culpeper's Complete Herbal*, which was about the medicinal and occult properties of plants.[13]

2009: *Pride and Prejudice and Zombies*, by American author Seth Grahame-Smith, is a rehashing of Jane Austen's 1813 Pride and Prejudice. But with zombies.

2015: American writer of *The Outsiders*, S.E. Hinton, claims that she has posted anonymous fanfictions of her own novel, as well as at least four *Supernatural* fanfics, being a huge fan of the show and of the paranormal.[14]

This is not an exhaustive list by any means, and it's often weighted toward Western examples of proto-fic or modern fanfiction, based on my personal exposure to stories. However, this list is a small taste of how plots, characters, settings, and syntax have been passed around and transformed throughout history. Without the innate human love for the 'what ifs,' a solid portion of well-known literature wouldn't exist. No story has been created in a vacuum of originality.

So, the next time someone tells you to stop writing fanfiction, or tells you that it's not a valid form of art, tell them that they obviously have never read the most important historical works of fiction, or even many popular modern stories, which are all rehashed fanfiction stories, borrowing characters and names and setting and even syntax.

Today's easier access to entertainment and publication has only increased the opportunity for stories to evolve in the minds of others. If you're writing fanfiction today, know that fic is the legacy of literature. It's a tradition spanning millennia, and it's resulted in some of humanity's most beloved stories. Maybe yours will be next!

This essay was adapted and expanded on from L.S.' original 2018 Tumblr post, "In Defense of Fanfiction."[15] L.S. writes and edits for clients across too many industries to count, and she usually does so with a puppy on her lap and a cup of tea on the table. She has been published in poetry books and literary magazines since 2004, but her next goal is to finish novel-length works.

WORKS CITED

1. The Editors of Encyclopaedia Britannica. "Gilgamesh." *Encyclopaedia Britannica Online*, 23 Apr. 2020. www.britannica.com/topic/Gilgamesh. Accessed 5 Aug. 2022.

2. Ong, Walter J. *Orality and Literary: The Technologizing of the Word*. London and New York: Routledge, 2002. *Monoskop.* monoskop.org/images/d/db/Ong_Walter_J_Orality_and_Literacy_2nd_ed.pdf. Accessed 6 Aug. 2022. PDF Download.

3. Cholmeley, R. J. "Poem 11." *The Idylls of Theocritus*. M.A. London, George Bell & Sons, 1901. *Perseus Digital Library.* www.perseus.tufts.edu/hopper/text?doc=Perseus:text:1999.04.0 069:text=comm:poem=11. Accessed 5 Aug. 2022.

4. Arntzen, Sonja. "The Heart of History: The Tale of Genji." *Education about Asia*, vol. 10, no. 3, Winter 2005, pp. 25-30. Association for Asian Studies. www.asianstudies.org/publications/eaa/archives/the-heart-of-history-the-tale-of-genji/. Accessed 5 Aug. 2022. PDF Download.

5. Meisfjord, Tom. "The Untold Truth of Dante's Inferno." *Grunge*, 22 June 2020, www.grunge.com/219819/the-untold-truth-of-dantes-inferno/. Accessed 5 Aug. 2022.

6. Scarci, Manuela. "From Mariotto and Ganozza to Romeo and Guilietta: Metamorphoses of a Renaissance Tale." *Scripta Mediterranea*, vol. 14-15 (1993-4), 2 Feb. 2015, scripta. journals.yorku.ca/index.php/scripta/article/view/39826. Accessed 29 Nov. 2022. PDF Download.

7. Courtilz de Sandraz, Gatin. *Memoirs of Monsieur d'Artagnan*. Translated by Ralph Nevill, London, H.S. Nichols. LTD, 1899. Internet Archive. archive.org/details/memoirsofmonsieu02couruoft/page/72/mode/2up.

8. Faraci, Derek. "Batman: 10 Things That Inspired the Creation of The Dark Knight." *CBR.com*, 13 Mar. 2020, www.cbr.com/batman-inspirations-movies-books-characters/. Accessed 5 Aug. 2022.

9. Kerven, Rosalind. "A Thousand Years Before Tolkien: The Original Evil Magic Ring." *Folklore Thursday*, 17 Jan. 2017, folklorethursday.com/legends/thousand-years-tolkien-original-evil-magic-ring/. Accessed 5 Aug. 2022.

10. Orth, John V. "Mirkwood." *Mythlore: A Journal of J.R.R. Tolkien, C.S. Lewis, Charles Williams, and Mythopoeic Literature*, vol. 38, no. 1, 2019, pp. 51-53. *SWOSU Digital Commons.* dc.swosu.edu/mythlore/vol38/iss1/31. Accessed 5 Aug. 2022.

11. Owen, Paul. "1984 thoughtcrime? Does it matter that George Orwell pinched the plot?" *The Guardian*, 8 June 2009. www.theguardian.com/books/booksblog/2009/jun/08/george-orwell-1984-zamyatin-we. Accessed 5 Aug. 2022.

12. Baehr, Ted, and James Baehr. *Narnia Beckons: C.S. Lewis's The Lion, The Witch and The Wardrobe and Beyond*. Broadman & Holman Publishers, 2005.

13. Pocock, Emma. "Harry Potter: A History of Magic and Plant Lore, Part One: J.K. Rowling and Culpeper's Complete

Herbal." *The Leaky Cauldron,* 4 Oct. 2018, www.the-leaky-cauldron.org/2018/10/04/harry-potter-a-history-of-magic-and-plant-lore-part-one-j-k-rowling-and-culpepers-complete-herbal/. Accessed 5 Aug. 2022.

14. Whitford, Emma. "Lev Grossman, S.E. Hinton, and Other Authors on the Freedom of Writing Fanfiction." *Vulture,* 13 Mar. 2015, www.vulture.com/2015/03/6-famous-authors-whove-written-fanfiction.html. Accessed 5 Aug. 2022.

15. thelightningstreak. "In Defense of Fanfiction." *Tumblr,* 10 Jan. 2018, thelightningstreak.tumblr.com/post/169549935563/rant-about-fanfiction-writing. Accessed 5 Aug. 2022.

I won the 2004 Hugo Award for Best short story for an H.P. Lovecraft/Arthur Conan Doyle mashup fiction, so fanfiction had better be legitimate, because I'm not giving the Hugo back. Or the 2005 Locus Award for Best Novelette. I'm not giving that back either.

— Neil Gaiman
Bestselling writer of *The Sandman*

CAN'T STOP THE SIGNAL
Anne Jamison

If you write fanfiction you know about Anne Jamison's book *Fic: Why Fanfiction Is Taking Over the World.*

At turns deeply scholarly and joyfully shouty, *Fic* is full of dozens of essays that in many ways made it mainstream to think of fanfiction as not only worthy of study, but worthy full stop.

Since writing an essay for that book, I've had the good fortune to meet Anne in person, chat with her on social media, and here we talk a bit about *Fic* and about fic.

Atlin Merrick: What is fanfiction to you?

Anne Jamison: To me personally, it is a really deep and multifaceted kind of fun. I have been gravitating to smaller or older or even defunct fandoms – but I keep them personal and don't write about them professionally, although in something like Hannibal my professional and personal interests coincide. I've become more of a lurker, though, because for a while I had a kind of outsized influence that I actually didn't want. I miss writing fic though, so I will probably take it up again soon.

Professionally – well, there are a lot of complicated technical and ethical issues involved in teaching and writing about amateur writers and contemporary digital culture that I am constantly grappling with. And if I want to stay current – I just blink and I'm behind! It is a very fast-moving target for research. I've been researching very early Sherlock Holmes participatory print culture and it's so relaxing when everyone you're writing about is dead, honestly.

You've said that writing fic can help novice writers build skills and confidence before launching their own publishing careers. Is apprenticeship a key benefit of writing fic?

Reading extensively, writing often, and having readers respond is the best recipe for improving writing, and that is exactly what fanfic writers do. I hope I make clear in my book that I do not feel fic's greatest value is as an apprenticeship to commercial publication, however. I think fanfiction affords writers, including professional writers, freedoms, creative opportunities, communities, and audiences that commercial writing can't.

"My writing career was probably saved by my love of fanfiction," *Rachel Caine writes in her Fic essay going on to write five million* *words of original fiction after 220,000 words of fic. Is inspiring writers* *to believe that if they can write good fic they can write good original* *work a boon of fic?*

It is a key benefit. But my caveat…commercially-viable original work and fanfiction come with different reader expectations and make different demands of writers. What makes a good novel does not necessarily make a good fanfic and vice versa.

I think this difference is often interpreted as fic being lesser, or 'training' for commercial fic. There are gatekeepers in publishing, so a lot of fanfic is not edited professionally (or sometimes at all), so fanfic writers should be aware of different standards for technical correctness. How much a fanfic community cares about grammar, spelling, etc. really, really varies. But I have certainly seen published writers write virtually-unread fanfics, while untrained amateur writers connect with thousands of readers.

In Fic you point out that most fanfiction is written by women and *marginalized people, while Kristina Busse says fic interrogates gender,* *sexuality, and cultural assumptions. Does fic empower writers and* *readers as people, as sexual people, as women?*

It certainly can. Not just because of who or what is getting represented, but because women and marginalized genders and sexualities are the dominant forces in the complicated networks of fanfic fandom. Though they are not the only ones! But fanfic is certainly an important venue for exploring, learning, confronting, and owning desire and pleasure, even when those desires and pleasures run counter to a person's community or even personal norms and beliefs.

"Fanfiction affords writers, including professional writers, freedoms, creative opportunities, communities, and audiences commercial writing can't"

Of course, there are plenty of instances of people criticizing others for their desires, or, on the other hand, people using desire to justify various representations that perpetuate stereotypes or exclusions. What makes one person feel desire may make another feel triggered or even harmed. Those issues are as old as fanfic, and are not going away any time soon.

Arthur Conan Doyle wrote to a devotee of his work, "Dear Sir, I read your story. It is not bad and I don't see why you should not change the names and try to get it published yourself." What are your thoughts on 'filing off the serial numbers' as a way to publication?

My feelings are complex. I think people should be able to do it, but I think they should consider community norms and assumptions, including how much the story/fic was helped by fan labor, the particular community involved, etc. Those norms are changing. There is not nearly the stigma that there once was, and I am completely against shaming writers who do this – but I do understand the anger in instances where other fans donate a ton of labor (beta-ing, maintaining websites, etc) to what they assume is a non-profit collective.

Tropes and conventions also circulate in fandoms and end up feeling like collective property. Fanfiction isn't just about the individual writer of the individual fanfic but, from a labor perspective, the writer is still doing the lion's share, and should be able to make the ultimate decision on what to do with their own creative work. I think now there is more of a sense that profit may happen, rather than it being the greatest taboo because it will make copyright holders come after you.

What would you say to someone worried that fic isn't 'real' writing?
Of course it's real writing.

Do you see fic becoming more mainstream, with people happily admitting to writing it?
Yes (see the title of my book).

In Fic's intro, Lev Grossman says writing and reading fic is a way of thinking critically about media – what are your thoughts?
Writing and reading fic can definitely mean pushing back against the status quo that excludes people like you from being the ones represented or doing the representing.

However, it can also be a way to experiment with representing or inhabiting or creating challenges for characters who are *unlike* you, or how people or characters who are unlike you could still overlap with people like you in various engaging, disturbing, or exciting ways. It can also be an exercise in trying to get more of the thing you love, or to get the thing you love to do more of the thing you love it to do.

'Should' or does canon affect fandom and its fan works?
I don't believe that canon ever has the power to validate or invalidate fanfic.

How do you think attempts to bolster corporate power over copyright might affect fanfiction's future?
Can't stop the signal.

Anne Jamison is Professor of English at the University of Utah, where she teaches and writes about literature and culture from the 18th century to the present. She holds a PhD in Comparative Literature from Princeton, and is the editor of Fic: Why Fanfiction Is Taking Over the World. One of the first things you'll see on her website about page – annejamison.net – is "Fanfiction is literature. Fight me."

AN INFINITE VARIETY
Jayantika Ganguly

Sherlockiana and fanfiction are my two greatest indulgences – and outside of work and family they constitute almost the entirety of my social life (an alarming degree of which is virtual). So, naturally, when the much-admired editor of this book asked me if I'd be interested in writing something which spanned both, it was only natural that I leapt up with a "Yes! I'd love to!"

Of course, Atlin, being Atlin, she gave me a beautifully-worded mandate: "This book is about the boon of fic, how it can give voice to groups often marginalized in conventional media – including female, LGBTQIA, and neurodivergent people, people of color, and others. While fandom is not perfect – it can be hidebound, heterogeneous, and full of bickering – the idea of *Spark* is to focus on the positive, including steps we as fandom and as writers can take to enhance our own creating and the creativity of others."

So, as general secretary and editor of the Sherlock Holmes Society of India, as a woman, an Indian, a person who has traveled and met so many across fandom, I've accepted the editor's challenge and here I hope to share my thoughts on how fandom expands us, and offers a more inclusive view of the world.

This is not an easy topic, to be honest, even though it seems so at first glance. It is not that I am unfamiliar with fanfiction – quite the contrary. After all, I've often admitted that fanfiction is my guilty pleasure the same way liquor-filled dark chocolate is. Personally, I'd estimate about a third of my reading material to be fanfiction (the other two being 'proper' books and manga/comics).

So – fanfiction. I think my first introduction to online fanfiction was while I was still in high school, and it was the Harry Potter fandom. I even wrote a few...in secret. But then, I've always written a lot in secret, even when I was a little kid. I wrote an entire fantasy novel in secret when I was thirteen, and it only got worse from there. If I'd somehow managed to keep all the random sheets of paper/notebooks/floppy disks/pen drives/hard drives of old computers that I wrote on, I'd probably have well over a hundred stories in various stages – and at least one third of these would be fanfiction – not only of Harry Potter and Sherlock Holmes, but many other characters that I liked. I wrote fanfiction before I even knew the term. I wrote crossovers and canon divergences and alternate universe stories years before I learned these words!

So, imagine my delight when, as a teenager, I stumbled upon this online world full of stories about characters I loved while waiting for the next book to be released! I could read as much as I wanted to, without driving the family into bankruptcy! (My parents are saints. Imagine having to raise a child that compulsively reads at least one novel a day – often more.)

And so I did. I read to my heart's content, and I found gems that were sometimes even better than 'real' books. One of my favorite series (an early discovery, thankfully, so I was able to read the entire trilogy before it was taken off-line) was so well-written that it blew my mind. The writer of that series is a bestselling fantasy novelist now. And it is most certainly not an isolated incident. Quite a few fanfiction writers have gone on to become professional writers, contrary to what the naysayers believe. This is one of my oft-quoted examples when someone says that the quality of fanfiction is not up to the mark (these are often people who have never read a single fanfic in their life). I can think of as many brilliant fanfiction works as 'proper' books. And conversely, I can think of quite a few badly written published books that make you wonder what the editor and publisher were thinking when they decided to waste paper and ink.

I have unabashedly referenced many fanfiction works in my own Sherlockian book *The Holmes Sutra*, and I'd recommend them any day. One common reaction I get is, "Oh, I didn't know you read fanfiction! You know the original so well!" or "You read fanfiction? But you love classics/literature/serious stuff!" – not only in relation to the Sherlockian fandom, but others as well. I find myself flabbergasted at these responses, honestly. Should it not stand to reason that I will not go looking for a fanfic unless I am familiar with the original and like the characters? Why should liking Shakespeare or Nabokov preclude me from enjoying a light-hearted fanfic of *Mo Dao Zu Shi?* I know for certain that I would not have enjoyed BBC *Sherlock* (or any other adaptation or fanfiction based on Sherlock Holmes) half as much if I had not read the original canon.

"I learned more about social norms and gender identity from fanfiction than I did in two semesters of sociology in law school"

Then there is the question of one's worldview. It is often said that people fear what they do not understand, and that being different from the crowd can make life very difficult. I know what it's like not to fit in, because I never really have myself. I read original classics as a pre-teen when everyone else was reading comics (and, perhaps ironically, I read more manga/comics now when people in my age group are supposed to read 'serious stuff'). I read murder mysteries when my peers were reading romance paperbacks. I was reading fantasy when the norm was autobiographies. You get used to it, and if you are fortunate, you find good friends who stick by you no matter how eccentric you may be. Because at some point or another, you need others. Even if you are reclusive by nature and tend to avoid crowds, there are times you want to assure yourself that you're not the only one. And I can think of no better antidote for that kind of loneliness than fanfiction.

That's the reason it has grown exponentially in such a short time, isn't it? Even if you are mostly a cryptid (I learned this word very recently and have been dying to use it) and won't interact with other fans online – I do that, I leave kudos on the works I like but I rarely comment and almost never get into discussions – it is encouraging, reassuring that there are like-minded people out there. And not only like-minded people, but such an infinite variety of people that you can't help but be interested. As someone who has lived in a largely heteronormative, patriarchal society all her life, it was a revelation. It was fascinating.

To be honest, I learned more about society and social norms and things like gender identity and presentation and such topics from the fanfiction world than I did in two semesters of sociology in law school. These concepts, expressed through different avatars of characters you love by people of all types who also love these characters, bring them home. So you read them and empathize. You think, *so what if Sherlock is gay/ace/sub/dom/omega/alpha/whatever, it's still Sherlock, and I love Sherlock!* And then as you read through the persecution they face because of this difference, you think, *oh no! I don't want Sherlock to suffer like this! So what if he's different? That's not a sin! He is what he is, just leave him in peace!* If that's not inclusive, I don't know what is. It broadens your horizons. That's the power of a well-written fanfic. It can affect your worldview in the exact same way a great book can – perhaps even more, because these are characters you already adore.

It is generally accepted that the more you read and the more you travel, the more accepting you become of different cultures and different people, even if you're not a xenophile. No one can dispute that reading fanfiction falls within the definition of 'reading' by any standards whatsoever, and I like to think that it is akin to virtual traveling as well. What is traveling if not assimilation of different people and different cultures?

Moreover, fic and fandom can build up a virtual support system for you if you're interacting with like-minded individuals all over the world. At a Sherlockian event before the pandemic made us lock ourselves in, I met a lovely lady, a Sherlockian, who spoke of her experience in the fandom and how it supported her through the most difficult time of her life. She had been going through a very hard time, not the least of which was looking for a job in vain and questioning her self-worth as a result. What kept her grounded was the support she received from her online fandom community, from all over the world. And then there was an incident with one of her fandom-mates, who was being persecuted halfway across the world, and this woman rose up in defense and wrote an opinion. This piece was found by an editor, piqued their interest, and this translated into a regular writing job for this lady, and now she's quite successful. Isn't that inspiring?

But most of all, fandom is supposed to be *fun*. It is supposed to be something to enjoy without being judged or persecuted, something to relieve the pressures and tedium of regular life. If a fanfic can bring a smile to your face, if a fandom discussion or thread can make your day a little bit brighter, if your fandom friends can make you feel a little less lonely – I'd say it has proved its worth in gold.

For what is life if not the pursuit of happiness?

Jayantika Ganguly, better known as Jay, is a consummate Sherlockian, the General Secretary and Editor of the Sherlock Holmes Society of India, and a member of several international Sherlockian communities, including the Baker Street Irregulars, the Sherlock Holmes Society of India, the Sherlock Holmes Society of London, Ceska spolecnost Sherlocka Holmes, Five Miles from Anywhere, the Bootmakers of Toronto, the Crew of the Barque Lone Star and the Studious Scarlets Society. She is a regular writer of traditional Sherlock Holmes pastiches for various anthologies, Sherlockian essays for various publications, and also has a non-fiction book "The Holmes Sutra" and an anthology of traditional style Sherlockian pastiches "A Continuum of Sherlock Holmes" to her name. She adores Sherlock Holmes in any avatar.

I've talked about being influenced by manga, fanfiction, and video games. I also love Cormac McCarthy, Shirley Jackson, and Flannery O'Connor. There is no contradiction here; they exist in the same space together. Never, ever be ashamed of the things that inspire you.

— Alyssa Wong
Nebula award-winning writer of
"Hungry Daughters of Starving Mothers"

STANDING OUT AND BEATING THE ODDS
S.H.

I'm asexual and agender (but female-presenting) in forensic chemistry – toxicology, to be exact. For those who aren't familiar with the term, it's the study of poisons. I currently work in a forensic lab that tests everything including hospital samples, drug court samples, date rape panels, and post-mortem samples from suspected homicides.

It's not easy. School was particularly rough. The old boys club in uni thought they were *very* progressive by teaching women and those who presented femme – and treating us like dolls, sex objects, or amusing eloquent pieces of furniture was perfectly fine because teaching us was progressive on its own merit.

Work is better, but even with that, there is definitely a boys' club, and I find that many of the people who have made it to and through grad school are men, so it's women doing the actual work, while they do paperwork in an office.

I'd be lying if I said I didn't get inspiration from fictional characters, often more than nonfictional. A certain fictional detective was a large inspiration. Tony Stark, Bruce Banner, and Jane Foster all gave me a mental boost through bad times in academia. Sometimes telling myself that they'd be proud of me for powering through was all that got me to the next day. Writing and talking about them, making them people in my head that could relate to my struggle, truly helped keep me sane sometimes.

I'm well aware there's a lot of judgment about things like fanfic and escapism like this.

Escapism and fanfic are *tools*. Like most tools, when used improperly escapism can be unhelpful. But when used correctly, they're tools specifically made for people like me!

My lack of gender compounded the struggle to find people

I related to in the field. I ended up looking toward people like Alan Turing and Isaac Newton, who, while cis, were at least queer, or very much suspected to be. Knowing there had always been someone standing out and beating odds gave me courage. Additional inspirations included Marie Curie, Rosalind Franklin, and Hedy Lamarr, who I knew had dealt with the sexism rampant in science.

But there was no-one truly like me: both agender and asexual! At least not that I knew of. Therefore, fanfic and fandom were lifesavers. Being able to *conceptualize* my journey – to visualize where I wanted to get to and what sort of person I wanted to be – gave me mental strength to get there.

This is something many people cannot understand. If you're a white cishet man, for example, most media is *catered* to you. You need look no further than what is on the page or screen to find someone like you. If you're a white cishet woman, there is representation for you as well, though less than the men, certainly. If you are outside those two categories…good luck finding well-rounded, relatable characters, let alone in your field.

Unless, of course, you look to fanworks.

In fanfic and fanart, anything goes. Captain America is agender, Robinson Crusoe is intersex, men have *pregnancies*, women have cocks. Trans and queer folk flourish in fan-made media. Fanfic takes art and puts it in the center of a diamond, and then insists on looking at it through every facet of the glass, every angle, every distortion. And it's incredible!

Fanfic challenges the assumptive norm and builds on it; makes it more accessible. And that access gave me the tools I needed to visualize my future and take steps to improve my life and make goals.

Sometimes escapism went too far. It's so easy to read and not do – in bad times, it's hard not to curl up with a fic and ignore the world. But that's where fandom stepped in! Friends I'd met through fandom all over the world encouraged me to keep going, to work through what was holding me back, and then get out of bed and move forward. So many people I've never met in person found the time to remind me I was worth the future I'd been working toward.

"Fanfic takes art and puts it in the center of a diamond, and then insists on looking at it through every facet"

As Corona took over the world, life changed; fanfic changed with it. New fic came out with adjusted perspectives that helped me process what was happening. Fandom friends stayed when some in-person friends did not, because we were already used to speaking online. I found strength in that community to continue with my future through the stress and mourning and fear, which is especially important in my line of work when I can't just work from home.

I still use fic to look at life differently. The same skills that allow me to put a piece of media in a diamond and look at its facets differently can be used to examine my own life: where am I? Who am I now? Where do I want to go? How do I want to live? And meanwhile the friends that I have continue to give me strength along the way. Fanfiction and fan media have become a tool in my mental health arsenal.

I found people like me – fictional and nonfictional – through fandom. It mattered, and now I have future goals: from academic (would be nice to have that PhD someday) to personal (PTSD is going to be a sidenote in my brain at some point; not now, but someday).

I also look around at those who are struggling to get to where I stand and endeavor to give them hope.

Because honestly? Where I now stand? It's pretty sweet. I can, if asked, write stories of how I've been treated or how cis white straight men have screwed with me – but I'd rather tell you the following:

I have studied overseas, and it was awesome.

I get to handle brains. It's whacky.

"What do you do for a living?" "Find poisons." It's so badass.

LCMS vial inserts look like tiny glass squids. Squinserts.

That tox report on Forensic Files? *Me.*

My professor told me to my face that I'm one of very few experts on a particular drug. In the world.

I don't have to work with retail customers anymore.

If you pronounce drugs with an Italian accent, they sound like pasta.

Every lab has a mythos. In my lab, we know exactly who has favor with the sample gremlins, who the fridge likes best, and if you put one particular co-worker on the GCMS that does volatiles, the curve works.

I always know that my work matters, and I'm doing a job that improves lives in my community.

My best friend from uni is doing her thesis on how dogs sense cancer. Dog chemistry. DOGS with JOBS. For university credit!

My colleague has, multiple times, informed me that the peaks on opiate curves were "erotic."

I have fun.

Honestly, that's it. That's the goal. As a wise man* once said, "Be kind, have fun." It's so easy for me to get caught up in "Did I make it, can I make it? Is there anyone else who did? How do I go further?" that I forget where I am, and what I achieved. I went from a little kid who looked up to my literary namesake (you get one guess, look at my initials above), and now? Now I solve crimes about poisons.

Live your dreams.

*John Finnemore, a genius.

S.H. is a chemist by workday and a fiber artist and writer by weekend. They enjoy history and dramatically destroying unnecessary social structures. You can find some of their fanwork under Aelfay on AO3, and other things on Tumblr at Alchemistdoctor. New friends always welcome!

I DON'T LIKE IT, I LOVE IT:
FANFICTION AS LITERATURE
Ann McClellan

My book *Sherlock's World: Fanfiction and the Reimagining of BBC's Sherlock*, starts with one basic premise: "Fanfictions are art objects and [this book] treats them with the respect, depth, appreciation – and love – which is their due."

Such a claim may seem revolutionary to literary critics and some journalists, but it's one I've found to be true in my years' experience reading and studying the genre.

Fanfictions come from a deeply held love and investment in particular stories and characters. Fans so love these creations that they are not satisfied with what the showrunners and producers give them; nay, they want more – more volume and variety and experimentation in the stories they consume. Sometimes that desire for more comes out of seemingly insatiable cravings, sometimes out of frustration at the writers' continued embeddedness in outdated gender, sexual, and social mores. Either way, fanfiction provides in-depth sociologically and culturally complex adaptations of character, theme, and worldbuilding.

While most fanfiction academic texts focus on the ethnographic and sociological motivations underpinning why fans author fanfictions, I'm more interested in the stories as literary texts. After all, I'm not a sociologist; I'm a literary critic. As such, I love to read, to talk about stories with friends, family, students, and members of my communities. With more than 30 years of established disciplinary history, I believed fan studies was ready to proceed beyond defining the what and whys of fan practices to what I like to call 'Fan Studies 2.0' (or even 3.0) where we delve more deeply into the analysis of fanfic as a cultural object.

Fanfiction is a popular culture genre, much like reality TV, sci-fi, games, and music. Yet while franchises like *Game of Thrones* or the *Harry Potter* books and films have long been considered 'serious' objects of academic study, fanfiction continues to be considered *less* – less serious, less polished, less worthy – though that is changing.

Much of the dismissal of fanfic as a serious academic discipline is based on three key factors, in my opinion: it's not 'original,' most fanfic is written by women, and people believe it's written by *young* women.

First, one common criticism launched against fanfic is that it isn't 'original.' Popular writers like Diana Gabaldon, George R. R. Martin, and Anne Rice criticize fans for writing about previously published characters, storylines, and worlds. Fans crafting stories about 'professional' authors' original characters and worlds implies a kind laziness and lack of creativity – as well as copyright infringement – the writers claim. Gabaldon, in particular, has written that she views fanfiction as 'immoral' as well as 'illegal.'

Explaining fair use and transformative works under copyright law is both beyond my capabilities and the scope of this essay, but many other, smarter people have done so on the web and in published research. The argument comes down to basic elements of character- and world-development, as well as plot. I would argue that most fan writers do *more* character development than the primary creators, simply because there are so many fans writing within the fictional world and producing so much. Sheer volume allows the characters and worlds to develop in ways perhaps not originally 'intended' by the initial creators.

Likewise, fanfic seems to relish putting said characters into unusual, unlikely, and even impossible situations that would never be viable in the 'original' world. While traditional writers are compelled to keep their characters and storylines consistent within the worlds they have created for them (even worlds that involve magic, time travel, and vampires!), fans face no such restrictions, other than consistent characterization (and even that can be skirted with crack!fic). Such freedom allows fans not only to place Sherlock Holmes and John Watson in Hogwarts, in the world of *Inception,* in Roman times, or in alien worlds, but it also allows them to develop the stories and canon/fanon in ways the characters' creators are contractually and economically unable. So, contrary to accusations that fanfic isn't as creative as 'real' literature, I would argue that it allows writers to be even *more* adventurous because they are not limited by established worlds, timelines, and strict consistency expectations.

Fanfic can be about *anything,* anytime, anywhere.

The dismissal of fanfic because it is assumed to be authored by young/women raises all kinds of assumptions and negatively conceived stereotypes. First, somehow (it seems impossible, but still) the American public continues to think that literature written by women is inherently bad. The fact that we still use disparaging genre distinctions like 'chick lit' and 'chick flicks' to describe books and films aimed either at women's interests, lives, experiences, and/ or audiences keenly illustrates how we, as a culture, continue to devalue women's stories.

> "The dismissal of fanfic because it's assumed to be authored by young/ women raises all kinds of assumptions and stereotypes"

To give one example from my personal teaching experience: about a decade ago I taught a class on Twice Told Tales that looked at past and present depictions of 'love and marriage' (sometimes tongue in cheek); in one case, we paired Jane Austen's canonical *Pride and Prejudice* with the immensely popular *Bridget Jones's Diary* by Helen Fielding. When it came time to discuss our first reading of Fielding's novel, the male students in the class (less than 50%) essentially staged a class rebellion. They refused to read or talk about "some stupid woman and her stupid life who only cared about getting fat and finding a man." The female students were shocked into disbelieving silence. In my previous 20 years of teaching experience, I had never had a student or group of students refuse to talk about 'male lives' or 'men's experiences' perhaps because we never label these as 'men's' lives or 'men's' experiences; they are just 'life.'

Even though women comprise more than 50% of the U.S. (and world) population, stories depicting their interests, their lives, and, most importantly, their desires, are separated out into a second tier, less-than category, automatically beneath any representation of men's lives.

Combine this cultural disdain for women's stories with their youth, and even more assumptions arise. Perhaps one of the biggest, and most problematic, accusations leveled against fanfic is that it's poorly written. Generalizing, qualitative judgments like these are primarily based on the assumed juvenility of fanfic: fic shows immature understandings of love, desire, and motivation. It is badly written with little understanding of basic grammatical rules and principles or the complex elements of storytelling. Fanfic represents young girls' poorly disguised fantasies about fictional characters or real life figures (revealing an immature understanding of the difference between fiction and reality).

Because it is assumed to be written by young people, it *must* be bad. But where did these assumptions come from?

Wolfgang Amadeus Mozart was revered as a musical genius when he composed his first concertos at the age of five. Both John Keats and Percy Shelley were considered rock stars in the Romantic poetry world before the age of 18. Heck, even Elizabeth Barrett Browning was a poetry phenom, writing her first poem when six years old and publishing regularly to great acclaim by age 15. So, women's writing = bad. *Young* women's writing? *The WORST*.

First of all, we don't know who writes fanfiction. That's one of the wonderful gems of the genre. There have been several amazing studies about fan demographics which claim that the majority is written by straight, cis, white women, but because most fanfic authors write under pseudonyms (and reply to surveys anonymously, thus protecting their 'real life' identities) we don't know whether respondents are reporting their age, gender, race, or sexual orientations 'accurately.'

Of course, there is also the issue of access. How do we know we're reaching all of the fanficcers out there? Where does the surveyed pool come from? How were they contacted? Are there other communities and groups we don't know about? It's a mystery!

Maybe this mystery is part of the reason so much of our culture rejects fanfic as a legitimate literary genre. Because we don't know who writes these stories, dismissing them as objects of study becomes much easier. Denigrating their authors, themes, style, and subject matter in elite publications like *The New Yorker*, *New York Times*, *Washington Post*, and other media outlets is easy because, if there are no 'authors,' no one's feelings can be hurt, right? Journalists mock fanfiction, fan art, and cosplayers in public forums like they would never dare if a 'real' author or actor was there to respond to such jibes. But because fanfic is 'anonymous' (and they suspect it is by women and by young people), it's easy to dismiss.

On the contrary, I would argue that because we *don't* know who authored the stories, we must treat them the same way critics consider anonymous fifteenth century sonnets or the most famous of classic English texts, *Beowulf*. We don't know the author of these, yet graduate students and scholars devote their lives to exploring the complexities and stylistic explorations of these literary masterpieces with the same care and devotion they dedicate to the plays of Shakespeare or the novels of George Eliot. All we have are the texts, and our analysis must treat them as such – as art objects open to deep literary study.

So how does one 'do' literary study? Well, we look at the specific language used in the text. Literary critics are deeply interested in denotation and connotation – what a word's dictionary definition and use are compared with the cultural, thematic, and metaphoric overtones a particular usage might invoke in the mind of the reader. Critics are interested in figurative language, elements like simile, metaphor, metonymy, hyperbole, and other techniques writers use to invoke associations between a particular word and a concept,

50

experience, or emotion. They are also interested in allusion – that is, implicit or explicit references to other texts, stories, and characters from literary history.

It was no coincidence that the cover for Stephanie Meyer's famed *Twilight* novel has an image of two hands holding an apple. The apple has *huge* literary symbolism in literature and religion, beginning in John Milton's use as the fruit of temptation in *Paradise Lost* and continuing through *Twilight* itself, as the apple symbolizes both Edward's and Bella's failure to resist the temptation of the other.

There are also the famous themes of 'great literature' we all learn in grade school: Man vs. Nature, Man vs. Society, Man vs. Man. (Sense a theme here?) Aristotle laid the foundations for basic, consistent storytelling (beginning-middle-end, protagonists vs antagonists, climaxes and resolutions) thousands of years ago, which contemporary post-modern writers have continued to challenge. All of these elements are tried-and-true, validated, and accepted methods for literary analysis. So what happens when we apply them to fanfic, without the culturally-conditioned bias against such writing already in place?

What we find are amazing, diverse, complicated, experimental stories about character development, love, desire, identity, conflict – all of the elements that make up truly great, life-changing literature.

In my research on *Sherlock* fanfiction, I found complex stories challenging the boundaries between 'reality' and 'fiction' in a postmodern, technological world. How can I tell whether 'Sherlock Hollmes' (sic) on Facebook is a role player or the 'real' character? Is this Holmes the same Holmes I see posting on Twitter? If showrunners can blog about their (fictional) characters and post them on the web (see johnwatsonblog.co.uk*), then how is fanfic any different from 'professional' writing? Fans explore complex concepts like the relationship between biological sex, gender identity, and sexuality, pointing out the ways Sherlock's and John's behaviors and actions on the TV show don't always match up with socially perceived understandings of 'masculinity' and in various sexswapped, genderswapped, and slash stories, experimenting with an infinite number of variations and possibilities.

They write about body shaming, eating disorders, sexual identity crises, self-harm, suicidal ideation, sexual (in)experience, as well as newfound love, desire, sexual experimentation, touch, romance, bonding, companionship, and friendship. Authors invoke classic themes, stories, and even characters from 'canonical' literature from the past, providing new takes on *Romeo and Juliet*, *The Great Gatsby*, and *Harry Potter*, among others.

Conversely, they write Sherlock and John into such 'real world' scenarios as contemporary Hollywood, with fictional transcripts from 'real' TV appearances on *Ellen* and other shows, as well as iconic magazine-style fan art for fictional movies such that it becomes virtually impossible to distinguish between reality and fiction.

Other fanfics explore the kind of technological and stylistic innovation and experimentation lauded in canonical works like James Joyce's *Ulysses,* with its use of stream of consciousness. How are typography and graphic design not sophisticated experimental elements of 'Literature' with a capital L? All of these elements – and more – are found in fanfiction.

Even with all of my arguments about how fanfiction fulfills and exhibits the same characteristics critics and readers value in 'good,' canonical literature, I often come down to one major reason why I read and study fanfiction: *anything* that garners that much support, that much cultural fascination, love, and following, deserves our attention and study.

According to the *New York Review of Books*, E. L. James's *Fifty Shades of Grey* fanfic forerunner, *Master of the Universe*, had over 37,000 published online reviews from fans, with lurkers numbering in the unknown thousands (Eakin). Her online success quickly transferred to profits in the marketplace, with *Fifty Shades of Grey* selling more than 125 million copies worldwide by 2015, making it the best-selling book of all time (Singh). Whether individuals like the story or not, anything that garners this kind of public following deserves our respect and attention.

Fanfiction has a huge following and growing influence, and the genre offers so much enjoyment, enrichment, and depth to the stories circulating in our world.

Fanfic is here to stay. And by Jove, I *love* it.

Ann McClellan is professor of English at Plymouth State University where she teaches 19th and 20th century British literature. She is the author of Sherlock's World: Fanfiction and the Reimagining of BBC's Sherlock (2018), How British Women Writers Transformed the Campus Novel (2012), and several articles on cultural topics ranging from servants on screen to social media, fanfiction, and Sherlock Holmes. She is currently writing a new monograph on Black Sherlock Holmes adaptations.

* https://web.archive.org/web/20221216014457/http://www.johnwatsonblog.co.uk/

Whoever it was trying to dump on fanfic today… Cut that shit out, let people enjoy things. Also, if you do write fanfic: awesome, enjoy it and don't let anyone steal your joy of it.

— John Scalzi
  Hugo award-winning writer of *Redshirts*

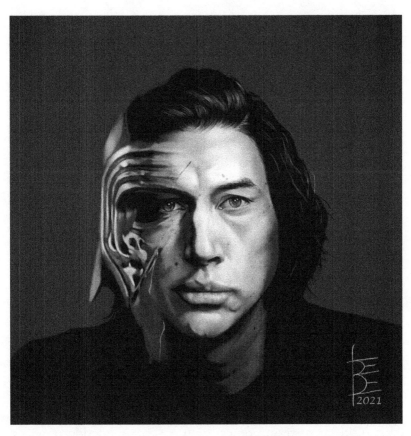

Where the Light Enters by Andrea L Farley (Altocello)

A LOVE AFFAIR:
WHY PROS AND NON-PROS WRITE FIC
Narrelle M. Harris

Fanfiction is fiction written by fans of films, books and even bands, about the further adventures of their heroes. It's a creative response to a text and is in many ways a love affair with someone's art. Some of it is even considered 'respectable' – Sebastian Faulks's recent *Jeeves and the Wedding Bells* is a splendid example, but Virgil, Shakespeare, and Charlotte Bronte can all be considered 'fanficcers' of their time. Neil Gaiman's *A Study in Emerald* is, by his own words, a Cthulhu/Sherlock Holmes crossover fic.

Many creators feel there's a place for fanfiction, as long as the writers aren't attempting to usurp copyright or make money from intellectual property that doesn't belong to them. Most fan writers are perfectly happy with this restriction.

Fanfiction has also been a training ground for writers. Some have gone on to professional success – and some of *them* continue to write fanfiction.

Writing in someone else's universe is not solely about creating further adventures for beloved characters. For many, the joy of fanfiction lies in a much more personal area – that of representation. People who don't fit the cultural, physical, sexual, mental or political 'norm' may struggle to see themselves reflected positively, if at all, in mainstream popular culture – but fanfiction provides opportunities for true diversity.

In this way, writers use existing characters to express a range of experiences, including gender fluidity, asexuality, consensual kinks, and other aspects of gender and sexuality, in a 'mainstream' context. Known characters can be recast with physical disabilities or mental health challenges, or with different cultures or ethnicities.

Many of these stories are written by people whose experiences are at best marginalized by the mainstream.

This ability to explore – respectfully, frankly, and openly – more inclusive aspects of being human is a strong attractor of both readers and writers.

But what draws professional writers to play in someone else's established world?

Besides the opportunity to write about a more diverse experience of being human, fan writing can be rewarding in other ways.

Several years ago, I began writing fanfiction to prompts as a cure for a debilitating bout of writer's block. A reader's request sparked a fun short story idea that simply flowed out of my fingers to the screen – and garnered immediate, positive response. I'd begun to fear my writing mojo had died, but I had just written 3000 words in an afternoon. *I could still write!*

Now, I've completed and sold not only the troublesome, block-inducing book, but many other novels and short stories.

I still write fanfiction. I revel in the freedom of writing without the weight of deadlines, the need for commercial viability, or the rigid demands of the editing process. I've experimented with form and style and improved areas that were weak. At least three professional projects have arisen from my experiments in the fannish realm. I've had a lot of *fun*.

I'm not alone.

Australian novelist Foz Meadows wrote fanfic in her teens, and returned to it in 2014. She also found it a very rewarding experience.

"At a time when I was struggling to write original fiction due to self-doubt and fears about the marketability of my work, giving myself permission to simply write something enjoyable, for its own sake, which I could nonetheless share with an interested audience, was immensely freeing.

"Not only did I find myself writing more and faster than I had in months, but where I've historically had a problem with over-description, the act of writing in a context where I could assume a certain degree of audience knowledge about the characters and settings, taught me how to streamline the details."

"Given the time between creation and circulation in traditional publishing, the immediacy of the feedback in the fanfic community feels supportive and validating"

Meadows's fanfiction isn't just an echo of her usual writing. Within it, she has been expanding her skills.

"Not only has it challenged me to go outside my usual comfort zones, but it's had something of a restorative effect, too, both creatively and in terms of boosting my confidence. Given the time between creation and circulation in traditional publishing, the immediacy of the feedback in the fanfic community feels both supportive and validating, and while the lack of editorial oversight and the speed of output can sometimes weaken a work, they can also strengthen its originality, with less need for the author to second guess themselves."

Jenna Braid, an American non-fiction writer living in London, has made many professional fiction sales that sprang from her fanfiction efforts, including books, and short stories included in *Year's Best* anthologies.

"These all came because I love writing fanfiction so much that I write hundreds of thousands of words of it a year – even though I'm a writer by profession and write for a living," says Braid. She has no doubts about the professional benefits of writing fic.

"Through writing all those words I've become a *better* writer, with more focus, and the ability to sit down and do it, on deadline."

The focus on romance and erotica in fanfiction is widely known, and for all it is mocked by the mainstream, it's a focus that has value and enjoyment for its readers and writers.

"The sexuality of the medium is appealing, too," says Meadows. "Not just in terms of containing far more sex-positive, affirmative, diverse and interesting sex than 99% of what I've seen in mainstream publications, but because there's no unspoken rule that explicit sex is the sole province of romance-centric narratives; that is, that stories which are predominantly mysteries or fantasies (for instance) can also contain sex scenes, and that positive sexual encounters can be just as narratively engaging and relevant as negative ones."

"Bottom line," says Meadows, "fanfiction is a sandbox filled with someone else's toys: they choose the participants, but you choose the parameters, and in an industry where the opposite is so often true, it's an extraordinarily satisfying – and, I would argue, creatively necessary – reversal."

Braid praises fanfiction for its personal impact as well.

"It's given me friendships and joy…so much of each that I can't imagine a future where I won't be writing fanfiction, no matter how many books or short stories I'm fortunate enough to sell. I hope to always be part of an inclusive, fantastic fandom, and in less than half a heartbeat I encourage anyone who wants the same to do the same."

Like Braid, my personal life has been enriched by the friends I've made in fandom. I've also been encouraged and deeply touched by feedback on some of my fan stories. As a writer, you always hope you'll write something that moves someone. In fanfiction forums, you often get to hear about it.

Fanfiction gets a harsh rap, but there is much more to it than meets the mainstream eye. It's where new writers can learn their craft in a safe and supportive environment. It's where people outside the mainstream can find stories that reflect their unique experiences. It's where an established writer can take risks and maybe strike a chord with a reader.

Just like traditional books.

Narrelle is an award-winning writer of crime, horror, fantasy and romance. Her 40+ novels and short stories have been published in Australia, US and the UK, and include vampire novels, erotic spy adventures, het and queer romance, fantasy, horror and crime fiction, traditional Holmesian mysteries, and Holmes/Watson romances. Narrelle also writes music, sings, and enjoys all kinds of creating.

2

REVELATIONS, FRIENDSHIP
&
OTHER BIGGIES
How fic and fandom shape us

THE PERFORMANCE PSYCHOLOGY OF FANDOM
Tei

It feels like I'm dying.

I know I'm not dying. It's just the bright lights and churning stomach and the shaking hands and the tunnel vision and the furiously pounding heart. I've felt this way for my entire life, every single time the lights go down on a performance. The fact that it's a predictable, almost unavoidable occurrence, doesn't make the physical manifestations of performance anxiety any less alarming as they happen.

I'm a professional classical musician; playing an instrument in an orchestra is my full-time job. When I tell people that, two major themes emerge. Firstly, almost everyone has an experience of performing that they want to tell me about – whether it was the debate team, drama club, or that they, like poor John Watson, were forced to squawk around on the clarinet in school.

Secondly, almost everyone has had an experience of performance anxiety that they believe to be unusually severe, maybe even unique. They believe that anyone who's gotten far enough to perform music for a living couldn't possibly have experienced something like *that,* let alone experience it constantly.

They couldn't be more wrong.

Managing performance anxiety is almost as big a concern in conservatories and university music programs as actually learning how to play. The area of psychology known as performance psychology started its life mainly in the realm of sports – athletes being another class of professionals who train for many years to perform their best in short, incredibly high-stress events. Sports books like *The Inner Game of Tennis, The New Toughness Training for Sports,* and *The Champion's Mind* are common topics of discussion in violin lessons and student orchestra rehearsals. The performance psychology industry has realized there's a market there; former navy SEAL Don Green has made a second career out of helping musicians prepare mentally for auditions and performances, and blogs like *The Bulletproof Musician* aim to take the entire psychological approach of top athletes and re-package it for musicians.

That's not what I'm going to write about, though. Because these days, when I step onstage, it's not sports mantras or advice from music professors I hold first and foremost in my mind; it's the lessons and attitudes I learned from fandom, and the fanfiction community.

Fanfiction has been a part of my life for a long time.

I first discovered it when I was a teenager, and kept reading casually and very occasionally writing for years. It was only when I discovered the BBC *Sherlock* fandom, though, that I really started writing; writing almost every day, publishing on Archive of Our Own (AO3) every few weeks, and for the first time, making friends in fandom. So I suppose it's unavoidable that the lessons from one area of my artistic life would carry over into another.

Fandom is the consummate nurturing artistic space. It is – both by circumstance and by design – set up to encourage and even enforce the very principles which make up performance psychology's foundation. I'd like to lay out the links between fandom attitudes towards artistic endeavors, and performance psychology; not only because it's helped me, but because there's a growing recognition that performance psychology isn't just for athletes, or musicians, or high-powered CEOs. Everyone has events where they want to be able to perform their best under pressure. Performance psychology is for everyone.

And if we can learn it through fandom, so much the better.

YOU CAN'T BE BETTER THAN YOU CAN

It's a basic law of the universe that in any area, you have to suck before you get good. Acceptance of this fact is very important in performance psychology, because the best performances happen when you accept the level of skill that you have and demonstrate it to the best of your ability. The worst, fall-flat-on-your-face performances happen when you're too conscious of where you want to be to show where you are. The band director at my music school referred to this idea with the advice, "you can't play better than you can."

It's hard to avoid the temptation, though; because in most artistic areas the early, sucky efforts of people who eventually got really good aren't *visible*. I don't get to hear a recording of my music teacher when they were seventeen. Most professional authors don't publish their writing assignments from school. Artists paint over canvases they aren't proud of with later efforts.

Fanfiction authors, though? Behind almost every incredible fanfiction author is a veritable treasure trove of early work, charting their artistic path. Thanks to the ease of publishing things online, and the long memory of the internet, the necessity of allowing yourself to unabashedly, enthusiastically *suck* is easily demonstrable by clicking back through your favorite author's AO3, LiveJournal, fanfiction.net, adultfanfiction.net, deadjournal, insanejournal, journalfen, independent archive, Geocities snapshot, or messages to an email group. The internet is littered with bad fanfiction, as our detractors are fond of pointing out. What they don't like to acknowledge, though, is that bad fanfiction has a purpose. Bad fanfiction serves the joyful, glorious purpose of allowing good fanfiction to happen.

> "when I step onstage, it's not sports mantras or advice from music professors I hold foremost in my mind; it's the lessons I learned from fandom, and the fanfiction community"

Not only is bad fanfiction far more visible than the early efforts of the greats in any other genre, fandom culture has come around to the point of view that bad fanfiction should be not merely tolerated, but celebrated. In the midst of a mainstream culture that says that trying too hard, or trying your best and still coming up short, is the ultimate embarrassment, fandom values simply *trying* for its own sake. That's why many fanfic authors are not only accepting of, but perversely proud of, the years or decades of flotsam they have lying around the fannish internet. It shows how hard they tried, and that makes every piece of work all the more valuable.

So, what I try to carry with me into the world from the vast underbelly of fandom: the paradox of needing to accept your current limitations in order to surpass them is no paradox at all. Be proud of your humble beginnings, terrible mistakes, and cringe-worthy missteps for their own sake.

AIM FOR THE YESES

If you want to be a professional orchestral musician, here's how you get a job. First, you spend several months meticulously preparing a selection of snippets of all the most difficult music written for your instrument. Then, you audition: you're sitting all alone, anonymous on one side of a blank screen, and the panel (made up of members of the orchestra you're auditioning for) judges you from the other side. After each candidate, the panel votes. Each panelist can vote yes or no on the person they just heard. If you get enough yeses, you get to move on to the next round, and the process repeats until eventually only one person is left standing. If you get too many nos, you head to the bar with all the other rejects.

Naturally, this process creates a lot of anxiety in jobseekers. It also leads to quite a bit of guessing; everyone wants to guess correctly what the faceless judges want to hear, because nobody wants to do something that will cause a panelist to vote 'no.' But one of the best pieces of advice I received about auditions was this: don't worry about the nos. The nos will always vote no. Aim for the yeses.

What does that mean? It means that some people are simply never going to be interested in what you have to offer, no matter

66

how hard you try to win them over. Instead of wasting your time with them, you should focus on impressing the people who *are* available to be your yes-voters; the people who are interested in what you have to say, and open to convincing.

This is a hard thing to accept in the real world, because most job-seekers – in any industry – want to believe that they could win over the recruiters for any job they have the right qualifications for. It's hard to accept that, even if you do your very best, someone else might decide you're just not the right fit, and send you on your way without even telling you why.

But the absurdity of expecting yourself to be able to appeal to *literally anyone on the planet* becomes obvious when you compare it to the way that readers select and consume fic.

Fandom, more so than any other artistic community, has developed incredibly complex and refined ways of connecting people with the content that they want, and helping them avoid the stuff they don't want. In large part, this is because the fact that fic is free (in both the 'free beer' and 'free speech' senses of the word) means that a lot of it is *weird*. The weirdness means that, as a fic reader, you're likely to find a story so niche and perfectly tailored to your worldview and desires, that it would never have found a publisher. However, as sure as the existence of that story, is that of its opposite – the story so perfectly suited to horrify, revolt, and discomfit you that you would have never even imagined something so awful could exist. But of course, nobody can quite agree on what these two stories are.

So we have learned, as a culture, that the central tenet of the fan experience is individuality and choice. 'Your Kink Is Not My Kink But Your Kink Is Okay,' 'Don't like, don't read,' 'Ship and let ship' – all of these phrases acknowledge that there are some differences in taste that are best navigated by simply avoiding what you don't like. And with Archive of Our Own having developed possibly the most advanced tagging system in the online world, it's possible to filter according to your tastes with incredible accuracy and reliability.

If you're posting fic on AO3, it's intuitive and obvious that you're wasting your time trying to win over people who don't like the thing you're doing, for the simple reason that those people will never even see it. You could write the most incredible alpha/beta/omega story in the universe with the goal of winning over people who think they hate ABO, but guess what? Those people will never even click on it! You *have* to ignore your nos. In the fanfic world, you are left alone with your potential yeses – all the people who share your taste, the people who subscribe and kudos and comment to you, the ones who (for some crazy reason) like the shape of your brain and want to read more from you.

What I realized, after writing and posting fanfic weekly and sometimes almost daily, was that this is an attitude you can *learn*. It hurts a little, at first, to realize that there's nothing you can do to convince someone else to like your stuff – even if your stuff is just crack fanfiction. But after a while, with practice, it hurts less. With even more practice, it can be extrapolated to other areas of your life. Someone doesn't like my playing? Doesn't want to hire me? Okay. I hope they find the thing they do like. There's something out there for everybody.

ONLY THE SELF

Here's the terrible, awful truth about doing something difficult well: the best way to achieve the kind of success that aligns with conventional metrics, is to let go of the need for success as defined by anything other than your own performance relative to your abilities.

Why do I say 'awful?' Because, despite the woo-woo sound of it, letting go of the need for external success is the most difficult and necessary thing that a person can do in pursuit of excellence. The necessity of it is visible in the sincere attitudes of almost all the world's truly outstanding achievers. Simone Biles – unquestionably the world's best gymnast, and arguably the most dominant athlete in the world in any sport – stated, two months before the 2016 Rio Olympics in which she won four gold medals, "A successful competition for me is always going out there and putting 100 percent into whatever I'm doing. It's not always winning. People, I think, mistake that it's just winning. Sometimes it could be, but for me it's hitting the best sets I can, gaining confidence and having a good time and having fun."[1] She's not just being modest. Over and over again, the world's top athletes state sincerely that the only opponent they truly need to best is themselves.

In daily life, however, a lot gets in the way of truly being able to embrace that idea. First and foremost is how much we all care. No matter what you do daily, if it makes you at all anxious, chances are that's because you care deeply about it. How can you care deeply about what you're doing, while not minding whether or not it lives up to conventional standards of quality?

In Anne Jamison's book *Fic: Why Fanfiction Is Taking Over the World*, venerable Holmes/Watson author Katie Forsythe sums up her motivation to write fanfiction: "The stories aren't for readers, they're for me and my noisy, noisy head, and then when people read them and enjoy them or even come away feeling a bit better, that's a completely unexpected bonus. Charging money for them would be like having heart surgery and then billing the doctor for the privilege of working on me."

This is a common attitude in fandom, or at least an attitude that everyone knows represents the *ideal* relationship to fanworks: that they should be written for you and you alone. Although of course it's still not as simple as it seems, writing fanfiction for you alone can feel easier than doing other kinds of artistic work for you alone, because the entire setup of the fandom community leads to fic-writing being as consequence-free as possible. Nobody gets rich or loses their shirt over the popularity or obscurity of their fanfic. Readers are actively encouraged to stop reading a story that they don't like the instant they realize they don't like it, so you as a writer can be sure that you're not forcing your work onto anyone unwilling.

Competing with and creating for yourself is a difficult skill that gets easier with practice. Not caring what other people think of you is a muscle that gets stronger with exercise, and writing fanfiction is the best exercise in the world for it. I have found that since starting to write fic regularly, and especially after getting comfortable with the type of fandom fest that involves prompts or quick turnover times, I am less self-conscious in general. Every time I hit post on a fic while thinking, "Hey, if everyone but me hates this, they're free to not read it!" it makes it a little bit easier to do the same in my career, my other hobbies, and my social life.

When most people think of sports coaching or performance psychology, they imagine pressure: high expectations, no second chances, and little tolerance for failure. The reality, as I discovered in music school, is exactly the opposite. The fandom community was right all along. Being kind to yourself gets better results than being cutthroat, you have to enjoy your own work if you want anyone else to, and embracing failure is the path to success.

Tei is a fan, professional musician, and hobby gymnast in the Canadian prairies.

1 Axon, Rachel, "Simone Biles doesn't let expectations overwhelm her." USA Today, 2 June 2016

FANDOM AND FINDING (OR ACCEPTING) YOUR SEXUALITY
Jamie Ashbird

I'm not sure if there is a better playground for exploring sexuality, gender, or identity, than fandom. Play is an integral part of learning and that is what fandom is to me. A place to enjoy, play, learn, explore.

Let me tell you a little story about entering puberty in the 1990s, in the middle of Italo-Hellene suburbia. When the high school computer room was full of decade old Apple Macintosh IIs and a couple of Commodore 64s. A time when dial-up was dependent on whether your parents were waiting on an important phone call and how patient you were for a single grainy picture to download. Wikipedia was called Encarta, was on a disc, and came with a trivia game set in a medieval castle that held far more appeal than anything the internet had to offer to the uninitiated.

A kid like me would have loved the unbelievably creative outlet that is fandom now. I would have had a Tumblr feed full of X-Files gifs, and probably would have written a ton of Faith/Angel/Buffy fic after having cut my teeth on some solid Rimmer/Lister. Maybe I'd have kept writing after high school instead of giving it up. Maybe I'd have kept drawing. Most importantly, maybe I wouldn't have spent more than twenty-five years of my life drifting, depressed, bitter, lonely because there was something wrong with me and I didn't know what. How can you fill a chasm when you don't know what's missing?

When puberty struck and I witnessed the burgeoning sexuality of my friends and peers around me, I had nothing – no point of reference, no information, certainly no representation to guide me into realizing I wasn't a mutant, or slow, or broken.

A female friend snuck into the loos with a male friend and asked me to keep watch. Innocent little me had no idea what they were doing in there. Maybe they were inspecting the taps. Turned out they were just having a snog. I couldn't understand the appeal.

Later in high school when everyone started pairing off and whispers of "they *did it*" went around, my main thoughts were that people should mind their own business, and more distantly, ew.

Compounding my lack of sexual desire for anyone, was the fact that I had a pair of working eyeballs and an appreciation of aesthetic beauty. I knew I tripped some happy brain chemicals staring at pictures of Eddie Vedder and Chris Cornell and their perfect grungy hair, hell I even dressed like them. I knew that I enjoyed watching *Don't Tell Mom The Babysitter's Dead* because I loved looking at Christina Applegate who was just as pretty as Josh Charles. Alyssa Milano was clearly the most beautiful girl in the world in *Who's The Boss*, but I neither wanted to be her or do her. Or anyone else for that matter.

It was getting on well into my university years when I began to despair that I hadn't developed that part of me that wanted to have sex with someone, anyone. Something was clearly wrong because all the evidence around me said so. I remember wishing so hard to be 'normal.' Crying myself to sleep some nights in despair that I would never be. I remember watching Edina in *Absolutely Fabulous* wishing Saffy was gay, because that would make her interesting. It was a silly joke but the thought stuck with me. I started wishing I was gay because that would be *something*. It was a known parameter, it was a thing that existed and would put me on solid ground. Alas, no amount of wishing makes a thing so.

But then the door to understanding was suddenly unlocked. Not opened, but all I had to do was give it a shove. It was some time in 2009 when in a discussion about writing, a young whippersnapper explained to me what fanfiction, fandoms, and Tumblr were. I began to dabble. Jokingly at first, I wrote a *Supernatural* crack fic as a writing exercise, began reading some Harry Potter fic (stumbling on the legend that was "My Immortal"). The door handle was turning.

After a trip to London to visit my sister in 2010 and a very enthusiastic appeal from her to watch this brand new show that had just aired with that guy from *The Office* in it, I flew off home to the antipodes with a suitcase full of tea, chocolate, and a note to check for when this *Sherlock* show would air here. It seemed never (read: months), so I did what any self respecting Martin Freeman and Sherlock Holmes fan would do, and bought the DVD from Amazon UK.

I loved it. The show was slick, and new, and clever. The new Sherlock was a strange beautiful alien creature and he was clearly in love with his Watson. Even I could see that. But unlike many, I took Sherlock for his word when he said he wasn't interested in that kind of thing. Why? Because I know what it's like to have people assume they know my mind better than I do. The ones who tell you, about anything that deviates from society's norm, "Oh you'll change your mind one day." How about, fuck off. So I listened to this Sherlock.

> "For the first time ever, I'd encountered words describing things I had felt and thought...and in a way that gently took me by the hand and said, this is okay. You're okay"

And that was it – I fell head over heels into my very first fandom. And what a fandom.

I was in my early 30s and had no idea, no understanding of why I was the person I was, nor who I was. Why couldn't I just be 'normal' like the people around me were? So I took my new-found love for a brilliant, innovative TV series, my new-found knowledge of the existence of fanfiction and fandom culture, and dived deep into anywhere the stories existed. LiveJournal, Fanfiction.net, Archive of Our Own (AO3). It was in the rather more organized latter that I found the thing that stunned me. Asexuality.

Listen, I studied biology and microbiology – I knew the word asexual but not in any way that pertained to me, or human people in general. Maybe I was asleep that day, my lectures were stupid early in second year anyway.

Fact is, until I began to read fanfiction I didn't know. I didn't know there was a name for me. I didn't know there were other people who were like me. I didn't know I wasn't a disappointing and freakish anomaly. Now I can say, years later, that labels don't define me, I'd rather not be boxed in, but holy shitting arsing fuck did I need something, *anything* to grab onto back then.

This, this is why when speaking about the asexual experience, it often starts with finding out, 1) you are not a broken thing, and 2) you are not alone. Because if there's one thing growing up like this was, it's lonely – especially pre-internet, especially pre-this amazing connectivity we all have today. Fucking lonely as all hell. And hand-in-hand with the loneliness comes the terror of feeling like that forever.

Because you look at a room full of your peers, all of whom are paired off and think, *why don't I have that,* at the same time as thinking *I'm not sure if I want that.*

Because a boy you've never spoken to at a high school party asks if you want to be his girlfriend and you don't know what to say because a) you've never been kissed and you think you ought to have been by now and b) god you really don't want this person to touch you.

Because you think you might as well give sex a go when you have the chance, just to see, even if you have zero *sexual* attraction to this person who is kind of fun to hang out with and, hmm, no.

Because you're constantly bombarded by the social constructs that tell you you ought to want this, desire that, feel this, strive for that and you simply do not.

Because you mistake wanting to be 'normal' for wanting the sort of relationship you don't actually want.

It's exhausting and terrifying, and it's so so lonely. And I'd been tired and terrified and lonely for more than twenty-five years.

So, imagine. Imagine floundering in the open ocean, keeping your head just above water. You long for your feet to find something solid beneath you, you've been treading that water an awful long time. Suddenly, just as your arms and legs have given up and your head is going under for the last time, a life-raft smacks you in the face. That was what discovering the existence of the spectrum of asexuality was like. And that life-raft was BBC *Sherlock* and its fanfiction.

I won't go too far into my annoyance at the difference between the restaurant scene in the unaired pilot and the first episode A Study in Pink, when John Watson is probing Sherlock about his relationship status. When Sherlock emphasizes "I'm really not looking for any *kind* of…" and in A Study in Pink only mumbles it. That emphasis in the pilot said to me, he's kind of like you. He's busy being all detective-y and getting his clothes tailored. He's not interested in that sort of thing. At all. Any *kind* of it. That's what he said, that's what you'd say! And then in A Study in Pink they snatched that away from me. That one miniscule bit of representation. Sure, I didn't know until the DVD extras were in my clammy little hands, but I retroactively felt it was stolen from me, just like Katniss Everdeen was, damn it. Shush you, just let me have this one entitled thing!

Now don't get me wrong, I was a happy little demon for all things Johnlockian. For femlock, translock, all the head canons. But that was the joy of the fanfic and fan theories. Fanfic was a party everyone was invited to. But the show for me was a love story between a probably bisexual man and an aromantic asexual man. It was the most beautiful thing I'd ever seen. Okay, maybe not. But it was close!

I can't remember now, exactly, when it first hit me. Back in 2010 and 2011 I was devouring this new fangled thing (to me) called fanfic like a starving whale shark. There were after all, only three episodes of *Sherlock* to hang onto and damn it man, Sherlock and John needed to Sort Themselves Out! But I know within a certain tolerance just what and who it was that hit out at me and made me seek more and more. Crazy as it sounds, these were proper stories. Good stories. Great stories.

First off the rank (because I have certain tendencies and like to read chronologically for peace of mind) was mresundance's "Unusual Symmetry" series on AO3:

> *"And I do like – certain kinds of touching. Just not – sex. Or anything sexual. And kissing for me is not like kissing is for you."*
>
> *"It's not sexual?"*
>
> *"Correct. It's more – tactile. Enjoying sensations and enjoying that you enjoy them. But it isn't connected to desiring you. Not sexually."*

You can see what happened here right? To poor sad naïve little me in my tiny little mind? For the first time ever, I'd encountered words describing things I had felt and thought. Or didn't feel and think. And in a way that gently took me by the hand and said, this is okay. You're okay. You exist and you're not alone. And it didn't stop there.

> *"Desire is in here for me," he tapped his head. "Not the body. I love your body because it's yours, because it's part of you. But I'd still love you if you were a woman who smelled like – boiled cabbage –"*

(mresundance, Luminosity, Archive of Our Own)

Talk about dizzy making. Desire…can just be in the head? But… but that's me, she cried. And I did. Cry that is. Maybe not at this specific fic but I was being inundated with new information that I never considered existed. That chasm inside me? I thought maybe I'd found what was missing. So yeah, I did a lot of crying.

After came the exquisite "Thermodynamics" series by entanglednow, also on AO3:

> *"You're comfortable," Sherlock offers at last, slowly and quietly, as if admitting the fact that he caved to sensation is something scandalous.*

This series that was like a slow warm rain of comfort. What revelations! What a notion! That there could be the possibility of people who would love me and just...let me be me? It couldn't possibly be. Books and television and movies never said so. Or did they? Was my only choice to be the Spinster Aunt? The ridiculed and pitiable Old Maid? But enough about poor representation in mainstream media, fanfiction has my back.

The learning and revelations didn't end there. Oh no. Because then came "In the Body" by aceofhearts61 on AO3 and yes!

He doesn't need to think of another person, he doesn't need porn, he doesn't need any kind of sexual fantasy. His pleasure is self-given, self-evoked, self-contained.

Yes, exactly, yes! I wasn't incapable of arousal, but past a certain point it didn't require anything other than me. Which is not to say the ideas of others – these stories – weren't arousing. Boy, is this hard to describe!

He is absolutely, ineffably in love with Sherlock Holmes.
And he never wants to shag him.
Which is fortunate – because Sherlock feels just the same
(aceofhearts61, A Love with No Name, Archive of Our Own)

And he never wants to shag him. And he never wants to...and Sherlock feels just the same. Right. Okay. Right. So. People could ostensibly be in love with one another and not be shagging? A couple, together in loving companionship and no sex. This...is this real? Is this? What? I was shaken to the core. This all seems so very obvious now, I'm sure will evoke a few eyerolls. But before this I was in utter darkness, naïve to be sure. From what society had shown me, everyone had or wanted to have sex. Whatever the genders of the participants, society told me it's what people do.

Yes. Kissing John. That, he wanted to try. Now that John said he wanted to as well. It was allowed. And maybe after, his curiosity would be sated and he wouldn't want to again. And maybe he would. It was interesting not to know the answer to something.
(221B_Hound, Unkissed, Archive of Our Own)

Now what? What here now? Being unsure is allowed too? Wanting to try something to make sure, and being okay either way? These are also allowed? Again, perhaps my naiveté was off the scales but just like Jon Snow, I knew nothing. Everyone else seemed to be loud and proud about anything and everything. Here I was not knowing that not knowing was okay. That growing and learning while doing is perfectly fine.

"The Unkissed" series by 221B_Hound, the "Unbiased Observations" series by theimprobable1 and anything anything *anything* by aceofhearts61, a smattering of others so gratefully consumed – I read these reeling at the recognition and the possibilities and the hope they gave someone as information- and community-starved as I was. They were the kindling that helped me seek out more information – though that itself was a long and timid journey. I had the link to the AVEN website saved for so long. It was the opening of that link that was hard to do. I was scared. Actually physiologically frightened to do it to the point of anxiety-induced nausea. I've often wondered why and I think it's because it was all so new and fragile – this seeing myself in fic – that I was scared to find out I was wrong. That this wasn't who I was. The thought of going back to that state of being nothing, a non-entity, terrified me enough that I couldn't even click a god-damned link. So I kept on reading fic and eventually I got braver, in more ways than one. After years of lurking, I finally found the courage to message and talk to other humans in the fandom. Imagine that!

It may have taken me a long time, but with a little help from one of the most open and friendly fandoms I've ever encountered, I got there. And I'm still going. First 'asexual' was like a revelation, then like a Magic Eye picture slowly coming into focus, demisexual became a possibility. I'm not sex-repulsed, maybe I could be sexually attracted to someone I got to know and love. And then the idea of aegosexual came drifting into my periphery and I thought hmm, yeah okay maybe. But in truth, I think I've found a balance and a peace in not being entirely sure of everything, in being okay with whatever feeling or emotion or desire pops up at any given moment. The growth and learning are constant.

"I abhor society's need to stick a label on every little thing…"
(tocourtdisaster, The Naming of Things, Archive of Our Own)

Maybe the term I prefer most is fluid. It leaves room to just damn well *be* whoever I damn well am. Whether that's framed by sexuality or gender. And there's another thing. I'm trying to understand more about gender fluidity and gender norms. Because I just don't seem to understand or experience 'womanhood' as it's portrayed at me. I never have. Does that mean anything? I don't know yet, but I'm willing to find out.

Maybe there's a fic I could read.

Jamie Ashbird is a polymath (because she likes that word) and a writer (because she says so) who haunts Melbourne. She had her very first published story – a 221B – included in the Improbable Press anthology A Murmuring of Bees, *and went on to write* A Question of Time *for Improbable. You can find Jamie checking under mushrooms for fairies, coveting moss, staring at sky kittens (clouds), squinching her eyes shut as she walks past a book shop, adding more projects to her pile of craft ideas, learning Norwegian for when she retires there as a small troll in the woods, and doing her gosh-darn best not to eat ice-cream.*

Hope is the whole point of fanfiction.

— Seanan McGuire
Hugo award-winning writer of
Down Among the Sticks and Bones

BOLDLY GOING WHERE NO AMPUTEE HAS GONE BEFORE: OR HOW I LEARNED TO STOP WORRYING AND LOVE SELF-INSERT OCS
Sebastian Jack

I'd never enjoyed self-insert original characters in fanfiction. I'd never enjoyed the way they always seemed forced right into the center of the action, lacking any and all flaws, as unconditionally beloved by every in-world character as they are by the author themselves. They were *obviously* self-insert. *Obviously* out-of-place.

As a teenager, I ran to fanfiction because I wanted to read about what happened before the story, or what happened afterwards. I wanted to know what those fascinating, underrepresented secondary characters were up to while the protagonists were locked in mortal combat for the fate of the universe. Did they not also triumph, suffer, laugh, and love? Who cares about what the author thinks they'd do, benefitted by knowledge of the meta-narrative, when the doomsday clock is ticking down at the climax?

No, I couldn't abide self-insert original characters (OC), not one bit.

And then I got my legs ripped off by a train.

Let me be clear: I was asking for it. Every single person in my life told me explicitly *not* to jump onto moving freight trains for fun. But I was 17, caught up in the vicious cycle of suicidal-yet-indestructible, and I was lured in by the good old-fashioned, all-American romance of the rails. For about two weeks, I was Jack fucking Kerouac. I was Patti Smith, I was Iggy Pop. I was a gonzo punk-poet hobo in platform combat boots, draped in chains, with a set of brass knuckles confidently in-hand. Riding the rails I'd never felt more alive, or more dead.

Then, one blistering summer night, I overheard a stranger talking in a coffee shop about train hopping across the state, and I asked him to take me with him. Of course, he refused. His exact words were, "No, I'm not taking you with me. Do you know how many people get their legs cut off, trying to jump trains?" (Incidentally, this is as good an illustration as any that foreshadowing, while often quite obvious to the reader, is seldom as obvious to the characters.) But I ignored his warnings, and after enough time, I wore him down.

Eighteen hours later, that stranger would save my life when a failed jump sent me stumbling beneath the wheels of a freight train. Just as he'd warned me, both of my legs were severed above the knee.

Yes, I was awake. Yes, I remember. Yes. It hurt.

No, I didn't know a human body contained that much blood.

In those minutes when I was bleeding out onto the tracks, I heard Tyler Durden tell me, "This is the greatest moment of your life, man, and you're off somewhere missing it."

So, I kept my eyes open, and I watched as the stranger from the coffee shop stopped my bleeding with a pair of improvised tourniquets that he carried in his backpack. I kept my eyes open when the paramedics gathered me up in three distinct pieces, neatly piling my severed limbs onto the gurney with me. I kept my eyes open for the entire ambulance ride, each bump in the road triggering a fresh jab of terror and agony.

They had to anesthetize me in the ER, just to get me to shut up.

When you're lying in a hospital bed, shifting deliriously from surgery to surgery, with a feeding tube taped to your face and your body bandaged from the waist down, even a month-long stay feels like an eternity. Awareness was agony, in those days. But every time I closed my eyes, I dreamed of white splinters on a red background. No distraction. No relief, no shield. Just loneliness, and the crushing knowledge of the permanence of what I'd done.

As it turns out, all the rooms in that particular children's hospital came equipped with an Xbox – a fact I only learned years later. My parents had strictly forbidden the nurses from telling me. So, in a way, this is really all their fault.

Devoid of any other entertainment, *desperate*, I did what any right-thinking person would've done: I became a Trekkie.

I wasn't a fan of the show prior, not by any stretch. But I'd been meaning to watch Next Generation for months. I'd seen the memes. So, stuck in the hospital with nothing else to do, I watched it.

And I watched it.

And I watched it.

Over.

And over.

And over.

I learned every word, every beat, every plotline by heart.

> "Devoid of any other entertainment, *desperate*, I did what any right-thinking person would've done: I became a Trekkie"

Because, amidst the parade of yellow, red, and blue on my laptop screen, I saw a world that I longed to inhabit.

Much in the way that Star Trek: The Original Series provided women and people of color (and women of color) a dose of long-overdue and much-needed representation in the 60s, Next Generation gave representation to people with disabilities. This is a world where the chief engineer of Starfleet's flagship is a blind, Black man. When the show begins, Geordi La Forge uses an assistive device to see (his VISOR), but by the end, he has prosthetic eyes. This is a world where Dr. Crusher et al manage to *grow a new spinal cord* when Worf is paralyzed in an accident. Even the Borg Queen, villain though she may be, is just a human head in a prosthetic body.

Maybe Q could just…snap his fingers and give me my legs back.

Gradually, the dreams of red and white splinters began to fade, replaced by the calm tan of Picard's bridge. My dreams glittered with stars, refracted through pale pink dilithium crystals. I crafted

Romulan peace treaties, and crept silently along the liminal, green corridors of Borg cubes. I shielded my gaze against the light of 40 Eridani A, craning to glimpse the L-langon Mountains as they shimmered in the blistering heat across Vulcan Forge.

But, when I opened my eyes, when I looked away from the screen, I was still in my hospital bed. Still in agony. Still broken. And there was still no one to blame but myself.

I couldn't handle being who I was, or where I was. So, I opened a Word document, and I invented someone who could.

I was not a writer. I still don't think I am. But I *was* the star pupil of my AP Literary Analysis course in high school, *and* I got a 5 on the final exam and essay. (A perfect score. I know, I know – please do hold your applause.) And isn't that the most important piece? Understanding what makes great writing, before you even begin? I certainly believed that.

So began the saga of Commander Citlalic T'pal Scout, tactician and chief of security to the Enterprise-D. Half-Vulcan, but her name comes from the Aztec Nahuatl language. It means "rising star."

Listen, I never said this was a story about a *good* story.

But the main element of this particular story that I've come to appreciate over the years, the one thing I've found myself picking apart and psychoanalyzing, is that it's written in first-person, present tense. (*"When I am notified of an unauthorized shuttlecraft departure, I attempt to lock on with a tractor beam. When I find that the tractor beam has been disabled, and my personal command override is nonfunctional, my heart plummets in my chest. Only one person aboard this ship would be able to do that."*)

I realize now that I wrote it that way because I couldn't bear to look backwards, and I couldn't begin to imagine my future. All I knew was a series of inescapable here-and-nows.

I realize now that I wrote it that way because I couldn't stand those here-and-nows, and fanfiction provided me with a way to journal. *Without* journaling.

Commander Scout's journey begins around the end of Season

1, when she replaces Tasha Yar as the bridge tactician and chief of security aboard the Enterprise-D. A main, recurring plot element in this saga involves the fact that our protagonist is a de-assimilated Borg drone; sort of a beta 7 of 9. On the off chance that you don't know (I'll forgive you), and in my character's own words, "*The Borg are a hive mind… They move from planet to planet assimilating cultures and technologies into their collective consciousness. Selected humanoid life forms are mechanized into drones…via cybernetic implants… Once someone has been assimilated, the Borg knows everything they know. So, when you fight even one drone, you're fighting an enemy with all the knowledge and experience of millions, perhaps billions of individual life forms.*"

This is where her cybernetic legs came from, you see. From *trauma*. Because there was no way in hell that I was going to let *that* goldmine of self-relatability and wishful thinking slip through the cracks.

Citlalic hails from a small, industrial planet in the Gamma Quadrant, far from Federation space. When the Borg attacked, only a handful of her people survived, and even fewer were untethered from the collective. But, after extensive de-programming and microsurgery, our protagonist was liberated. But the legs, she kept.

"*What is it like, to depend on them every day?*" [Picard] *gestures towards my legs.*

"*Difficult to reconcile, at first. But I've come to think of them as a trophy of war.*"

He smiles faintly. "*Not a very Vulcan attitude.*"

I shake my head. "*No. But it's what gets me by. They tried to kill me. They tried to suck the life out of me…*" *I linger on the words, tasting their bitterness on my tongue,* "*But I survived, despite them. And now I walk around, every day, dependent on their technology… Battle scars,*" *I insist,* "*I'm stronger for having them.*"

The Captain nods, brow knitted together.

"*I have my demons,*" *I tell him,* "*You will too. Most of the time, they're silent. But when they talk… How they can howl.*"

I think, like me, Citlalic is quite tortured. She wonders why *she* was the lucky one who got rescued, when there have been so many countless others who deserved it more.

After the attack on her home world, she made her way Earthward, and was sworn to secrecy by the Federation.

"Why?" Picard asks.

"Starfleet felt that the Borg were too far from Federation space to pose any reasonable threat, and they determined that it wasn't worth causing a panic over. Why frighten people on Earth into preparing for an apocalypse that may never come? That's why my records had been sealed, until now.'"

Sound logic. If you're a 17-year-old on a ton of painkillers, pretending desperately that you're a Vulcan.

As I sat, hunched over my laptop in my hospital bed, I found myself falling into every single trope and cliché that I thought I despised. Citlalic is good at all the things that I'm not: math and science, primarily. And her culture has taught her to view emotion through an objective, logical lens, and discard the feelings that are of no utility to her.

That skill was especially idealized for me, at the time.

I wrote myself into all my favorite episodes. Q Who, The Offspring, The Best of Both Worlds. I, Borg. Time's Arrow. Descent. (I was a fan of the season-spanning two-parters, clearly.) And that's only scratching the surface. Whenever there was series-defining action, Citlalic was there: right in the middle of it. I put subtitles on and pressed pause over and over, transcribing hours of dialogue. I re-assigned lines upon lines of script to my original character, and added even more. A decade later, I'll admit that Citlalic's integration into the show is rather forced – in all the ways I despised as a reader. But in the moment, it felt entirely seamless. *I* believed it.

I *had* to believe it.

Even after her admittedly rocky start (arriving to replace a dead woman, her sealed service records, and the first encounter with the Borg when the truth comes out) everyone on the Enterprise gradually comes to love and respect Commander Scout. I think there was a part of me that was yearning desperately for a clean slate – for someone to look at my scars and my mistakes and agree to let me move on from them. I needed someone to see me and understand that *what I've become is not about them.*

And then, after a month, I was suddenly back at my parents' house. In hindsight, it all happened so fast: the accident, the hospital, the wheelchair, and then…home. I learned very, very quickly that home was not where I wanted to be. There's this association that I think every healthy, able-bodied person holds that being released from the hospital means you're better. You're cured. But I was released from the hospital because there was no cure. I was as good as I was ever going to get.

That was my life.

I was home, and I still had no legs.

Forever.

No. I wasn't ready to be *me*, yet, not in this world that's so frightening and so painful.

I kept writing.

Citlalic got promoted. She learned Klingon. A horrifying encounter with Lore (an evil android with a penchant for liberated Borg drones) saw her re-fitted with newer, better legs. She set foot on Vulcan for the first time, only to learn that her father had been considered something of a black sheep, and that the scarcity of "half-breeds" like her and Spock had led to some strange prejudices among the citizens.

Meanwhile, in the painful, real world, my girlfriend of three years left me. This wasn't what she signed up for, she said, and I was different. I *was* different. *Of course*, I had been changed by this. But then again, *I absolutely hadn't*, and *why couldn't she see that?*

That's how Citlalic fell in love with Lieutenant Commander Data, the Enterprise's resident android.

At one point, he asks her, "*Is that to say that, if I were to change, you would no longer love me? Is your affection contingent upon my current state of being?*"

"*No*," she replies, "*What I'm saying is that I will always love you, as you are, whether you change or not. I don't want you to be any different, nor will I ever ask you to be. But I'll love you no matter what."*

Incidentally, I adore writing Data. I adore getting to think like him, and predict his reactions. He's probably my favorite person I've ever gotten to pretend to be.

Eventually, he does ask her to marry him.

I think that, in those hard, first months, I craved consistency. I craved predictable, on-sided emotional support, unclouded by the emotionality of the people around me. I didn't have time to worry about how everyone else was coping, and it was so, *so* draining to pretend to be strong for their sake. That's a selfish thing to admit, I know. And it's a thought I've kept entirely to myself, until this exact moment in time.

But Citlalic knew. She understood.

"I suppose... The emotionlessness is what I need," she says of her partner, *"I'm part Vulcan, and a very self-sufficient person. I always have been. I don't often have emotional needs that I can't handle by myself, and when I do, I've found that Data is... Perfect. He puts things into perspective for me, and keeps me grounded when I'm losing focus."*

Wishful thinking, on many, many fronts.

When Data's latent dream program is activated by an accidental burst of energy from an alien machine, Citlalic is there to help him understand. When he builds himself a daughter, she's there to help him teach her. She's there when he meets his brothers (prototype androids of the same design), and when his emotion chip is finally installed. She saves his life more times than I can count, as he does hers. And, yes: it does get fluffy. (As fluffy as a naturally-emotionless robot and a Vulcan can get with one another, anyway.)

"'I have noted that you are exceptionally concerned for my safety," Data says. *An awkward attempt to acknowledge my feelings.*

I continue to move around the room, inputting commands into the computer, running pre-diagnostics, establishing a baseline reading.

"I've come too close to losing you, too many times," I explain, *emotionlessly, "I'd like to marry you someday, Commander."*

Slowly, reality became more bearable. *My* story went on, despite me. (Resistance is futile, as any ex-Borg can tell you.) And, by the time I'd started my first real job, post-legs, Citlalic had been promoted to Captain.

But her true test comes when she finds herself re-assimilated during First Contact. That's the only piece of the writing that I'm genuinely proud of. It represents a stark facing of very rational fears, and a confrontation of the dark crucible in which all of Citlalic's strength and all her vulnerability had been forged.

There are no passages that I can bring myself to share from that section. What happens, and the meaning behind it, will remain between Citlalic and me.

I worked on that story for six years, off and on. Whenever I felt weak, or out of control, I relinquished the bridge to Citlalic and let her drive for a while. As it stands, the story is 87,818 words – easily the length of a novel. To this day, no one else has ever read it. You won't find it on Archive of Our Own, or Fanfiction.net, nor will you ever. The excerpts I've included here are the most I've ever shared. Not even my wife has read it.

Instead, the story remains as a 175-page word document saved to my laptop, entitled simply, "*Citlalic*."

I haven't added to this particular fanfiction in years. I doubt I will again. I don't *need* her, anymore. But the story will remain as a private chronicle of those hard, terrible times; the times when that 17-year-old amputee was too frightened to face his own world, so he asked Citlalic Scout to do it for him.

I think, like so many people, I sought solace and belonging in fiction when there was none to be found in reality. In fiction, the problems are already solved for us. Even if the solutions are messy and imperfect, we can trust that everything will be all right in the end because *it has already been written*. Someone else slogged through the hard parts for us, and the conclusion is assured.

To create fan works, on the other hand, is to sacrifice that comfort and familiarity and instead face your own reflection in the stories you love. It's like climbing into someone else's sandbox for a while, and daring to knock down a few of the castles to make room for your own: new creations, just as perfect and terrifying and assuaging as you need them to be. It's an act of defiance and bravery, and a fierce re-taking of agency for those of us who have, for too long, been denied it.

Rather, think of it this way: through fiction, we can fall in love with brilliant, impossible people, and watch in awe as they do such brilliant, impossible things. Through fanfiction, we can join them on their quests. A hospital bed becomes a Captain's chair, and a trip to the physical therapy room is an away mission. And then maybe, even if it's just for one beautiful spark of time, the boundary between the fictional world and the painful reality fades entirely from sight. It's a form of magic we all have the capacity to wield. And if you're careful, you can catch that spark in your hands and cling to its warmth forever.

To this day, I still see Citlalic when I look at the stars.

Sebastian Jack is the legless offspring of a Victorian chest containing untold secrets, and a very noisy piece of industrial machinery. He's never met an android, cryptid, gentle forest boy, witch, glam rocker, or Sith he didn't fall in love with. He lives on the top of a mountain with his wife, and their hairless cat named Chuck. This year he's also a first-time published novelist with his book Electric Blue.

Xena and Gabrielle by Lucy W

TRANSFORMATIVE
Andrea L Farley (aka Altocello)

Since I knew I had hands, I've painted and drawn. But to call myself an artist seemed to imply a mastery, a depth of skill and experience, that I didn't feel I had, and wasn't sure how I could, in my daily life as a wife and mother, ever achieve.

So it's not an exaggeration to say that my participation in fandoms over the years, creating transformative works, eventually led to my own transformation, helping me remake my self identity.

That's because fandom gave me the opportunity to explore the idea of myself as an artist, and, critically, fandom gave me a space where I had *permission*.

Permission to make whatever I wanted, for whatever reason. I was allowed to play with my creativity, like kids do. What I made didn't need to be tied to some sense of "artistic purpose;" it didn't have to mean anything, other than that making it made me happy. It didn't have to make any money; I could make as much or as little as I had the time and inclination for, and I wasn't dependent on the approval of anyone else to create income from it to pay the bills.

Freed from the stress of those expectations, I found myself more than willing to experiment with subjects, materials, and techniques that I never would have attempted otherwise. I've never taken a figure drawing course, but I played with full body poses, clothed and unclothed. I drew lovers embracing, men in corsets, played with mirroring poses, symbolic representations, line art a la Art Nouveau, photorealism…pencil, ink, chalk pastel. I even did a couple of pieces where I drew line art with a sepia pen and used coffee as a watercolor. When I got tired of the effort it took to take and edit photos of my traditional art pieces in order to share them online, I taught myself how to paint digitally, and discovered a whole new world to explore.

All of this meant that, when art was the only way I felt like I could hold onto my sanity in 2020, I knew I could paint a nearly endless series of portraits of one actor, just because it made me happy, and nobody would chastise me for having an inappropriate hyperfixation, or look at me like I had grown a second head. One of the many beautiful things about fandom is that what makes you happy, probably makes someone else happy too. And thanks to the wonders of tagging and searches, it really literally is, "if you make it they will come." I made it, it was found by those searching for it, and the joy reflected back to me via comments and replies inspired me to make more. A lot more!

Whereas my singular focus would have been tolerated, at best, by those who happen to be around me in "real life," fandom welcomed it with open arms, thrilled to have someone consistently creating new art of the subject they also found captivating. At my busiest, I was making and sharing a portrait study every couple of days. Andy Warhol had Campbell's soup cans; I have Adam Driver. It turns out that, with sufficient motivation, I did have time in my life to begin a daily art practice. And, as any teacher will tell you, practice is what hones the skills that talent lays in your hands; it's not an exaggeration to say that I'm almost exponentially better at portraiture after the last couple of years.

It was the artistic equivalent of releasing a goldfish into a full sized pond; by imagining myself as a fully realized artist, I became one.

Back in 2009, if you had asked me if I was an artist, I would have said, "I'm artistic, but I'm not an artist," in the same way that I still correct "musician" to "musical," and "writer" to "not terrible with words." In truth, I probably am all of those things. I'm still coming to grips with musician and writer, but, after thirteen years of consistently creating fan art, I feel like I can finally claim the identity of *artist* for myself. All of those pieces that I made for myself and shared, just because I thought someone else might like to see them too, became a de facto portfolio. And that portfolio caught the attention of someone who asked if I might consider making a book cover, which in turn led to me being asked to make three more covers, and some internal illustrations, and lo! Suddenly a dream I had as a child, something I thought could never actually come to pass, is now a reality. I can say that I'm a published, professional, artist.

Of course, I was an artist all along; getting paid to make a piece doesn't make someone more of an artist, or a writer, or a musician, it just means they got paid. What makes someone a creator is the act of creation, and money has nothing to do with that. But to have somebody eager to exchange something of value for a piece that you made, that is a special feeling, an extra cherry on top of the external validation cake; not only did they *like* what I made, they wanted to *buy* it.

"practice is what hones the skills that talent lays in your hands"

It's a failing that society suffers from this perception that to make any kind of art one must, with very little training or practice, have somehow perfected all the skills associated with producing it. That you have to be 'talented.' As adults, we're not allowed to be imperfect, to sing the song with gusto and out of key simply for the joy of singing, to make the endearingly crooked painting of the dog. It's an embarrassment to produce anything other than polished pop perfection, an embarrassment so severe that we won't even try to produce *anything*.

This relentless rejection of work that doesn't fit the ideal is an incredible disservice to young people, because kids learn by mimicking the adults they love, and they learn by playing; by trying, and failing, and trying again. Kids with family members who sing or play instruments around the house are given the opportunity to see impromptu music making; they see their loved one having fun making music and want to play too, and in doing so, they gain the musical competency they need to become musicians themselves. Not everyone has someone in the house who sings, or paints, or writes (or all three!), and so they don't get to explore those sides of themselves as children. And even those who did still have so much room for growth through their lives; learning doesn't stop when we graduate from school, it's a lifelong adventure, and so is acquiring and practicing skills. We give kids permission to be imperfect when they're learning; we should extend the same grace to ourselves as adults.

Thankfully, fandom exists as a place that enables this kind of creative growth for folks of all ages. Instead of fostering an attitude that considers art something to only be consumed by the majority of people, I've found that the best parts of fandom view creativity as the open conversation that it can be, where joy sparks creativity that sparks further joy and further creativity in an endless beautiful giving circle.

Fandom gave me the chance to imagine myself as an artist. It gave me the space to try, and fail, and try again, and again, and *again,* while the people I found there gave me helpful hints and cheered me on. It provided the motivation I needed to prioritize my time so that I could keep creating. It encouraged me to fully be my entirely too enthusiastic self in a way that I didn't feel I could in my real life as a wife and a mother.

And so, I am proud to be able to say, "I am an artist." And it's all thanks to the incredibly positive, uplifting, enabling, and transformative wonder that is fandom.

Andrea L Farley is an artist, writer, and amateur musician with a license to practice pharmacy who fell into her dream job of illustrating book covers and interiors by way of creating a series of over 100 portrait studies of her favorite actor as a way to not lose her mind during the COVID pandemic. She lives in the Pacific Northwest with her family and a rather large, very friendly, black cat. You can find her online at www.altocello.com and as @altocello on Twitter and just about everywhere else.

Fanfiction is what literature might look like if it were reinvented from scratch after a nuclear apocalypse by a band of brilliant pop-culture junkies trapped in a sealed bunker. They don't do it for money. That's not what it's about. The writers write it and put it up online just for the satisfaction. They're fans, but they're not silent, couchbound consumers of media. The culture talks to them, and they talk back to the culture in its own language.

— Lev Grossman
Screenwriter of *The Map of Tiny Perfect Things*

LOSING AND FINDING MY VOICE
Dannye Chase

Fandom is a lifeline. It's a miracle. It's an upward path out of disaster. It's very human, and it means everything that we share it with each other.

Let me explain.

I didn't know what fandom or fanfic was when I began to produce it in the early 1990s. My best friend and I bought several blank notebooks and passed them back and forth in the hallway between high school classes, updating our stories as the day went through. We wrote for the 1990 TV show *Zorro*, but also for our original characters: superheroes and psychics, enchantresses and elves, and so many, many vampires. It was the age when *The Vampire Diaries* and *Roswell* were books, and there were no internet fandoms because there was no real internet.

I was always a little embarrassed about the writing, because it was high school, and because it was only ever romance. If I thought someone might be observing what I was working on while I was supposed to be paying attention in class, I would switch into my high-school-level French to evade them. I used to do the same thing in grad school. Because the love of writing, especially romance, only grew in me as I got older, but I didn't know how other people would react to it. I certainly didn't know many other people who would share it.

In college, I began to write paranormal romance novels, plotted with care and written with all my heart. But it was very private, at least until I met my husband. We married young, and I am happy to say that he has always been my faithful beta, even as my writing has changed from closed-door male/female vampire/human suggested smut, to full-on male/male monster sex. (The internet has been a very good influence on me.)

We had children, and when those children were in high school, I gave them my novels to read, edited to be teenager-appropriate. My daughters loved them and they passed them on to their friends, who also loved them. That gave me some confidence, but I wasn't sure where on earth I would find readers who weren't related to me.

A few years later came *Good Omens*. We watched the TV show as a family while my oldest child was home on break from college, and I was overwhelmed by how much I loved the romance between an angel and a demon. I was devastated that there were only six episodes, and my children, now young adults, informed me that there was this website called AO3, and on it was something called fanfiction.

I promptly realized that all those years ago I had been a fanfic writer, for *Zorro, Roswell, Scarecrow & Mrs. King,* and *Lois & Clark*. But there had been no way for me to find fellow fans. Now, in the time of *Good Omens,* everything was different.

My children were very helpful. They introduced me to Tumblr, though I quickly began to annoy them by recognizing their meme-sharing and vine-quoting. They helped me make sense of Discord channels. On AO3 I started as a reader, and then became a commenter, and then I thought, *I mean, I write things, don't I? I write romance. I've done fanfic. Maybe I should write for* Good Omens.

A couple of months later, I wrote a 70,000 word *Good Omens* fic and posted it to AO3, hoping for 10 kudos. My children, although they had noticed with some trepidation that the last chapter was something I'd discovered was called *smut with feelings,* lovingly assured me that people would like it, and they were right. The fic took off in a way that floored me. I had found an audience for my writing for the first time in my life.

And then – then I *met* people. We connected on social media and through AO3 comments. I read their fics and gushed over them, and they did the same for me. I wrote fic for art and received art for fic. I started to join zines and to collaborate with artists.

This strange romantic land that I'd always had in my head, populated with masked heroes and vampires, now included *Good*

Omens, and I realized that the same thing was true for so many other people. Of course, we all put our own spin on things. There were people who liked a dark, demonic Crowley; people like me who leaned toward a less-bastard-and-more-angelic version of Aziraphale; people who built themselves a palace of complicated narratives and historical detail; people who surrounded themselves with sweet, domestic fluff; and those who wrote the raunchiest, and often quite loving, smut.

Most of us are a combination, and that is a miracle unto itself. We sneak pieces of other people's head canon kingdoms into our own like transplanted cuttings of trees, making our own gardens. I even found people who liked to do crossovers of the same unrelated fandoms as I do, such as *Good Omens* and *Jurassic Park.*

"It's amazing to share a world of fandom and imagination with people. You can go to that world anytime and find your friends there"

Because this was my first internet fandom (at the age of 42), and my introduction to AO3, Discord, Tumblr, Dreamwidth, and so on, I learned as I went along. For example, I found that the *Good Omens* fandom is largely a friendly place, but that not all fandoms are. I saw the pain caused to fan creators by nasty comments, and I learned how I like to deal with such things (I ignore them. And of course, I don't leave them). I learned the two cakes rule, which I adore. This idea looks at fandom from the perspective of a fan presented with treats made by different creators. Writers and artists often worry about how their work compares to that of other creators using the same basic ingredients, but the fans are just excited to have so much cake!

I became filled with gratitude toward everyone involved in the fandom, not least to the people who helped me figure out things like Instagram stories and multi-fandom exchanges, but also, of course, to the creators of the original works, the actors in the show, other fan creators, and other fans, the ones who comment, the ones who leave kudos, and the ones who just silently read. Because we are all part of this same world together.

And I was especially grateful that this unexpected fandom world dropped into my lap at what turned out to be one of the most difficult times of my life: I went through treatment for oral cancer at the age of 37. The cancer runs in my family at a young age, even for those of us who don't use tobacco or alcohol. I have been cancer-free since then, thank heavens, but the effects of radiation to the mouth and throat are not something that I will ever be able to leave behind.

I used to be a singer. I grew up with it; my mother would play the piano and I would sing, and we did church performances, and music therapy at hospitals and hospice memorial services. I continued to do music therapy as an adult, and when I was diagnosed with cancer, I had a steady once-a-week gig at a cancer lodge (of all places), plus a great deal of solo and choral work at my church. I sang with a Dixieland jazz band, and I had once done a couple of years with a swing band that played weddings. I loved to sing. I loved it like pilots love to fly and gymnasts love to climb. It was me. In some ways it was all of me. It was how I defined myself.

But my singing voice did not survive cancer treatment. I can talk – it's a bit strange sometimes, and I have a hard time being understood over the phone or behind a mask – but at least I can communicate. But I am lucky if I'm able to sing even one middle-range song with my old, clear tone, and I can no longer sing louder than any accompanying instrument. It hurts to talk. It hurts worse to sing, and sometimes when I try, I find that part of my range is utterly silent.

I was attempting to come to terms with this loss when we first watched *Good Omens*. I am a religious person, and I honestly believe that the writing was a gift from God to console me through this terrible loss of self. Because it was also a loss of audience.

I did music therapy at nursing homes and sang with bands because I don't like formal recitals. I like interacting with an audience, and getting questions like "What is the weirdest old song you know?"

I have to digress because that was one of my favorite gigs ever. In case you are curious, my contributions were *Last Night I Saw Upon the Stair, The Little Blue Man, You Can't Get to Heaven (On Roller Skates),* and whatever that one is that starts "One bright morning in the middle of the night." (I looked it up, it's called *Two Dead Boys.*)

As a writer on AO3 I got my audience back. I got kudos and comments. I got regular readers who would joke with me like the staff at the hospital used to, the ones who were there every week and became my friends. I was able to collaborate, like I would do with audience members at the cancer lodge who also liked to sing, or who had brought along their flute to treatment, or who could play piano better than I could (that's not hard). On AO3 I got to follow writing prompts, which are just the same as requests from the audience to sing *Danny Boy* or *Amazing Grace,* or for the band to play *Moonlight Serenade.* That was one of the most fun things about those kinds of gigs, and about fic prompts – you never know what you are going to end up producing.

One of the main things I lost along with my singing voice was my church choir. I used to go to rehearsals anyway, just to listen (and cry, sometimes). The choir was my group of friends. We were irreverent and silly, and very queer (it's a friendly church), and we all loved to sing. It was like a little fandom of its own for beloved Episcopal church hymns. I lost the choir when we moved out of state, and I am not sure how to find another one, because I am no longer a singer.

But I found friends in fandom, and I carried with me the lessons that I learned from choir and singing, and discovered that there are also sacred fandom rules. One is that you are kind, and value other people's contributions (no nasty comments). You don't get snooty with inexperienced newbies, you sit by them and help them make sense of everything that's confusing, like that one hymn with all the repeats that we always urged new members just to learn by ear.

You don't hold auditions for your fandom (one of my bands did, but they were trying to actually make money from music, the fools). Everyone of every level is welcome, you just have to love what we love. Two cakes indeed! And you definitely do not hog the cantor parts (those are the solos) or the microphone. You don't ever stop someone else from singing.

After a long while in the *Good Omens* fandom, I started to think more about the original characters (OCs) who had lived in my head for so long. I didn't know if any of my fanfic readers would want to meet them. But with the support of my kids (who, it turned out, aren't much embarrassed about me writing my own sexy vampires or writing smut for a character who looks like the 10th Doctor), I gave it a try. I put a couple of original works on AO3. They didn't get much traction, but a few people liked them. Then I started to do original zines. (Fun fact: many original fanzines have such a hard time attracting creators that they don't have an application process. You can join at will.) I experimented with different fics and started to get a handle on what *Good Omens* fans were interested in – and of course, it was beloved tropes that attracted us to *Good Omens* in the first place: enemies who can't help but be friends, friends who become lovers, a forbidden romance that makes things like good vs evil look petty in the face of love.

So I wrote an original fic that was like fanfic: a super-tropey m/m best-friends-to-lovers story. And it was popular. So then I held my breath and wrote a fic for some vampire OCs that I'd had in my head for twenty years, since my children were infants. And people liked my vampires. It was exactly that romance writing I'd tried to hide from my classmates, and now people wanted to read it.

Fanfic and trope-heavy romance writing, I realized, are like music therapy. It's not the sort of formal concert that I always found so lonely, instead it's me competing with *M*A*S*H* on the TV in the dining room of a cancer lodge, looking up chords for *Finian's Rainbow* on my phone so I can sing *When I'm Not Near the Girl I Love, I Love the Girl I'm Near* (hilarious song, by the way, and a real crowd pleaser). It's connecting with an audience and giving them what they want to hear.

Eventually I got the courage to submit an original fic to a small press – a soft, sweet, paranormal romance – and it was accepted. Being a published writer, and one with readers, was a miracle of creation and a miracle of timing, coming just when my world of singing was shutting down. People talk about God shutting a door and opening a window – the loss of singing for me was the whole building falling down. But miraculously, I stepped outside and found myself in my old writing kingdom.

It's amazing to share a world of fandom and imagination with people. By definition, it does not exist, and yet it exists everywhere. You can go to that world anytime and find your friends there. And in that way, it's very like the music I used to produce.

It's not about being a singer, in the end, because most people at the gig aren't performers. It's not about having 10,000 screaming fans (I never had any screaming fans), or even being listed on the program. It's being asked if you'll provide background music in the lobby while people are filing by on their way to the actual show, and being very excited about it because then you get to play your music. (The Dixieland band had a standing lobby gig for a fundraiser every year.) It's about sitting together in the audience while the other bands play and cheering with the stranger beside you.

You're just happy to be there. You're happy that other people know what you're excited about, and that they're excited about it too.

Fandom really is a lifeline and a miracle, an upward path out of disaster. It's so very human, and it means everything that we share it with each other.

Dannye Chase is a married mom of three who lives in the US Pacific Northwest. She writes original queer romance, fantasy, and horror, as well as fanfiction, mostly for Good Omens. *Her pieces have appeared in over 25 original and fandom zines, and she has a short story in the anthology "Dark Cheer: Cryptids Emerging (Volume Blue)" with Improbable Press. Find Dannye at DannyeChase.com, on AO3 as @ holycatsandrabbits, and on Twitter and Facebook @DannyeChase.*

FANDOM SAFE SPACES
AND THE LIMITLESS IDEAS OF FIC
Monica Micio

I've wanted to write since I can remember. One of the best gifts of my childhood was a typewriter I used incessantly, until the first computer came.

I haven't stopped yet.

When I asked an employee of my neighborhood library the secret to becoming a good writer (she lived surrounded by books, back then I thought she couldn't not know), she said: "You have to read a lot, and then a lot more."

At first I was puzzled, but she was right; reading is the best way for writers to find our own style, the topics and setting we prefer, and what isn't our cup of tea.

Humans learn by imitation, looking to people who already know how to do things, and repeating their gestures. Why should it be different for writing?

Through reading, a new author learns how to move the characters, balance dialog and description, the differences between past and present tense, the wise use of the third or first person, how to write long stories without getting lost, how to concentrate an emotion in a few lines.

My first writing model was Agatha Christie. Her novels were published in a small and cheap format, you could afford to buy many and read them everywhere, and so I did.

They were suitable for a 12-year-old girl, because even if someone always died, the story wasn't frightening, focusing more on investigation and suspense. The conversations between characters were interesting, and the descriptions of places like old houses were so vivid I had no trouble seeing them as photographs in my mind.

I wanted to reproduce those images myself, so, sitting at my desk with my typewriter, I imagined I was like Agatha: mine was a real process of imitation. Obviously, being very young, my attempts were clumsy, but having a model to look at gave me the right inspiration.

Some years later, Stephen King helped me to work on the details of stories, and to not be afraid of the length of them, because if each element has a reason to be there, there's nothing superfluous.

Banana Yoshimoto taught me that feelings have a shape and a color, and that a single sensation (nostalgia, tenderness, pain) can be the foundation of an entire novel.

Fandoms too, are ideal environments in which to learn: a fanfiction archive brings together many types of writers, and it's full of classic tropes, clichés, unique settings, periods from prehistory to the remote future, and diverse interactions between characters. An environment so varied is a real gym to train the minds and hands of new writers.

And this training is not one-sided: even veteran writers learn from beginners, who bring new ideas, renewed enthusiasm, revitalizing old or stale fandoms.

Being in the BBC *Sherlock* fandom as a writer since 2012, I consider myself almost a veteran, and one of my biggest fears is exactly that of running out of ideas. I'm sure that if I wrote in a vacuum and not in a fandom, I would have long exhausted my creative streak.

But within such a large fandom the ideas virtually run forever: every day there's an author who writes a crossover, AU, headcanon, or trope I hadn't thought about. In the last few years a couple authors wrote stories that have nature and mountaineering in the background, and reading them, I said to myself: "Hey, I am a hiker, I know the mountains, I could write something. How is it that never occurred to me?"

Because a spark was missing, and if I wasn't in a fandom, I wouldn't have found it.

In the long run, this interaction between old and new writers becomes like the passing of the baton during a relay: while some leave for other fandoms or hobbies, new people take over, carrying on the writing, preparing the ground so in the future new people will be attracted by the fandom, enter, and interact.

In this way the collective voice of a fandom never dies.

Some fandoms have been going on like this for many years. Just think of classic Star Trek or the Star Wars movies: their fans have carried these franchises on their shoulders for years, and it was their enthusiasm that made it possible for each new series and movie to come to life. If, after 1966, the fans had abandoned Star Trek, the producers wouldn't have risked carrying on a forgotten television show.

The next time someone tells you that fandom is silly, show them the numbers of these two franchises alone.

Some writers can be afraid to make their voice heard in a fandom because their story is about a common trope and they fear they're just copying stories already written.

It's not like that, though. Even with the most common tropes there's a point of view and a story that's never been written: the one in *your* mind and keyboard.

"Fandoms give shelter to women, queer people, and other marginalized communities"

It doesn't matter if there are already a thousand other stories about, for example, vampires: your story is still missing.

This is why a fandom should always be a safe place, where everyone has the opportunity to make their writing voice heard, whether they have been writing for ten years or just started.

A fandom is also a place where a writer should feel free to write about any subject, to pursue their point of view, to explore and share desires, fantasies, and sexual kinks.

It's a place where you can say, clearly and aloud: "I like this, these are my fantasies, and I'm not afraid to say it."

We know the world out there doesn't have a positive attitude towards fanfiction, so some people try to silence this writing voice in particular, intolerant of free and different points of view because of agendas and narrowness, because they've a fragile ego and are terrified by people talking freely about sensuality and sexuality, especially if it's women doing it.

According to some, it seems a person must drop all hobbies and interests that aren't related to work, home, or family – especially after a certain age.

Fandoms and safe online spaces managed by fans offer a refuge from this stupidity, and give people the opportunity to continue to make their voices heard. It's no coincidence that the more oppressive the society, the more people find refuge in these places.

Coming from not one of the most progressive countries in the world, I've always been very aware of what the society around me approved or disapproved of, and I knew that my opinions would find a hostile environment.

A woman who speaks aloud about sexuality, who decides to be active and not an object? Are you crazy?

The LGBT+ community? Hm, yes, it exists, but please, I don't want to hear about it.

Why are you wasting so much time writing a story? You're not making a living out of it.

I can't sit at a cafe table in front of a coffee cup and talk about sexuality or fic writing with anyone without earning a dirty look; but fortunately, within fandoms, I found a virtual table, where other people with the same struggle can take a break, talk with a happy-go-lucky attitude about a naughty kink, and even ask for suggestions on the best way to write about it. The reason I feel so comfortable in fandom is because I feel I'm among people who speak my language.

Fandoms give shelter to women, queer people, and other marginalized communities, so it's very important to have a safe space, where every writing voice is free to express itself without constraints, a space protected from censorship.

Fanfiction can also become a place for people to talk about depression, mental illness, disability, and neurodiversity, subjects that can still be taboo.

Being able to write fanfiction then becomes an opportunity for some to talk about their condition and life experience without boundaries. It's not easy, because through a story these authors end up talking about themselves, but when fandom is a safe space they can feel free to do so, no longer marginalized or judged.

This is so important and fandoms must never lose it.

Once you find a safe space to express your writing voice, it's important for it to evolve and improve with time and experience.

If a writer isn't satisfied with their style or stories, yearning to improve what they feel doesn't work, wanting to make their writing a more important part of their life, fandom offers the chance to increase commitment and ability, such as taking part in writing challenges, story collections, gifts for festivities, charity projects, and raffles.

Within these events, our writing voices become part of a choir, part of something bigger.

Participating in a writing challenge, for example, can lead an author to write things outside their comfort zone, expand their experience, and encourage them to research new subjects to enrich their stories.

Discovering from which parts of the world pineapples come? Go ahead.

Spending hours researching Aztec ritual knives? Why not.

Research stimulates the writing process. I remember not knowing anything about poker, as I dislike gambling, yet this game became crucial for one of my stories, so I spent days on online forums which explained the game's strategies and winning combinations; I even watched matches, to better enter the spirit of the game.

Other times, I've researched poisons and toxins, especially mushrooms, borrowing library textbooks, following lectures by mycologists, and became good at distinguishing edible mushrooms from poisonous ones. I'll never poison anyone, I swear, but I can now prepare a mushroom risotto without fear of dying later!

Another important aspect of fandom safe spaces is that many organized fandom projects have deadlines.

At the beginning deadlines frightened me, and for my first fandom years I refused to participate in events because I thought, "I will never manage to do it before the deadline." I was afraid to fail.

This is a common fear I think, because when you participate in group events there are consequences to missing a deadline which can affect the whole project. It's okay to be afraid to fail, but over time I tried to have a more positive mindset. I looked at what other authors did and said to myself: "Listen, there are many writers participating in fan projects and respecting the deadlines. Maybe I can, too."

So I tried. I started with the Secret Santa, because the idea of gifting my fanfiction to someone was a further incentive. Dedicating half an hour every day to the story, I managed to finish it without a hitch, so the following year I decided to repeat the experience. I'm still doing it seven years later.

The key is moving forward with baby steps, because nobody learns to run if they don't walk first. My advice: start with one project, maybe an easy, small one.

From there, it's *planning*.

Many of us have other commitments: study, work, children, home. A day unfortunately has only 24 hours and we haven't yet learned to manipulate time, so it's important to organize your time when you start a project with a deadline.

It's useful to draw up a schedule, look at the things you already have to do, move something aside, find time – ten minutes a day? an hour a week? – to devote to the writing project. And stick to it.

It requires commitment for sure, but is it not like that for the other things in our life? Studying and work require commitment, so writing projects can too.

Helping us with safe spaces isn't all fandom does: it can help in a broader sense, too.

With the social platforms accessible from every part of the world, a fandom can bring together people who come from every corner of the earth, each with their own life experiences, social and cultural background, ideas. In perhaps what's one of the few, authentic global experiences we can have, fandom becomes an invaluable opportunity for interaction and personal growth.

Maybe a foreign author has taken inspiration for their story from a book famous in their country, maybe they use lines of dialog in their native language – and that sparks in you the desire to learn more. What an opportunity to expand your cultural interests!

In turn that cultural enrichment can wrap back around and bring new life and ideas to your writing, giving you a fresh perspective to observe characters and plot, a new point of view to reawaken your imagination, curiosity, and to make plot bunnies hop in your mind!

Meeting, discussing and debating with people different from us can lead to the discovery of new customs and habits, show us how to be more open and less fearful about what we don't know, teach us about people who live a life far different from ours.

It's no coincidence that many fanfiction authors and fandom members are also people who are mindful of social problems, active against racism, xenophobia, and homophobia.

Obviously, finding a common ground between fans of different nations requires a common basis to understand each other, and there is no doubt that English is a passport to access fandoms.

For a moment I'll speak as a non-native. As English is not my first language, at the beginning fandom wasn't easy to me, I felt isolated and it was a bit discouraging and frustrating, but with some effort on my side, I knew the interaction with other fans would become simpler.

So I dusted off my high school English textbook and dictionary to review the most important grammatical rules, I avoided online translators, making the effort to write my piece in English and check if it was correct later. An online translator is useful in many situations, but it hardly helps you get better – it does all the work for you.

I also began watching movies and TV shows with subtitles in my native language, but later I switched to English subtitles, trying to look at them as little as possible and concentrate on the sounds of words. After several years, I can say I have improved, even if I am far from perfect.

Being able to easily read fanfiction written in English helped me in the process of widening horizons, but also put me in touch with other non-native people, so today I can talk in the same way with a Russian or a Canadian. I've then used my renewed knowledge of the language in the workplace, so I have another reason to be grateful to fandoms.

And all of this started from a common interest in a book, a movie, a TV show.

Many are the entertainment media that have brought me closer to this world, but if I have to rank them I'd say Star Trek showed me what a fandom is in all its aspects (cosplay, fanzines, fanfiction, fan art), anime and manga fandom encouraged me to interact for the first time, while Harry Potter and Sherlock helped me grow and improve as a writer.

Fandoms are much more than a gathering of strange nerds, they're safe spaces where the writer's writing voice can find the ideal environment to be born, grow, and improve, but since the writing voice isn't an abstract concept, but a part of us, those positive changes are reflected in us, too.

Isn't it extraordinary?

About herself Monica says: I am an undying nerd. I survive by working in a law firm and I live by being into fandoms, as my mind is constantly full of prompts that demands to be written.

The vast majority of what we watch is from the male perspective – authored, directed, and filmed by men, and mostly straight white men at that. Fan fiction gives women and other marginalised groups the chance to subvert that perspective, to fracture a story and recast it in her own way... It often feels as if there isn't much space for difference in the dominant cultural narratives; in fandom, by design, there's space for all.

— Elizabeth Minkel
Hugo award-finalist and culture writer
for *The New Yorker*

SYMPATHY FOR THE DEVIL: ATTACHMENT THEORY AND FANFICTION
Angela Nauss, LMFT

Many fanfiction authors are drawn to fictional attachments as much as the characters themselves. In psychology, 'attachment' usually refers to an early childhood relationship with a caregiver. Childhood abuse, neglect, prolonged separation, or anything else that damages the attachment is called an 'attachment wound.' Attachment wounds can manifest throughout the lifespan as maladaptive beliefs such as: "I'm not good enough" or "There is something wrong with me." Attachment-focused therapists model healthy relationships by establishing boundaries and validating the client's emotions. This type of therapeutic relationship is a prerequisite for attachment repair. Fanfiction authors explore attachment repair by writing therapeutic relationships into their work.

Fanfiction authors process attachment wounds using fictional characters as proxies. The ideal character for this process has many damaged relationships and a history of destructive behavior. Authors are sometimes drawn to characters with coping skills or relationship patterns similar to their own. In the context of the original canon, characters who meet these criteria are usually villains because heroes are commonly written without character flaws. Fanfiction authors have been criticized for omitting villains' most problematic behaviors and focusing on redemption. However, the character's role in the original canon is irrelevant. An author who identifies with a villain might believe that a part of their identity is similarly problematic.

Art therapists believe that a complete therapeutic art piece integrates conflicting information such as past and present, or good and bad emotions. Uniting conflicting parts of the artist's experience is a prerequisite for catharsis.

FUNERAL FANFICTION: AN EXAMPLE OF DYNAMIC CHARACTER QUALITIES IN CATHARSIS

An author shared a fanfiction with me, inspired by parental attachment wounds during their teenage years. The author said they grew up in an environment where it was outside of cultural norms for parents and children to express verbal affection for each other. They wrote both parents into their story as the recently deceased father of the main character. According to the author, the father in the story is: "a stand-in character that's an over-exaggeration of both parental roles, basically the negative parts played to the extreme."

The story allowed the author to process and understand the origin of the problems encountered during adolescence. The story's main character acknowledged her father's expectations were a show of love and apologized for her part in their arguments. The eulogy allowed the author to verbally express love for their parents. They said that writing the fanfiction was "somewhat cathartic" because "I don't often express my love or gratitude for my parents in spoken words."

POLITICAL FANFICTION: AN EXAMPLE OF ATTACHMENT REPAIR

Sometimes authors explore relationship repair that's impossible in real life. For example, an author shared a fanfiction about their relationship to their country of birth. The author has been living abroad for several years due to an unsafe political situation. However, they wrote a fanfiction that allowed them to explore "the what-if situation if the country could change."

To this end, they wrote a fanfiction where two characters have a Socratic dialog about an analogous political situation. The author allowed themselves to defend their attachment to their birth country via the character of a passionate revolutionary. At the end of the story, the revolutionary writes an optimistic letter about the possibility of change.

FANFICTION CONVENTIONS FOR THERAPEUTIC RELATIONSHIPS
The most common therapeutic relationship in fanfiction is the one between the main character and a love interest. This relationship creates stability that does not exist in the original canon. As a result, the main character builds self-esteem, self-worth, and even experiences changes in mood. The love interest co-regulates the main character while they process their attachment wounds and repressed trauma. The process of co-regulation is similar to infant co-regulation, where caregivers soothe an infant who has not yet developed the skills to calm themselves. The love interests co-regulate until the main character develops the skills to do so on their own.

> "Some authors write fanfiction to humanize uncomfortable aspects of their identity, grieve and repair damaged relationships, and process attachment wounds"

Another vehicle for introducing therapeutic relationships in fanfiction is the 'alternate universe' trope. Using this trope, the author processes attachment wounds by exploring how the character would behave in adaptive relationships. For example, villains are assigned a new role in the alternate universe. They do not experience their canon trauma and are able to develop emotional regulation skills. The villain processes their attachment wounds with help from a stable support system.

FANDOM SPECIFIC CONVENTIONS: KYLUX
The *Star Wars* fanfiction community is known for writing dramatic attachment wounds into stories with high sexual content. Common tags in this fandom include: hurt/comfort, abuse, and mental health issues, in addition to tags for kink and sexual content.
    Some art therapists believe that unplanned sexual or aggressive imagery in art are defense mechanisms. The symbolic imagery

indicates that the artist has accessed unconscious material too painful to be made conscious. The defense mechanism activates while the artist represses the painful content.

When reading fanfiction, take note of what was going on immediately prior to the initiation of sexual content. Often sex scenes are preceded by moments of high emotional intensity, such as the main character describing their repressed trauma or attachment wounds. I've noticed that authors will disclose past trauma but get uncomfortable when they talk about themselves in the present. For example, maybe the author was ready to talk about their past, but not ready to re-live or acknowledge its effects on the present. Abrupt sexual content may be a way of derailing further exploration into present emotions. It's important to distinguish this type of sexual content from planned erotica, which is conscious material and not a defense mechanism. However, a formal analysis would require observing the author's process.

One of the most popular pairings in the new Star Wars franchise is 'Kylux,' or Kylo Ren and General Hux. Kylo Ren's most commonly cited attachment wounds are the relationships with his parents, who are typically written as emotionally withholding or incapable of forming attachments with their son. In the original canon, Kylo Ren kills his father on screen. General Hux is written as the victim of child abuse and he kills his father off-screen. Both are prime candidates for fanfiction because authors sympathize with the way the villains are treated by other characters.

Fanfiction authors project their unconscious trauma onto the characters. General Hux and Kylo Ren become love interests who co-regulate while they process damaged attachments from childhood. The characters gain insight into their behavior and no longer feel responsible for their childhood attachment wounds. Through their writing, the author incorporates repressed trauma and attachment wounds into their conscious experience and achieves catharsis.

CONCLUSION: HUMANITY

Some authors write fanfiction to humanize uncomfortable aspects of their identity, grieve and repair damaged relationships, and process attachment wounds. I would encourage any fanfiction author to re-read their own work and explore whether they are processing relationship trauma or challenging a part of themselves. Writing fanfiction is a valid form of therapeutic self-exploration. The authors who contribute to online communities are doing more than making social connections, they are supporting each other through a process of personal growth.

Angela Nauss is a trauma specialist certified in EMDR and licensed as a Marriage and Family Therapist. She has more than half a dozen years of experience in substance use and trauma. She also specializes in men's issues and sees clients in private practice. Mrs Nauss also has an undergraduate degree in design. She is an accomplished watercolor artist and a published fiction author. Her website is nausstherapy.com.

3

GOING PRO IS UP TO YOU
Thoughts on how and why

YOU'RE MORE TALENTED THAN YOU THINK
Emily

Here's the thing.

I read a lot of scripts. A lot. From professionals to aspiring writers to complete newbies. Features and pilots. Specs and treatments.

And eight times out of ten the fanfic that I've read over the last, oh, 15 years is *leagues* better than this stuff. It's more inspired. It's more compelling. It's genre bending and creative and heartfelt. It's well-paced and intense and funny and sexy and *meaningful*. It's smart and thoughtful and *good*. It's novel quality. Better than, sometimes.

Rare is the script I don't want to put down, but how often have we stayed up until 3am to get to the last chapter of a 100k fic? And it's not even a fan fic author's day job. This is what they do on the side. In their spare time. For free.

So my point is, fanfic authors, you're *good*. You're good writers and great storytellers. I know it doesn't always feel like it, especially if you're one of the authors who's not a big name fan and doesn't get the notes/hits that a few do. And because some people still view fic as 'not real writing.' You guys know the shit that gets made into movies. You're better than that. So *be* better than that. If writing is what you think want to do, then just know you're already doing it. You've already started.

And you're more talented than you might think.

Emily (she/her) is a longtime fandom enthusiast and fic writer who has spent far too much time thinking about the inner lives of fictional characters after watching "The X-Files" at a very young age. In a previous life, she worked in film and theatre development and somehow managed to wrangle a Tony award. She can currently be found gardening, drinking coffee, and thinking about hiking.

WHAT IF I FLY?
Amy Murphy

Fanfiction changes lives. Atlin Merrick wrote that in a Tumblr post, and she's not wrong. It has certainly changed mine significantly and irrevocably, in ways I could never have predicted. In 2010 I was a suburban housewife with children who had transitioned from public-school-at-home to traditional brick-and-mortar school.

They weren't involved in the predominant local activities; I wasn't a soccer or dance mom, nor did I want to be. But I was desperately, achingly lonely. I took to watching television when the house was too quiet, and one day I saw an advertisement for a modern adaptation of Sherlock Holmes. "Might be interesting," I said, and suggested to hubs that we give it a try. The first moments grabbed me and by the opening theme, I was utterly consumed.

This was the repeat showing, as nearly as I can figure out the timeline, so I didn't have quite the same wait as everyone else between series one and two. Enough of one, though. I wanted more. Could the internet tell me anything about the new season? Not so much, really. There was fanfiction, of course. But everyone knew about fanfiction, didn't they? Like that pointy-toothed book series with the crepuscular name? I'd heard enough about *that* to shake my head and hover over the back button.

But...Sherlock.

And honestly, who would even know? Just a taste, just one little story. Our little secret, me and my monitor. I'm sure you can relate to what happened next. One story became two became thirty, became hours spent reading about my favorite characters falling off of bridges. Into rivers. Falling in love. It wasn't long before I had a mental list of favorite authors. Atlin Merrick was one of them. She was publishing stories on her blog: sweet things and spicy things and oh-my-sweet-lord things. After each fic, there was a section for comments. People responding to the story, to each other. Even Atlin was part of the conversation: an author in community with her readers. Fans all, creators and consumers in beautiful symbiosis, spinning theories and bouncing ideas and sharing the joy of exploring 'what if.'

I was flabbergasted and envious. These people all had the courage to read what they were reading *and* to comment on it in a public forum. Not me, though. Anyone might find out, no matter how cagey my username. More than anything, I dreaded the taunts of my childhood: freak, weirdo. In the more modern vernacular, cray-cray. I lurked, and read, and watched over my shoulder in case anyone happened to see me sitting in my basement reading fanfiction instead of folding laundry and lamenting over the state of my carpets.

Things might have continued that way forever: Atlin's community of readers joyfully talking about Sherlock and John, and me watching through the proverbial window. Perhaps it was exposure to the sort of interaction I craved, maybe it was a particularly touching story that made me push myself to comment. I knew exactly what I wanted to say. But would the fans welcome me, these clever and intelligent and sparkling people? Who the heck was I, thinking that I had anything remotely interesting to say? What would they think of this slow-thinking, overly cautious housewife chiming in on their celebration? If an online voice can shake, mine did. But I made my comment. The response was generous: I was welcomed, and folded into the community without pause. These passionate and brilliantly creative people thought that what I had to say was interesting. They didn't think I was weird, or pretentious, or trying to squeeze in where I wasn't wanted.

I didn't know it yet, but in dancing through the give-and-take of a fan community, I was approaching a cliff.

Season two of *Sherlock* came. And went. I kept reading. Thousands of words, dozens of authors. The fandom was awash in angst and reunions, in heartbreak and healing and kisses and punches and hope. It was glorious. In August I got my long-awaited

AO3 invite. A few people in my day-to-day life found out about my fan activities, and they were confused but not aghast. "What will they think" was answered: they thought I was a fan. Odd, but I'd always been odd. It was amazingly freeing, not having to hide that part of myself.

> "Would the fans welcome me, these clever and intelligent people? What would they think of this slow-thinking, overly cautious housewife chiming in on their celebration?"

And then an idea tapped me politely on the brain. "No," I said. "That's lovely, but I'm not a writer. I could never do it properly." You know how it is with ideas, right? To paraphrase Sherlock, you can't kill an idea, can you? Not once it's made a home in your head. This idea just didn't stop. Images and emotions floated around my head. An opening line shouted in my ear. Dialog shaped itself until it fit in the character's mouths.

Here was the cliff I hadn't seen coming. But I didn't need to jump, did I? I could stay here on the edge, just try to write this story. I didn't need to actually *share* it. Getting the words out would be enough, right? In hindsight, I can see that I was being an idiot. Delusional; the story didn't want to just be typed and left. It wanted out. It wanted to be read. But what if it was awful, the idea too preposterous (was this before Tuna!lock or Bat!John? I don't remember). What if nobody read it? Worse, what if they taunted and teased and left unpleasant commentary? Just how far did the welcome extend? What if, in stepping off that cliff of creativity, I fell?

"But, darling," the voices on the blog asked. "What if you fly?"

I took courage, braced by the community that urged me forward, buoyed by the sheer exhilaration of creating, and leapt. My first piece was published on AO3 on November 24, 2012. Seven hundred seventy six words that I spent three months editing, tweaking, fixing. When I'd copied it into AO3, I sat staring at it for a long time. In a moment that felt a lot like utter insanity, I hit the post button. It was done. For better or worse, I had committed. Right before bedtime, as it happens. I still don't know how I fell asleep. I woke up in the middle of the night, and couldn't help but open my Kindle and refresh my page (I've since learned that this isn't an uncommon occurrence among writers.) The hits were into the double digits, the kudos an impressive percentage. There were comments. Comments!

I wrote another story, and more after that. And now I was a writer.

Eventually, I owned it to people in my day-to-day life, and the world didn't end. To date, I have written 66 fanfics in three fandoms. The quality varies, there are some I'm downright embarrassed by, but I was proud of each one when I hit 'post' so they live on AO3 in honor of the person I was at the time.

And in that time I've done so much more than just claim the title 'writer.' Reading fanfic has taught me more about human sexuality than I knew I didn't know; a good thing for anyone, I think, but particularly for someone raising queer teenagers in this conformity-happy culture. The act of writing and sharing has brought me cherished friends. I'm still not a soccer mom, but I am a whole lot more okay with that than I was in 2011.

This would be proof enough of Atlin's assertion that fanfic changes lives, but it doesn't stop there.

I tried my hand at longer, multi-chapter pieces. One of these was an urban fantasy alternative universe, combining as many ideas as I thought I could get away with. Lots of research, world building, and lengthy discussions with my beta reader. Outlined, drafted, then edited and posted serially, it was the biggest thing I'd ever done. A major project, that I saw through to the end. The feedback was positive and encouraging. There, I thought. I've peaked. That's the best I can do. I toyed with the idea of scrubbing and self-publishing, quickly realized I didn't have the skills or contacts, and let that dream go before it was more than a hint of a whisper.

Then one day I saw a post from a newly formed publishing company. "No," I said. "That's for other people. I'm happy doing the fanfic thing." Of course, the company posted again. They were interested in helping fan writers become published authors. Seeking submissions; willing to take a link to the archive. I could do this; it couldn't be made any easier. But what would they think?

Taking the step of submitting it felt a whole awful lot like posting that first fic. My hands were sweaty, my chest tight. Perhaps it was muscle memory, but I like to think I've gathered a bit of courage, too, that enabled me to hit the 'submit' button. Only after I'd sent it off did I realize this wasn't just a case of being afraid I'd be called names, or my story would be rejected. It wasn't about the story: it was about a dream I hadn't dared to acknowledge. I wanted to do this. The wait wasn't long, only about three hundred years. And the result? My novel was accepted. The project has since fallen through, but the fact remains: My novel length fic was accepted for development.

In 2012, that would've been it. Dream over. But it's not 2012, and I've grown and flown so much since then. There are other stories that sing within me. Maybe I'll revisit self-publishing, maybe I'll try other roads. The point is, I can. I haven't crashed and, even if I'm doing a bit more flapping than soaring at present, I'm still airborne. I'm looking for the next cliff.

And now that I reflect on my journey, I have to say that Atlin got it wrong; fanfiction didn't change my life. It changed *me*.

That lonely woman in 2011, sitting in her basement and fearing someone would find out she was reading fanfiction? The one in 2012, who worried that people would mock her for daring to write it? More recently, the one who mumbled 'it's just romance' when asked what her novel was about?

Those women were me, and of course they still are, but I'm not them anymore. I don't hide. I read in the living room. I write in the dining room. And when asked about my writing, I am able to say "I write gay romance. I started in fanfiction and am in the process of developing an original novel that I hope to publish."

What do people think when I say that? I don't know. It doesn't matter. What matters now is simply this question every time I come to the edge of a new cliff:

What if I fly?

A prolific crafter, Amy enjoys doll making, sewing, and weaving. Amy lives in the suburbs of Minneapolis with her husband, children, and far more pets than is reasonable. She writes as Kestrel337 on the Archive of Our Own (AO3).

People wonder why I still write fanfiction. Part of it is that fanfiction is like being in a community. You're literally doing it in the context of a fandom community of other people who are all your peers within this one writing universe. But the other piece of it is that it's just play…people forget that people start writing for fun.

— Naomi Novik
Nebula award-winning writer of *Uprooted*

FANFICTION DOESN'T PLAY BY THE RULES (OR: WHY YOU NEED NEVER MAKE MONEY AS A WRITER)

Rosalyn Hunter

Commercial fiction is boring.

Commercial fiction has no guts.

Commercial fiction equates money with virtue. It tells you *"Good writing is writing that sells!"*

But if you ask me, money distorts your writing. It leads you away from complex topics, away from controversial characters. It leads you to follow the norms, to write like everyone else.

One look at Hollywood is enough to show you that. Films get made because they look like films that sold. Sequel after sequel comes to the screen while more exciting original works are passed over for production. The message is clear.

"Don't be too weird, because weird doesn't sell."

But I tell you, weird is wonderful!

Dare to be weird!

Write non-commercial works.

Write things editors will hate.

Write a story that will make one person laugh instead of a thousand.

Write a story where expectations are dashed.

Or write the fluffiest, warmest story in the world with no conflict and no pain.

I guarantee you, someone will love you for it, if only yourself.

Fanfiction didn't become big because it played by the rules. Someone made a rule that they could own stories, own characters. That was never true in the past, when everyone could tell stories of King Arthur, or Odysseus, or Hercules. The Brothers Grimm didn't write those fairy tales. Women, men, and children, old and young made them; they told them back and forth by the fireside. They changed them to fit the times. Wrote themselves in. Misunderstood 'fur' slippers for 'glass' ones. The Brothers Grimm were a great commercial success, but they just recorded stories that had been passed down and changed for thousands of years. Modern research supports it! *(Some fairy tales may be 6000 years old.[1])*

You don't require anyone's permission to dream, why should you require it to write down that dream? Dare to write the story that will never sell. The song fic with your modified lyrics. The crossover fic where your favorite character becomes a little pony. You're not selling it so it doesn't matter. It's enough that reading about it might make someone's day.

What would it be like if the only stories we could tell each other were ones that could sell?

If commercial interests blocked the production and distribution of fanfiction, what a sad world it would be.

A world where greed wins.

Where sharing stories and playing with characters is banned.

A place where imagination is chained. Creativity is drowned.

Such a world would break my heart.

Luckily, right now, that world is only fiction, and I won't write about *that*. I don't care if it would sell or not.

When did we begin thinking that commercial works are the only good writing? Do you remember what it was like to tell stories when you were a kid?

Kids aren't afraid of stories, they live them. To a kid, a trip to the store can be an epic poem. Just listen to a child for five minutes. Set a timer and make yourself shut up and sit still. What will you hear?

"...then a dog came by, and he had bushy ears that stuck out and they were white, well they were brown, he was a brown dog, but the ears had hairs that stuck out the inside and they were white, like angels' wings, you know when I wore that costume for the Christmas play with the white fabric that you could see through? Well, his ears were like

that and he came right up to me and licked my hand. Then I dropped my bag, and he picked it up and gave it back to me. Can you believe it! He gave it back, and..."

Children can be great story tellers.

Well no. They are repetitive, redundant, and they don't know the right words, but their enthusiasm betrays how much they love their stories. Once upon a time you loved your stories just as much.

Do you have a novel under the bed?

"You don't need anyone's approval to write what you love. Once you realize that, you're free to write for your own reasons"

It doesn't have to literally be under the bed, although mine was for years. It doesn't matter where it is, the thing that matters is that once long ago you wrote a story that you never shared.

Why not?

I can't say exactly why you didn't do it, but I can tell you why I didn't.

"It isn't good enough. It isn't finished. It's cliche. There are so many other better books. Someone might say something bad about it. The story logic is all wrong. It's too melodramatic. No one would like it. No one wants to read it. It's embarrassing. It's too personal. It's been so long, there's no use trying to write-it-finish it-show-it now."

How did we go from those first excited thoughts to the sadness, regret, and doubt of the second?

We grew up, and growing up means learning what you can and can't do. So much of that has to do with the commercial world. You grow up and they tell you that to be published, a story has to be just the right length, and in the right font, and follow good structure, and have good grammar. And suddenly it isn't enough what you've done. Somehow it doesn't matter that you have lived inside this world and loved it for so long. That you understand the characters better than you do your own family. You learn that if you want others to read your work, it has to be different, cleaner, better, more mainstream.

As a youth, I read paperback books. They were way cooler than hardcover books because they were cheaper. I meant both money-wise and in seriousness. A paperback could be a quick read. It could be silly. It could be over-dramatic and stupid. I aspired to be a paperback writer. Okay, in truth I wanted to write hardbacks. To have people look at my work in all seriousness and praise it to the end of time. However, I learned that such futures weren't for everyone. The hardbacks were reserved for *great* writers, and by definition, I wasn't one of them.

So I settled for wanting to be a paperback writer. My story wasn't yet good enough, but with a little work it could become a paperback. Couldn't it?

Somehow, though, that story never got finished, and although I had enough (according to the countless writing books on my desk) to send in a first chapter and an outline, I never did. Why not? See the paragraphs above.

But then something miraculous happened!

The internet happened. Fan sites happened, and people shared stories that they couldn't sell!

And one day I posted one of mine. No one noticed, but I didn't care, because it was one of my stories, and it was up there for the world to see! I posted it *because* I couldn't sell it. Not being commercial made it safe. I was just playing around. The characters belonged to someone else. I couldn't sell it, so the goal became not to sell it, but to show it off. To share it with others.

Then one day I wrote something that people did like, and it felt good. It was like being a kid again. I was talking, and maybe what I was saying wasn't in the right order, and maybe some of the words were poor, and it was a bit rambly and confusing, but they listened anyway, and they liked it.

I was writing fanfiction, and fanfiction has a right to be bad.

It has a right to be absolutely awful.

You can write your worst story. You can write about unexpected things, like men having babies, or your favorite anime character and your favorite celebrity kissing, or even put yourself in the story. You can be silly. You can play. You don't have to convince an editor that your work is worth the paper it is printed on, because it isn't printed on anything.

And you can read silly stories, stupid stories. You can compete at who can write the worst one. And the best thing about it is that we are all doing it together!

That novel under your bed was likely read by you alone. (Congratulations if you had the guts to show it off. I never did.) But fanfiction is different. It's okay to show it off. It's okay to write it even if your writing is bad.

So you write fanfiction. And somewhere along the way, you may find that the works you write now are better than that novel under your bed. You may find that now you have the words, and know the structure, that now you have the maturity and the skills to write that story you held in your heart for so long.

But…you don't need to write it anymore, because all that you really wanted from that book was for someone else to listen to you, to tell you that they liked it, and for you to know that you were appreciated and that you were good at what you did.

You are good.

You are appreciated.

Your work *now* is worth writing.

Even if it never earns you a dime.

You don't need anyone's approval to write what you love. Once you realize that, you're free to write for your own reasons. The only ones you have to please are yourself, and the friends you made along the way. Friends who you write for to make them happy, or to help them when they are sad. You will write what inspires you, what challenges you, what gives you joy, because when you take away all the fears about what your stories *should* be, writing becomes play.

And if you choose then to publish it commercially, or as the next great fanfiction epic, you'll know that it's worth the pixels it's printed on, because it truly comes from you, and your stories are worth telling no matter how weird or how ordinary they are.

Remember, fanfiction didn't become big because it played by the rules, it became big in spite of them.

So take a seat next to the internet fire, and write stories the way you want to write them.

And here's a time-tested ending that you can have for free.

And we all lived happily ever after.

The End.

Rosalyn Hunter writes fanfiction as Alessnox, and has written fiction since the age of twelve. Rosalyn lives in a little house on the prairie with her husband, children, and four cats. She is working on launching an animated series that she wrote and her husband illustrated called LUNATICS: No Children in Space, *about a family moving to the moon. She likes sunshine, wildflowers, thunderstorms, salsa music, and your comments.*

1. Shultz, David, "Some fairy tales may be 6000 years old." *Science,* 22 Apr 2016

Plot Bunnies by Khorazir (Anke Eißmann)

THE BEST OF BOTH WORLDS: FANFIC & LICENSED FICTION
George Ivanoff

Without fanfic, I don't know that I would have a writing career now. WARNING: Explaining this means featuring gratuitous fanfiction excerpts of questionable quality.

"Shields up. Go to Red Alert."

The shields were raised just in time, as the Enterprise rocked under the first barrage of Romulan torpedos.

"Shields down to seventy percent," reported Worf, "and three more Romulan ships decloaking behind us, Sir."

Captain Wesley Crusher could feel the beads of perspiration forming on his brow as he ordered, "Ready photon torpedoes Mr Worf."

[George Ivanoff: aged 25. "To Be Captain," SPOCK #65, AUSTREK: The Star Trek Fan Club of Victoria, 1993]

Star Trek, Doctor Who, Battlestar Galactica, V, The Professionals... these are just some of the universes I've played in. Unofficially. By writing fanfic. Dozens and dozens of stories. Some published in fanzines and club newsletters, others best left unread in dusty folders, triple boxed and locked away in an underground bunker.

My adventures in officialdom have been much less prolific. Licensed short stories for *Doctor Who, Lethbridge-Stewart, UNIT, Deadworld* and *The X-files*; and novels for *Lethbridge-Stewart* and *The Lucy Wilson Mysteries* (a spinoff from the *Lethbridge-Stewart* books, which are themselves a spinoff from *Doctor Who*). I consider myself to be extraordinarily lucky to have made that transition from fanfic to licensed fiction written for publications approved by the license holder. A long, slow, meandering, unplanned transition.

How does one go, as an author, from fanfiction to licensed fiction? Can one lead to another? Is there a pathway? Is it inevitable? Is it even desirable? So many questions. Sadly, I do not have definitive answers. Heck, I'm not sure I have even the vaguest of answers! But what I can do is relate some of my experiences, and tell you about the things that writing fanfic has taught me and how those things influenced my career as a professional writer. Will that do in lieu of answers?

Fanfiction does not necessarily lead to licensed fiction. Nor should it. Despite similarities, they are quite different. Yes, both are essentially equivalent to playing in someone else's sandbox. But with the former, there are no rules. The owner of the sandbox isn't there. You can do whatever you want. In the mood to kill off a main character? Sure, go for it! Want to play with a character's motivation and raison d'être? Retcon to your heart's content. How about introducing a major shift to the universe? Why not? What's the worst that can happen? Other fans might complain that Wesley Crusher would never make Captain. But…pfft to them! They can go write their own fic, damnit!

Licensed fiction, on the other hand, comes with rules. *Lots* of rules. Because the owner of the sandbox is watching you. [Insert ominous music.] Firstly, it comes with the same rules that the creators of the main media adhere to. Secondly, it comes with requirements not to change anything or introduce elements that could alter the status quo – so you can't kill Spock, turn Buffy into a vampire, or amputate Commander Adama's pinkie. Thirdly, it can come with other rules depending on whether you are writing a stand-alone story or a story that needs to fit in with a series of stories. *Doctor Who* is a great example of all of these. Licensed fiction for this property has always needed to be in line with the existing television series. But, the Virgin series of New Adventure novels, which were published in that hazy era between the original series and the new series, were quite free and easy with making changes. The novels continued on from the canceled series, without any upcoming episodes of the series to worry about, so companions could come and go, relationships could change, and the status quo could be played with. Having said that, this series of novels had its own progression, so writers had to work within that framework and the rules it entailed. Things are now different with a series of *Doctor Who* in production. Current licensed fiction must again take into account the ongoing source material. Of course there are always exceptions, and novelizations of series episodes are a different kettle of fish again.

Let's simplify the kettle by saying again, fanfic can be an end in itself. It doesn't have to lead on to licensed fiction. Certainly, while I was writing fanfic, it was a creative outlet in its own right. While I may have dreamed of writing it in an official capacity, it was never a serious goal. It was not something I was striving towards, or even attempting. I didn't set my sights on that until after I had a writing career. So the fanfic was all about fun and exploration and storytelling, without any sort of greater motive.

> "Even after I discovered the joys of writing my own original fiction, I stuck with fanfic for many years. It was fun!"

So...while fanfiction did not warp speed me towards licensed fiction, it did help me with my writing career as a whole. And it was having that writing career that then allowed me to stick a foot in the licensed fiction door and pitch ideas. (I should also point out that I've pitched way more ideas than have been given the go ahead – I particularly lament the publishers' lack of foresight in neglecting to pick up my *Doctor Who* story about exploding sheep or the *Spiderman* novel with interdimensional, super-intelligent spiders forming a gestalt super-villain.)

How did writing fanfic help my professional writing career? Let me tell you about that...

Most obviously, it taught me how to craft stories. Initially, I didn't need to worry about world building or character creation as those elements were already there, provided by someone else, waiting for me to use them. I could just focus on telling a story within an environment that I knew and loved, with characters I knew and loved. Then slowly, I started adding my own characters, using what I had learned from the existing ones I played with. I also took existing characters and yanked them out of their universe, putting them elsewhere, building my own worlds. I discovered so much about the craft of writing. Fanfic was a great training ground. The more I wrote, the more I learned about storytelling, structure, and how to string words together into a vaguely-pleasant reading experience.

Once I started submitting my fanfic to fanzines, I discovered there was an editorial process – rejection, feedback, and rewriting. All valuable lessons that have stayed with me, in part because these lessons were learned in a gentle way. The editors were fellow fans, and often friends, who were encouraging, even when being critical.

After becoming comfortable in the fanfic arena, I started to experiment and push boundaries, doing things that would never happen in the official version of the universe I was writing in. I wrote a *Next Generation* story from the perspective of a sentient plant that is ripped from its home and family by the Enterprise's botanist Keiko O'Brien as she collects vegetation samples from a planet that the starship is visiting. [GI: aged 25. "In the Name of Science," SPOCK #64, AUSTREK: The Star Trek Fan Club of Victoria, 1993] Within the universe of *Doctor Who*, I wrote a story about the Doctor reaching the end of his final regeneration, dying alone and lonely, haunted by the memories of past companions. [GI: aged 19. "Death of a Time Lord," Multiverse #17, 1987] I tried to examine things from 'the other point of view,' often allowing the villains to win. In the *V* based story "The Traitor" [GI: aged 22. The Lizards of Oz #2, 1990, The V Fan Club of Victoria] I wrote about a Visitor whose husband has just joined the fifth-column movement, intent on helping the persecuted humans. She gets what useful info she can from him, before executing him.

The experimentation came from a desire to make my fanfic different. I didn't want to simply write the types of stories that would happen in the source media, and I didn't want to write the same types of stories other fans were producing. This approach has followed me in my writing career. Whenever submitting a story to a themed anthology, I try to find a different way of approaching the topic. That could be as simple as submitting a story about a cat statue to a kids' cat-themed anthology [GI: aged 48. "Guardian of Tears," Cat Stories, Penguin Random House, 2016], or a story about playing footy on a far away planet with weak gravity for an ALF anthology [GI: aged 50. "Dreaming the Win," *Speccy-tacular AFL Stories*, Puffin Books, 2018]; or it could be about subverting expectations with a fairy-themed story told from the POV of a troll who wants to cook himself some fairies [GI: aged 45. "Fairy Pie," *Stories for Girls*, Random House Aust., 2013].

The greatest lesson I learned from fanfiction, was that writing could be fun!

I began by writing wish-fulfillment stories in primary school, giving me the things that I would have liked to see in the actual source material – writing *Doctor Who* stories and scripts with titles such as "The Daleks versus the Cybermen" [GI: aged 11. 1979]. Thankfully I never let anyone other than family read these awful pieces of fiction and, having found some of them a few years ago, I can confirm that they were, indeed, *really* bad. Case in point...

The K.9.s lead the Doctor through many corridors until they finally reached the room in which everyone was waiting. The Doctor opened the door and walked in.

"SURPRISE," yelled everyone, "HAPPY BIRTHDAY DOCTOR."
The Doctor looked very surprised. Romana, Leela and Andred walked up to him.

"Hello Doctor," said Leela. "Do you remember me and Andred. Oh, and K.9. Mark 1 of course."

"Yes, yes, yes, of course I do, but what are you doing here?"

"Well," said Andred, "Romana wanted a surprise birthday party for you. With my help she was able to get the coordinates of most of your past companions, and, well here we are."

The Doctor still looked a bit surprised. "Doctor did you forget," said Romana, "you're 764 today."

"You made a mistake Romana," replied the Doctor.
Romana gave a gasp. "Oh no."
"Oh yes," said the Doctor, "I'm only 763." The Doctor burst out
laughing and went to join the party.
[GI: aged 12. "The Big Surprise," 1980]

It was a long, convoluted four-page story, all because I wanted to give the Doctor a birthday party. Now…forget that you read the above extract as I'm about to misplace it again.

In the end, it didn't matter how bad these stories were, because the writing of them was so much fun. Prior to this, the only writing I had done was what I was instructed to do by teachers at school. That sort of writing was the furthest thing from fun that I could imagine (with the possible exception of maths). I didn't like doing it, and I only ever did the bare minimum I could get away with. Discovering that writing could be fun was quite a revelation. And, although focused on fanfic, it overflowed into all my writing. The school writing, while still not necessarily fun, gradually stopped being the burden it had been. I began to look for opportunities to find enjoyment in it, or at least to make it not too boring and onerous a task. I then took an interest in writing my own original stories in high school. It began with stories written as creative writing assignments for English class, then extended to stories written for my own pleasure and eventually to stories that found publication in general SF fanzines. And finally, eventually, that leap into the professional arena.

Even after I discovered the joys of writing my own original fiction, I stuck with fanfic for many years. Because it was fun! And I looked for new and exciting ways to extend the fun. So I wrote stories that played on my favorite elements of a franchise – like living out Holmesian fantasies in the *Next Gen* holodeck [GI: aged 22. "Q Dun It," SPOCK #59, AUSTREK: The Star Trek Fan Club of Victoria, 1990]. And I mixed things up a lot, introducing genres that were not part of a franchise into said franchise. A *Professionals* story with a sci-fi flavor saw CI5 dealing with a telepathic and telekinetic opponent [GI: aged 24. "It's All in the Mind," *Wild Justice*, Private Madness Ink, 1992].

I loved cross-over stories, perhaps even going overboard with "Beverley Crusher: 90210," a humorous *Next Gen* holodeck adventure that crossed over with *Beverley Hills: 90210, Get Smart,* and an obscure kids' television series called *The New Adventures of Beans Baxter.*

Beverly smoothed down a wrinkle in the skirt of her pale grey business suit and smiled with pride as she glanced at the sign which adorned her door.

"Beverly Crusher, 90210: Detective Agency," read Picard, and then frowned at his C.M.O.

"Well Jean-Luc," she said, "if you can run around the holodeck pretending to be Dixon Hill, then I'm also entitled to play detective every once in a while." [GI: aged 25. SPOCK #65, AUSTREK: The Star Trek Fan Club of Victoria, 1993]

As I said at the beginning, I think it's fair to say that without the fanfic experience, I don't know that I would ever have taken an interest in writing. Without it, I don't know that I would have a writing career now. And to this day, because of that fanfic starting point, I still have fun with my writing. I write the sort of stories I love reading. I write sci-fi and fantasy and horror and over-the-top action/adventure. I try to push boundaries and mix things up and subvert expectations and generally have a jolly good time. As a fan, I put hidden *Doctor Who* references into my books and, whenever possible, I chase my favorite franchises (actively looking for opportunities, submitting pitches, and sending unsolicited "please let me write for you" emails). There's a lot of running and only a limited amount of catching, but the occasional successes are worth every minute of effort.

"There are numerous cases of alien abduction where body parts have been removed. Eyes, fingers, toes, an entire hand. Sometimes internal organs are extracted, leaving no discernable scars – liver, kidneys, even appendixes."

"Hmm," mused Scully dryly. "Alien appendectomy."

"Mock if you will, Scully," said Mulder. "But there are documented cases. I have slides."

"You always have slides. But this current case, Mulder, is all about eyes. Four people, four removed eyeballs. Left eyeball in each case." Scully shuffled through the paperwork. "All four victims still alive. All with short-term memory loss."

"Memory loss," insisted Mulder, "is another classic symptom of alien abduction."

"Mulder," said Scully, dropping the papers onto the desk, the tiniest bit of frustration creeping into her otherwise smooth voice. "There are no reported UFO sightings even remotely connected with this case. No one saw any lights in the sky. No one heard any strange noises. You are clutching at straws. This is just a case of missing eyeballs."

Mulder smiled. "You say that as if missing eyeball cases are run of the mill."

[GI: aged 48. "An Eye For An Eye," The X-Files: Secret Agendas, IDW Publishing, USA, 2016]

As I mentioned earlier, licensed fiction comes with lots of rules. But that's okay. The sheer joy of writing within these universes is enough to weather any limitations thrown at me. And finding ways to tell the stories I want to tell, while staying within the boundaries I'm given, can also be heaps of fun.

So, let me take this opportunity to doff my cap and say a hearty *thanks* to fanfic. It has been a creative outlet, a training arena, and a playground for me, and for that I will be eternally grateful.

With no family or friends to comfort him, he was alone in the twilight of his life, as he awaited the approaching darkness.

With painful slowness the old man closed his eyes for the last time. The already dim lights began to fade away. The transparent cylinder at the centre of the console slowed to a stop as the green light winked out of existence. The cloister bell sounded a lamented farewell, and then all was silent.

[GI: aged 19. "Death of a Time Lord," Multiverse #17, 1987]

George Ivanoff is an author and fanboy residing in Melbourne, Australia. He has written over 100 books for kids and teens, occasional short stories for grown-ups and a few pieces of licensed media tie-in material. He drinks too much coffee, eats LOTS of chocolate and collects sonic screwdrivers. If you really want to know more about him, you can always check out his website: georgeivanoff.com.au.

I used to write Halo and Star Wars fan fiction for fun. About a decade later, I was reviewing Halo Wars 2 for Rolling Stone and writing features for Lucasfilm. Don't ever believe that writing fanfic disqualifies you from being a 'serious writer.' You're writing; be proud of that.

— Alex J Kane
Journalist and senior writer for *USA Today*

DOWN THE BARREL OF SOMEDAY (3 KEYS FOR ACTUALLY DOING)
Darcy Lindbergh

"Nevergiveuponadreamjustbecauseofthetimeitwilltaketoaccomplishit. The time will pass anyway." - Earl Nightingale

I've always been a writer.

Some people really struggle with whether or not they can call themselves that – do they write enough? do they write *seriously* enough? – but to me, storytelling has always been innate, instinctive. I've always had stories to tell and always tried to tell them. There's too much going on inside to keep it tucked away; I need to put it *out there*.

A lot of stuff I've written has made it *out there*. There's been some really earnest poetry, some really bizarre short stories, quite a lot of dry, intentionally sterile professional writing, and a great deal of fanfiction.

I'm a writer. That's what I do.

But I knew that someday, I wanted to do *more*.

ON ACTUALLY COMMITTING
Someday is a fake concept. It's an illusion. Time is happening now! And if you're waiting for *someday*, it's passing you by. And while time may be an infinite resource, you and I are not; we have lifespans that will, eventually and inevitably, end. I say this not to be depressing, but instead to set the mood. We are looking down the barrel at our own mortality.

It's a pretty tenuous position to be in while talking about the things we'll do *someday*.

But you don't think of it that way, right? *Someday* is out there because we're trying to reassure ourselves about the things we aren't doing now — that they aren't lost to us, only postponed! Someday you *will* take that Alaskan cruise, even though you can't afford it right now. Someday you *will* learn how to cross-stitch, even though you need new glasses first. Someday you *will* watch a full marathon of all of the *Lord of the Rings* extended editions, even though you can't spare fifteen consecutive hours this upcoming weekend.

But when it comes to writing, and what we're writing and what we're not writing, and the risks we're taking or not taking, *someday* is usually not so much a daydream as it is an excuse.

Then, a few years ago, Improbable Press offered me an opportunity to take the next step with my writing. This was a bit of an unusual situation because IP happened to have my email address — I'd written a short story for them in the collection *A Murmuring of Bees* — so they emailed me asking hey, do you want to write a book for us?

The same basic thing happens to you every time you scroll down Twitter or Tumblr and see calls for submissions from all the publishing houses out there. I want to make that perfectly clear here. My situation was unusual in the sense that it was directed specifically to me, but it's not unusual that publishers are, in fact, in the business of finding writers to write things so they may publish them. This is not in any way some kind of industry secret. Publishers need writers to publish. They're always out there, looking for writers who want in on this with them.

But in this particular case, I was lucky, because IP knew of me and they had my email address. So when they asked, do you want to write for us? I couldn't just scroll on by. I had to actually stop and think about it.

Someday was here, knocking at my door.

And since I am a writer, and always have been, and very likely always will be, I was *completely blindsided* to realize how afraid I was of *someday*. How very afraid I was to take that next step with my writing.

The 'next step' looks different for every writer. In this case, the next step for me was writing and publishing something professionally, but that may not be the case for you. Maybe for you, it's the step from writing fanfiction to sharing fanfiction. Maybe it's the step from writing short stories to writing long-form fiction. Maybe it's going from writing fluffy kisses to writing explicit smut, writing in a new genre, or trying a new format.

"Here's the thing about the next step: I was never going to be perfectly ready to take it"

Whichever way, as writers, we always know there's a next step. It's the one we're afraid of taking.

I had always told myself I would write a book *someday*. Once I finish this project, and after this event is over, and when I have time to get more organized, I'll write that. When I can devote myself to the research, I'll write that. When I really get a handle on understanding the process, then I'll be able to write that! I just want to do it *perfectly!*

I have wanted to write a book pretty much since the time I learned how to read books, and here I was, about to turn down the opportunity to write a book.

Here's the thing about the next step: I was never going to be perfectly ready to take it.

I wasn't. I was never going to be ready. The idea that taking the next step can be done perfectly – or even *gracefully* – is a lie, and even more so when we're talking about something as intimate and personal as writing. There's no manual for taking the next step; there's no *proper* way of doing it. There's never going to be 'the right time' to start writing. There's never going to be 'organized enough' to start writing. There's never going to be 'enough research' to start writing. And if I think I can ever fully understand the process before I go through it, I'm going to be sorely disappointed.

So I had to ask myself: if it's never going to be perfect, do I do it at all?

The answer, obviously, was *yes*. If circumstances were never going to be perfect, I have to stop holding myself to the standard of the perfect circumstances.

I wanted to write. I wanted to take the next step. So I just had to do it. I had to do it *right now*. I had to admit that I was not going to do it perfectly and find my peace with that. I had to admit that I might write something unexpected, or something uninteresting, and then write it anyway. I had to decide that I would write in five minute breaks here and there if I had to, because that would be five minutes worth of work I didn't have before. I had to decide that it was okay if it took me two weeks to research the answer to a question, because it would be an answer I didn't have two weeks before. I decided that if I wanted to know how the process worked, I would just have to take the plunge and, as Ray Bradbury once said, build my wings on the way down.

So I emailed IP back and said, as a matter of fact, I think I do. (That's not really what I said – what I *actually* said was a little panicky and disjointed, but that's what it amounted to.) And IP said great! Let's do this.

And it *was* great! and it was freeing! I was committed to taking the first step of fulfilling a lifelong dream! I had Decided.

The problem then was that I had to actually write the damn thing.

ON LITERALLY, ACTUALLY DOING

The worst part about literally, actually doing anything is starting. There's nothing so intimidating as staring at a blank page and wondering what the heck you're going to put on it. It's just you and the void, and the void is honestly a little judgmental.

The only way to shut the void up is to write something, so if you're not sure where to start, start with the Shitty First Draft.

What makes a helpful Shitty First Draft is going to be different for everyone. Some people are nearly robots and can spit their shitty first drafts out in near-fully-completed form, check a few commas, and boom, final product, ready to go. Some people are very logic-minded and find it easier to start with a bit of structure – Act One, Part One requires A, Act One, Part Two requires B, and so on – and then they can build their outlines and then subsequently their narratives around those bones. For me, the Shitty First Draft is mostly a stream-of-consciousness exercise where I basically yell down a word processing document (or, on occasion, into a chat box with whatever friend was unfortunate enough to say 'hey' back first) with no care to spelling, grammar, punctuation, or general coherency until my fingers are too tired to continue.

It doesn't matter how you do it; it only matters that you relieve yourself of the burden of doing it *well*.

From there, you just have to trust yourself.

It's harder than I'm making it out to be, I'll admit it. It's uncomfortable. It's scary. It's like the first time you got into a swimming pool without your floaters on. You write a few things down, wonder what the hell you think you're doing, and nearly admit defeat. Then you write a few more things down, and a few more things. It looks like gobbledygook. You have no idea what you're talking about. You write a few more things down. You almost give up again.

Then you look at what you've written, and you think, *oh, hey! That's not bad, actually.*

And you learn, bit by bit, to trust yourself a little more. People who have taken lots of next steps will tell you that it's easier to trust themselves now than it was in the beginning. It's something you learn by practicing – which means you have to practice.

Which means you have to *do it*.

You can't learn what it is to fly if you don't first jump. Nobody's asking you to do an Olympic-level dive on your first shot. So what if you belly flop?

At least you were in the air.

ON LETTING GO

If there's one thing scarier than the next writing step, it's letting go.

We, as writers, are storytellers, which of course means we *tell* stories. Which implies that at some point, there's going to be someone you're telling the story *to*.

Which means at some point, someone is probably going to tell you what they think of it.

I personally prefer to do this in stages. When I was writing my piece for Improbable, I first sent everything to my SPAG-focused beta reader (spelling, punctuation, and grammar), then I sent it to my structure-focused beta, then I sent it to my Victoriana-focused beta. That was a fairly easy step, because they're cheerleaders as much as they are editors, and friends to boot. Their comments make me laugh and build me up even as they challenge me and make me reconsider a word, a line, a whole scene.

Then of course everything went to IP, and those edits came back, and that's when I got the hollowed-out anxious/giddy feeling that I always get when I get feedback from someone I don't know as well, who reads my writing without the benefit of being a little in my head. But these comments work, at least in part, to ease the writing away from myself a little: they ease me into another view, into seeing my writing from the Outside in.

The first time I read through those comments, I *only* read the comments, just to give this feeling a little space and to respect the Outsideness of it. Then I closed out of the document and let it sit for several days, and came back after the anxious/giddy feeling had subsided a bit and read them again, refreshed, and *then* I started working on addressing them. It's a bit uncomfortable, sure, but it's ultimately *fine*, because the goal of this commentary is to improve the writing for people who don't have the benefit of being me.

Someday that won't be true. Someday the commentary will be something I can't do anything about. Someday the commentary won't be intended to lift me up and support me. Someday the commentary might just be because someone doesn't like what I have to say.

But that's *someday*, and remember: *someday* is a little bit fake. The same way we can't put things off for *someday*, neither can we live in fear of it.

This goes back to trusting yourself. Find your peace with what you have accomplished and trust yourself that you wrote your story the way you needed it to be written. It's not going to be perfect, nothing ever is. That impulse toward perfectionism is the same one that almost stopped you in the beginning, before you ever started, and you already know how to defeat it.

Take a deep breath. Take the leap.

The time will pass whether you do it or you don't. The time will pass whether you take the risk or you don't. The time will pass whether you write or don't, whether you share it or don't, whether you take the next step or you stand, uncertain, hovering on the precipice.

The time will pass anyway.

Pass it in pursuit.

Darcy Lindbergh has been a Holmes enthusiast for years, devouring and enjoying every adaptation she can get her hands on. Aside from writing original fiction like The Watches of the Night for Improbable Press, as well as fanfiction, Darcy enjoys cross-stitching fine art patterns, compiling extremely long to-do lists, and blogging about life, the universe, and Holmes and Watson on Tumblr and Twitter. Darcy lives in the American Midwest with her dog, a beautiful good girl who is also called Darcy.

There are fanfic authors that write circles around published authors, and are so prolific they'll blow your mind. There are fics out there 10 times better than what hits shelves. 20 times. If I ever get [on Twitter] and insult fic as a whole medium, just know that I've been kidnapped or hacked.

— Tracy Deonn
Bestselling writer of *Bloodmarked*

FROM FANFIC WRITER TO SCREENWRITER
Melissa Good

Melissa Good is like a many fic writers: she works full-time (as a network engineer), lives with pets (lizards and a dog), and is technically inclined (with a BFA in technical theater and lighting design).

Missy Good is also a prolific author, with dozens of books on Goodreads and thousands of words of *Xena: Warrior Princess* fic across multiple websites. It's this last bit which led Melissa to that rarer achievement: writing two episodes of the TV show itself – "Coming Home" and "Legacy."

Here Missy talks with *Spark* about how she went from fanfiction writer to screenwriter, and in sharing this part of her origin story it's easy to believe that this is how *anything* amazing comes to be: we do, we share, we engage – and then sometimes stuff happens. Who knows which one of us may yet pen episodes of our favorite program?

From writing fic to writing for the show for which you were writing fic: would you recommend this journey or is it 'careful what you wish for?'

I would not trade one moment of my experience for anything on earth. I don't know that *recommend* is the right word, but if you do get to do something of that sort, my advice is go in with a completely open mind and heart and take what comes. Don't try to make it be something to fit a preconceived notion, just let it be.

How did you end up writing for Xena?

Well, you know one of the things about *Xena* is that it was on the television at a very specific time – the coming into being of the World Wide Web and the internet and, more importantly, the evolution of the internet from a narrow-focus technical oddity, into a broadly-used universal service. Everyone wanted to mess with it, and that brought together creators and fans in a way that just hadn't happened before.

Up until then, creators were behind a wall, one breached only by a very few. They did not get the broadside of the opinions of the internet, but in the first few seasons the *Xena* producers did, and they reveled in that contact. Then they came foul of it during season five for a plethora of reasons. The result was a 'war' with the fans after the tone of the show radically altered.

There were a lot of reasons for all of it, and there's no fault on either side really. Fans came to believe they had a piece of the *Xena* action, and the production team was behaving as though they owned all of it (they did).

So as they were going into season six, executive producer Rob Tapert thought he would maybe let one fan get to be a part of the writing of an episode – an olive branch as it were.

I think it was a quite unpopular idea, but Rob is a tenaciously strong-willed person. So he asked Steve Sears, who did then and does now have a close relationship with the fandom, if there wasn't someone he could suggest to maybe get involved.

I knew Steve, had met him at *Xena* events and at DragonCon where I'd led the *Xena* track for a few years, and one late afternoon I got an instant message from him asking if I was interested. I was, and I did write for them, and had a really good and really interesting time of it.

First came fic, then this interesting time. What got you started writing fanfiction?

I enjoy writing and telling stories and always have. There are notebooks somewhere full of long, hand-written stories I don't even remember. The internet and being able to type on a keyboard certainly helped, I have wretched handwriting. I started writing *Xena* fic because the characters caught my imagination, and still do, and so I continue to write them because it gives me joy to do it. It's like spending time with dear friends.

"I would not trade one moment of my experience for anything on earth"

What's been the biggest surprise for you in your fandom and fic journey, good or bad?

Bad: having thousands of people crash my website and get me kicked off an ISP after putting up a message board. Best good surprise is continually finding that people come to the fandom fresh and new even now, and they find something charming in the writing and the characters all over again.

What three things have mattered the most to your writing success?

I don't know that I can really define that because I never looked at writing as a success or failure. It's something I enjoy doing, something that engages the creative maelstrom in isolation of itself. It's like painting, in that regard. Creating expresses something very specific to the creator – sad, or happy, or thrilling, it lets you lift yourself up by shaping your own reality in words – how do you define success or failure in that, so long as you love it?

What are your thoughts on fic writers going pro?

I think sometimes, when you are under pressure to produce professional writing, you have a different layer of imperatives on you, not in a bad way, that can shape how you tell a story. If that's your goal and your passion, it can lift you to great success. But sometimes that also means you don't have the freedom to capture an idle daydream just for the pure joy of rambling on.

Do people you know and love know you write fic?

I have been posting Xena and Gabrielle stories on the internet for around twenty years now, under my real name. So yes, for sure people around me know. My staff at my last job knew, knew about the whole *Xena* thing, my new teams at my new job Googled me on the internet and knew, before I joined them.

Never mattered to me but that is an extremely personal decision and many writers, especially those who tell the hard stories, are not in a place where they feel safe doing that. Stay with your instincts. Don't let people push you into a light if you don't want to go there.

What's your take-away message to fellow fic writers?
Write for the love of it. Write because it nourishes the creative power inside you and let it let you take flight.

Melissa Good is a full time network engineer and part time writer who lives in Pembroke Pines, Florida with a handful of lizards and a dog. When not traveling for work, or participating in the usual chores she ejects several sets of clamoring voices onto a variety of keyboards and tries to entertain others with them to the best of her ability with books that include A Journey of Soulmates series and the Dar and Kerry series.

One tends to think of [fanfiction] as written by total fanboys and fangirls as a kind of worshipful act, but a lot of times you'll read these stories and it'll be like 'What if Star Trek had an openly gay character on the bridge?' And of course the point is that they don't, and they wouldn't, because they don't have the balls, or they are beholden to their advertisers, or whatever. There's a powerful critique, almost punk-like anger, being expressed there-which I find fascinating and interesting and cool.

— Lev Grossman
Bestselling writer of *The Magicians Trilogy*

FILING OFF THE SERIAL NUMBERS: A RAMBLING GUIDE
C. Veillon

Before we get started, first things first: it's okay if you never want to scrub your fanfiction and publish it, and I am not here to imply otherwise. Fic for fic's sake means the world to me, is the thing I enjoy most, and has been my constant companion since 1998. The writing of fanfiction is a labor of love, but still, it is *labor,* as well as a straight-up art form. Fanfiction is real writing, valid in and of itself. Scrubbing fic and publishing it does not suddenly make it more valid, real, or "serious" than it was before. Full stop.

Disclaimer over.

Now that's out of the way, what if you do want to scrub a fic and self-publish or submit it to a publisher? Hopefully I can help here! What I'm about to lay out is less a step-by-step instruction manual, and more a set of loose guidelines and encouragements. I have coordinated over nearly two dozen published or soon-to-be-published projects for Carnation Books, including guiding the scrubbing process. Over the last few years of doing this, I have learned the following universal fic scrubbing truths:

Some fics are easier to scrub than others, and alternative universes (AU) are a good place to start.

You have to let go of the fic.

The process depends on the author and the story.

FIRST THINGS FIRST – CHOOSING A FIC TO SCRUB
Selecting a fic seems like a pretty obvious first step, but I have seen a *ton* of fics in my day that are simply not scrubbable. They're *great* pieces of fic, *wonderful* writing, *amazing* plot, maybe *scorching hot* love scenes. But they only work as pieces of fanfiction, because they're so rooted in the canon from which they sprung.

This is not a bad thing!

Remember what I said about fic for fic's sake? These works are amazing, well-loved by so many, and I certainly enjoy reading them as much as I enjoy reading fic that would work as a scrubbed piece, and *way more* than I enjoy most popular original fiction. The fact remains that a fic which started as a fix-it for a season or episode of a TV show, or as a rewrite of the plot of a popular movie, or to fill in missing scenes from a novel, are really hard, if not impossible, to scrub.

The great news?

An author who is good at writing deep-into-the-canon fanfic probably has a *great* AU idea, or has one already written! And AUs? Those are your best bet. An AU, especially one that takes place in a totally different time or place (or both) will scrub up much more easily than one that is say, canon divergent. That's because it's pretty likely that in the process of dreaming up an AU, an author has already shaved away layers of the canon that would make the story recognizable as a fan work.

Does this mean *only* AUs can be scrubbed? Not at all. But they're a great place to start, and in my experience, the least intimidating to scrub. So start there, and see what happens!

Okay so you have a fic you want to scrub – now what?

ITEM TWO: MAKE LIKE ELSA AND *LET IT GO*

You are now taking your fic, with these canon characters that you love so, so much, and you're going to have to do terrible things to it. You have to gut it. You're going to have to be merciless. If you're thinking of it as your fic, this story you're super proud of, one all your friends read, and for which people left you kudos and comments, a fic you wrote after you heard that one song on Spotify and thought oh god, this song is about my one true pair (you get the picture), you might feel some things about changing it.

That's okay!

"There is no right or wrong."

But you *have* to let it go. Some publishers might require you to eventually remove a fic from the internet before a scrubbed version can be published, so now is a good time to make peace with that idea, as well as any stressful feelings about making such huge changes to your story. Take a deep breath. And think of it as making your own canon. You're the boss. You're the alpha. You can do this.

You now have a fic and the mindset, so now it's time to see how many more references to various fandoms I can squish into a basic explanation of the process, which, as I mentioned above in item three, is different for everyone.

THE THREE OF THIS PROCESS DEPENDS ON YOU

A good place to start scrubbing a fic is with a quick and dirty find-and-replace. Start with character names. Let's use John and Sherlock for this example. Find and replace every John with your new original character's name. Now do a find on Watson, and make sure his last name is the new character's last name. Same with Sherlock and Holmes. Now think of your most frequently mentioned supporting characters. Time to find and replace Mrs. Hudson, Mycroft, Greg, and Lestrade. If characters use nicknames, make sure you search for those and change them, too.

Next, start thinking of how you're changing these characters and their world. Are they older? Younger? If this isn't already a very AU story, are they still a detective and a doctor? Do they live in London or somewhere else? What parts of your story rely heavily on the reader having watched Sherlock to 'get' what's happening, even in an AU? Start reading through and finding any pieces of regurgitated canon.

For example, if you've written an AU about John and Sherlock where they're professional skateboarders who meet in Seattle in the 90s, did you re-use dialogue from the first episode of Sherlock as a cheeky easter egg? Highlight it. Make a note that this needs to change, and come back to it later if you need to. Look for places where the characterization might not make sense to a reader who has never heard of John and Sherlock before. For this example, let's say you changed Sherlock's name to...Kirk. Does Kirk seem too Sherlock-y? If a reader who has only known him as Kirk were to read the story, would they like him? Would they 'get' him?

This is where you will need to do the bulk of your new writing to bring this story into the realm of the original. How much new writing or rewriting an author has to do is different from story to story. Some folks add tens of thousands of new words. Some *double* the length of their story. Others don't need to, or they do a ton of rewriting and adding and then deleting, and it all comes out with the same word count as before. There is no right or wrong.

Adding words does not always equal adding value. Sometimes in the process of scrubbing a fic it can feel like more words, more backstory, is what will make the story an original piece. This is not always the case. Evaluate the universe you already have in front of you. If you started with an AU, you very likely have a well fleshed out world already. Maybe it's a space station. Perhaps a coffee shop. Chances are, if you took characters from one of your favorite shows and transplanted them to a new setting, you have already done a lot of explaining to the reader. Look for subtle ways to change the fic that might not require pages of additional material. Evaluate the characters. Can you tweak their appearance? Their family situation? A character who, in your fic, has a brother, might now have two brothers, or a sister, in your original story.

Don't forget to see where you can *take away* rather than *add*. A great example here is a fic with a large ensemble cast. A fic that spends time with every last Avenger is a thrill to a fandom reader who already knows the characters and their dynamics. However, in an original piece, you are now tasked with making *a lot* of characters feel whole and interesting to a reader who has no idea they were once known as Earth's greatest defenders. You may want to consider leaving some minor roles on the cutting room floor, or perhaps combining characters. I know it's hard. The thought of losing Coulson pains me, too, but he isn't Coulson anymore; he's a new character, and he's superfluous when you have that guy who used to be Nick Fury bossing everyone about.

(This truly pained me to write, dear reader, because I *adore* Coulson, but I needed an example. May Clark Gregg forgive me.)

On the other hand, sometimes we *do* need to add to a fic for it to make sense as an original piece. The most significant area you will most likely need to address is characterization. As mentioned before, the readers of your original story may need a little convincing to like a character as acerbic as Sherlock Holmes, for example. As the author, your job is to make the reader understand this character's motives and background, and this will probably take some additional writing. One great method for this is to write a whole new set of biographies for your characters. Keep these in a separate document. Then, during rewrites, make like that gif and just *sprinkle* the new information through the new story. This will help prevent front-loading too much information into your new manuscript.

A note here: Though you are changing these characters a lot, a great thing to remember is that the general framework can stay, if you want it to. There's a reason these character dynamics worked for you so much that you wanted to write about them. The archetypes did it for you, and will do it for readers of your original piece. So remember, while Sherlock might be Kirk now, Kirk can be a genius who gets into a lot of trouble. His best friend-turned-lover can be a bit of an adrenaline junkie who would follow him into hell itself. Some things are universally appealing, you know?

Through these first steps, my advice is to completely ignore your typos, spelling errors, and what your commas are doing. Save it for once you think the story is totally rewritten, and is no longer fic. Even when you're doing a final read-through once you've added fresh backstory and made sure you haven't left traces of John and Sherlock behind, ignore everything else. Get a friend to read it. Get a *few* friends to read it. Have someone beta it for spelling, punctuation, and grammar. Getting bogged down in word choice and flow gets really discouraging really fast, so let that be your last concern, if you can.

And here, intrepid author, is where you finish scrubbing.

Scrubbing is not editing, and it's not shopping a manuscript. It's just getting this fic to a place where you can move on to those next steps. Once your fic is no longer the fic, it will be time to give it a solid edit as the new story, which is why I recommend having a friend read and/or beta read it for you. If you have never worked with a beta before, now is a very good time to start, because if you are able to get your manuscript accepted by a publisher, you will soon be working with an editor. Practicing receiving criticism is a great idea, and a fresh set of eyes can help polish your story to a high shine.

As I mentioned before, the scrubbing process is different for everyone. Maybe your story is so AU it's practically already scrubbed once you change the names. Great! Maybe you just start rewriting the thing, page by page, like one amazing author I know has done. Or maybe you are extremely chaotic and save the find-and-replace for last. That's fine. You scare me, but it's all fine. You can probably still apply some of this advice in ways that work for you, you rebel you.

Good luck scrubbing, writers! I'm cheering you on!

Colleen lives in the U.S. with her family. She has been in fandom since the mid-to-late 1990s and will never, ever leave. She currently sails the good ships Neville/Draco, Mycroft/Lestrade, and Jack/Bitty. She manages Carnation Books (@carnationbooks), a fandom-based independent publisher of queer romance. You can find Colleen on twitter @meansgirlwrites for all your shouting and arm-waving needs.

ALL STORIES GROW
(A MYTHICAL 221B)
Carman C. Curton

All stories grow – towering tales boasted out to the gods in beer-y voices, occupying the hearing and attention of all within the Tellers' Circle, expanding until they draw the awe and respect stories command.

All stories grow – until one didn't. Unfit for the adoration of the audience, unable to fill the epic space of the Tellers' Circle, the small story's teller took her flutelike voice to the Makers' Circle, an uneven site filled with active hands making bread and babies and baskets and other ordinary things.

All stories grow – but this one, whose tiny tale was told by a teller sitting among busy women, waiting for them to take a break, a breath, was a mere 221 words, each perfect because necessary. Some kept working and some listened in the short spaces between Makings, smiling and nodding.

One of the listeners rested her hands on her son's head, pausing from braiding his hair, Here's a small story—. After her, a sturdy weaver said, Here's another—. And after her, a woman with sparkling green eyes wiped yeasty dough from between her fingers, Here's one to share—.

All stories grow – except those that don't. And those who had time in the Makers' Circle stopped, rested, listened. And at the end of each small, so small, story, the Makers breathed: *Beautiful.*

Carman C. Curton consumes caffeine while writing a series of microstories called QuickFics, which she leaves in random places for people to find.

4

WRITING NITTY GRITTY
Getting down to the business of doing

FANDOM TAUGHT ME TO FINISH
K. Caine

I went to see *Mad Max: Fury Road* in theaters when it came out. It's an odd movie – it's dressed up like an action film, and the action sequences themselves are phenomenal, but it's also a story about a group of people who go all the way across a hostile desert, only to realize that's not where they needed to be. It's a story of people who face an endless plain of salt stretching in front of them – and instead of pressing forward into an uncertain future, they decide to turn around, and go right back where they came from.

Huh, I thought. *That wasn't where I expected the story to go. That was a pretty gutsy move for a Hollywood blockbuster. I'll have to think about that.*

I didn't just think about it.

I let it change my *life*.

The first fandom I remember being really passionate about was *Robin Hood* (the Disney one, with the fox). After *Robin Hood*, there was *Star Wars*. At night I used to dream about going to the Jedi Academy, and training with Jacen and Jaina. Making new friends. Falling in love for the first time. Then I'd wipe that character clean, and start over again.

Hi, Jacen. I'm Anaya.

Hi, Jaina. My name is Isabell.

After *Star Wars*, it was *Titanic, Harry Potter,* then *The Terror.*

I knew what fandom was, but I didn't really get into it until after I moved away from home – and then I was into it in a big way. I devoured as much of it as I could, frequently staying up until three in the morning, just to keep reading people's stories.

I was writing them, too – but, you know. Not fanfic. Serious stuff. I mean, okay. It was genre. And I knew that genre wasn't the best use of my time, because that's what the people around me told me, but I loved it, so I could just, like. Practice with it, right? And then I could switch to better writing when I got older. Something that could be critically acclaimed. I was a talented writer, my partners told me. I could write critically-acclaimed fiction. That would be good. I could do that.

Except – I couldn't.

I just couldn't.

My heart wasn't there.

Though I did learn a lot of things about writing from a lot of places. I learned about story structure by reading voraciously – not just stories that succeeded beyond my wildest imagination, but stories which failed miserably. I read fanfic, I read genre, I read literature. I followed authors through fandoms where the source material was unfamiliar, I followed authors into their back catalog just to see how their stories had changed over time. I read stories that drew me in and absorbed me so fully that I lost track of time completely, and I read stories that threw me so abruptly out of the narrative that I got engrossed in figuring out *why* they threw me. I started to learn more precisely about craft by reading writing books, and later by taking classes. I learned how to talk about writing. I read blogs about revising and copyediting. I practiced giving and receiving feedback with friends, and later, with writing groups.

Yet all those things felt very surface-level to me. I understood the theories, but I couldn't put them into practice. I understood what I was supposed to be doing, but I didn't want to do any of it. I bought a copy of the Writer's Market, and I couldn't find a space that felt like a reflection of me.

I didn't know what I was looking for, and I didn't know who I was.

By the early two thousands, writing and I were in a weird place. I was writing a lot, but I wasn't finishing anything. Every time I moved apartments, I had more banker's boxes of writing to bring

170

with me. I drafted at least four novels – and it's entirely possible there are a fifth and sixth that I've forgotten about – and I finished none of them. Every single draft needed work, and I didn't even understand how to *start* that work, much less complete it.

"Once you trust there is a home for your work in fandom? You can trust there is a home for your non-fandom work as well"

All during this time, I was lurking around the edges of fandom, but I wasn't saying anything. I didn't know how to say anything.

I wasn't happy. I was isolated and alone. I was tired of being told that my work was good – so why wasn't I writing literary fiction? I was smart – so why wasn't I watching critically-acclaimed media? I was talented – so what was I doing with my life?

I knew the answer was *nothing*, so I quit writing completely.

And I stayed quit for ten years.

If there's one thing I love about myself, it's my ability to believe two conflicting things at the same time: namely, that the best part of *Fury Road* was that there was no romance in it between Max and Furiosa, and also, simultaneously, that the romance between Max and Furiosa would have been the best damn part of the movie.

For the record, I am endlessly grateful that the movie exists exactly as it does. But then – how did I fix the gap in my heart that also wanted to see the two of them working, slowly and cautiously, through each other's PTSD to see if there was anything else that might blossom?

Luckily for me, I remembered fanfic existed. After all, I'd been reading it in the early two thousands….it had to still be around, right?

Wow, was it ever still around – and in a big way.

When I came back to fandom, it was far more organized, and far more accessible than it had been when I left.

Then *The Force Awakens* came out, and I remembered about fanfic *even more intensely*. Wow, I was suddenly reading a lot of fanfic.

I still had nothing to say, though.

After all, I didn't know how to finish, so was there even any point in starting?

The thing that I love most about fandom is the depth of exploration. Not even the depth of exploration that's possible – they're stories, and any story can have that kind of depth – but the depth of exploration that is readily and quickly available. The way that fandom collectively churns through tropes, blending them together and inverting them, chopping them up into tiny pieces and sautéing them over a specific heat level, adding in the flavored syrup of a coffee shop AU (alternative universe), or the specific bitter sharpness of a Canadian prairie winter.

I love the way that we have defined scenarios – first time; there's only one bed; enemies to friends to lovers; sex pollen – and yet, every single time that we apply those scenarios to a different fandom, a different pairing, a different AU, we get to see entirely new facets of a thing that we thought was fully explored. *What if it's a coffee shop?* is an entirely different story than *what if it's a coffee shop and one of them has anxiety?* which is a different story again from *what if it's a coffee shop in the Middle Ages?*

There's a lot of writing advice that encourages people to believe that *our* story is unique, that our story is special, that our story has something in it that is uniquely inherently us, but for a long time I didn't believe it. I mean, how could I believe it? Outside of fic it wasn't easy to find more than one telling of a similar story, and it seemed like the unique things had to do with the plot, or something, and not anything the author was inherently saying – and I didn't know these authors anyways, maybe they were just – maybe they were just good like that, maybe they were–

But you know when I finally believed? You know when I finally understood that our individual stories are unique, just because they're written by us? It was when I got engrossed in fandom and saw it every single day. I can search through the tags, and I can find forty-five modern AUs of any particular ship, and I can watch those characters fall in love for the first time over and over and over again and *every single one of those stories is different.*

Eventually, I joined a writing group. Nothing had really changed since I quit writing a decade prior. There were new how-to books, and new blogs to read. People still wanted to talk about the Hero's Journey. Authors I used to really enjoy had turned out to be horrible people, but also, there were a lot of new authors, so it all worked out.

I still didn't know how to finish. I knew how to progress, but all I was doing was progressing. I was moving forward, but there was no end. My writing was never good enough. It was never smart enough. It was never detailed enough. I felt like I couldn't show anyone my fiction, because I didn't feel as though anyone had context for it. I knew that the worldbuilding was incomplete. I knew that the descriptions weren't good. I knew, I knew.

But I didn't know how to fix it. I didn't know how to ask for feedback on incomplete works, and I didn't know how to complete things. I didn't know what it would feel like to be satisfied with my work. I didn't know what it would be like to be satisfied with *myself.*

I was moving forward, but I didn't know how to reach my destination. How much did it matter that I moved three feet today, and four feet the day before, and one foot the day before that, if I never got to the end? If I never reached the Green Place, did it matter how fast I was getting there? Did it matter if I progressed at all? What does an ending even look like? How do projects get completed?

What do you move when there's nothing ahead of you but salt?

Then I started commenting on fics that I enjoyed. Why not, you know? I was having more fun reading fanfiction than I was trying to slog through novels that I should be reading that I didn't actually like, so I might as well reach out and leave some comments on stories I *did* like.

My technical skills were coming back after having stagnated, but I still wasn't any closer to finishing any of my own works. Even if I hypothetically managed to finish one, I didn't know what I was going to do with it. It would take me years to get an agent, if I got one. (I might not.) Years to be published, if I made it. (I might not do that either.) I'd have to move on and do another project, but then I would have to go through the same process there too–

Sometimes you need to go right back where you started.

One day I remember doing a careful evaluation process every time I thought about writing fanfic. "Do I have something to say about this? And if I do, is it important?"

The answer was *no*, for a long time.

I kept reading. I kept working on my own work.

I kept asking myself the same questions.

"Do I have something to say? Does it matter?"

The answer was *no*, for a long time.

And then, eventually, the answer was *maybe*.

Because, you see, the thing about writing fanfic was that I immediately knew what I was going to do with it when it was done. I knew where it was going to go. I knew the tropes that it fell into, the tags that I would use. I knew that *somebody* would read it. Maybe not very many somebodies! But there would be some people that would read it. I had been one of those somebodies. And maybe somebody would like it. Maybe they wouldn't like it, but the piece had a destination, and it had a potential audience, and setting the work in a specific fandom with specific characters meant that it would be safe – that people would read it just because of that, even if they didn't know who I was.

They didn't need to know who I was, because it didn't matter. And they already liked the characters.

Fanfic is all about taking characters that we love, or characters that we hate, or characters that we love to hate, and showing everyone new sides of them. New interpretations. More depth. Less depth. Fanfiction is about exploring something to a degree that moviemakers could only dream of – because we can use as few or as many words as we like.

We don't need to tell a two hour story. We can tell a story that takes five minutes. And we can tell a story that takes five years.

I look back on my own work now, and I can see this really fascinating thing with it: I always knew what I was trying to do.

I knew where my stories were going. I knew where the arcs were going. But I didn't know where the finished products were going to go, and so every time I closed off a draft, I just...started something new. I started something new because the prospect of revising something that didn't have a home was daunting. I started something new, every time, because I was scared to look at what I had completed. I was scared to see the breadth of the work that was required in order to polish it. I was scared that I would do all that, and it would still never have a home.

If I had turned around and looked backward, I would have seen the story. And I would have known that what I needed to do was to gather my belongings, and get back on my bike, and go all the way back to the beginning, so that I could finish what I started, right in the place I came from. But I couldn't stop staring at the salt ahead of me, so I didn't know where to go from there.

The thing about fandom is – someone is always there. There's always an audience. It doesn't matter how obscure or how narrow, there is somebody out there who will find your work and read it. And knowing that there's someone who will read it makes it much, much easier to sit down and do the work. Every time I stare at the first paragraph of a fic and think to myself "I'll never figure out how to edit this," I know I can reach out on social media, and I can find people who will connect with the story I'm going to write. I can find people to beta. I can find people to share head canons with. I can find people who are interested in my content. And knowing that there's an audience makes it that much easier to focus on the work that needs to be done once the draft is complete.

If you're sitting at your computer, and you're looking at an endless plain of salt, it's very hard to focus on the work that needs to be done, because it's salt today, salt tomorrow, and salt the day afterward, with no end in sight. But if you turn around, and you look at the place that you came from, and you know that there are people waiting for you there? The journey is much, much easier.

It doesn't matter what you write.

There is a home for it in fandom.

And once you trust there's a home for your work in fandom? You can trust there is a home for your non-fandom work as well. It may take longer to find – but it's out there. It's not just salt.

I do everything, these days.

I write my own fiction, I write fandom-adjacent fiction, and I write fanfic. I'm a proud genre writer – and I'm finally unlearning all the toxic attitudes I picked up when I was younger. I don't worry so much, anymore, about whether or not my work has a home, I know I'll find one for it.

I have enough practice in finishing my fanfic now that I don't feel that same pressure with my own work that I used to. I've finished multiple 100k+ fics. I *know* I can finish a novel.

I still ask myself whether I have something to say, but I don't interrogate myself, anymore, on whether or not it's important. Who gives a fuck, you know? I'm having fun, and I'm producing good work, and I'm learning a ton of new writing techniques I never would have been courageous enough to attempt in my own work if I hadn't already tried them in fanfic.

I fought my way to the edge of the desert, and I looked at the salt – and then I turned around, and I came right back to the place where I started, and this is where I've built my home. Fandom is where I build my skills, where I develop my voice, where I stretch out and test other writing techniques. Fandom is the place I can try different versions of the same tropes, where I can test a setting, where I can do an experiment of a specific way in which people fall in love. And I know, at any point, that I can gather up my gear and strike out in a direction, and there will always be a place for me to come home to.

I know how to finish, now, and I know how to finish because fandom taught me.

K. Caine is a queer writer, living and writing in the Canadian prairies. Their work encompasses multiple genres, including romance, erotica, horror, and spec fic, and is consistently characterized by deep POV, high emotional stakes, and layered foreshadowing. K. Caine's writing often includes themes of feminism, sexuality, gender, and non-traditional relationships.

The older I get, the more I realize I don't need to be the smartest, the prettiest, the richest, the most talented. I want to be the most alive. I want beams of HELL YES to shine out of my eyes and infect everyone I meet. I want to do the opposite of ossifying.

— Delilah S Dawson
Bestselling writer of *Star Wars: Phasma*

BICHOK
Meredith Spies

I admit it. I've tricked myself into writing.

Okay, just get this done. 1,000 words. You can do this. You can have that super fancy chocolate you bought once you hit 1,000 words.

I have to.

Oooooh, but Jessica Jones is on!

Okay, look, you have a deadline. If you hit your word count before the deadline, you can watch an episode.

I love writing though…once I get going.

Right, okay, let's have a race. It's one o'clock now…I bet I can finish writing this article before the clock strikes three. Winner gets to goof off on the internet for the remainder of the time left before three.

It's the *getting started* that's the hard part.

So. Many. Chores. Don't wanna write today… *flop* But…if I don't write, I'll lazy-spiral myself out of this novel-poem-article. Fine, how about 250 words? I can do that. That's the least I can do, right? Every day?

You know the story you want to tell, *I* know the story I want to tell, but getting that wheel turning… I've tried almost every hint and tip thrown out there by writer's workshops and helpful websites and authors on Twitter.

Yet I almost always fail miserably.

And still…

"Try using a prompt! Just to get the juices flowing!"

"Start in the middle of the story and work your way out!"

"Write a scene from the point of view of a different character/a bird who was nearby/the NSA agent monitoring their messenger accounts!"

I've tried those. All of them. And flopped. I was absolutely sure

I was a failed writer before I even got published. They'd find me buried under a pile of my own manuscripts, because apparently in my defeatist fantasies I'd have given up writing on a computer and reverted entirely to typewritten manuscripts stored in old boxes so that my demise could be more dramatic.

Just a sec – I need to write that plot idea down...

Right, so the problem with all that writing advice wasn't the advice itself – it was all solid, excellent advice. The problem was that it was *incomplete*. It assumed, in most cases, that the issue the writer was dealing with involved lack of ideas, or stalling out mid-plot, rather than a lack of focus, a crushing sense of *too much*.

Wait, wait, wait – don't get upset! I'm not saying you *or* I are scattered or messy! I'm trying to verbalize the problem a lot of us have and that's this: writing is freaking intimidating. Especially if you've managed to get your first story/article/poem out there and realize, *Oh Shit!* I need to write *more* because people are actually reading this but...

How?

How do that?

Words not work good!

"Butt In Chair, Hands On Keys"

Maybe we want that Instagram aesthetic moment, the one where we have a steaming cup of something on the desk, a nice soft light bathing us in a writerly glow, our fresh, blank screen (not dusty for once) ready to be filled with our fantabulous stories.

Yet.

It.

Is.

So hard.

To.

Get there.

Because the words don't always pour out, do they? Not when

you remember you promised to start dinner before six, or the cat is yowling, or that Netflix queue isn't getting any shorter...and it's all so much easier to do those than face down the possibility that your words aren't going to be perfect and will need the work of editing, polishing, more editing, more polishing, then the fun of getting your shit together for publication. Then, to get ourselves focused on what we need to do for that story, article, or poem, we try to follow the incomplete advice I talked about earlier, shouting Yes! I'm motivated! Yes! I have a story to tell!

And then instead we go watch *Anne with an E.*

So that trickery I mentioned earlier? Bribing myself to get writing done? Clearly it didn't always work and few things feel worse than cheating yourself, sneaking a treat you know you didn't earn.

So what did work?

It was deceptively simple, and ended up helping me reframe my entire writing approach.

Gather in, listen close.

All of that advice? The awesome prompt ideas, the writing in a different pattern, exploring other characters? All of the tips you've seen online or in books or workshops? None of it works if you're not actually sitting down to do it.

I know, I know, that sounds simple, right?

Let me explain with one single acronym: BICHOK.

Butt In Chair, Hands On Keys.

I'll say it again because it's important. I'll make it bold this time, too:

Butt In Chair, Hands On Keys.

I'm not the first writer to talk about this, and I'm definitely not the originator of the idea, but it's one that bears repeating. It's so simple but so difficult at the same time. Simple because it is a grilled cheese sandwich – the name tells you exactly what it is, no tricks or fuss. Hard because it requires effort to make it happen, also kind of like a grilled cheese sandwich? (Analogies aren't my strong suit.)

There's no one way to do BICHOK, but there are a few things to keep in mind. I call them the BICHOK bullet points. To make it happen, to get your butt in the chair with your hands on the keys:

- *Make reasonable goals.* Sure, it'd be awesome to crank out twenty thousand words in an evening but...start small. Try two hundred and fifty. Sail past that one and bump it up to five hundred next time.

- *Block out time.* It's easy to seat-of-the-pants this one, tell yourself you'll cram in some time between chores or before bed, but blocking out a *specific* half hour to BICHOK makes a huge difference, and is another one of those reasonable goals. You won't feel like you're flailing into the void of "I must fill all this spare time!" or "I don't have enough time to do this!" if you have dedicated half an hour, an hour, even ten minutes *just* to writing. You can change your block of time as needed. I've gone through months where I had to reduce my BICHOK time to just ten or fifteen minutes per day because my non-writer responsibilities got so hectic. But the beauty of using BICHOK and having that time blocked out, even for a handful of minutes per day? I knew I'd be getting my writing in there and I wouldn't stress away the day worried about not being able to do anything on my manuscript.

- *Unplug.* No, you don't have to be a Luddite but you should remove distractions. Netflix tempting you? If you're worried you won't be able to resist, try writing in a room without the television, or covering it up if you can't move rooms. If it's the internet that drags your attention away, try temporarily disabling it on your computer if you don't think you can ignore the siren call of social media for your dedicated BICHOK time. Unless you're expecting an important call or need to have it near you for potential emergencies, hide your phone away for your BICHOK time, too.

- *Don't edit!* Please please don't edit. You want to get your words out and you're not going to hit your goals if you spend your

BICHOK time analyzing every word choice you make, or rereading what you wrote last time. There will be time for edits later. So. Many. Edits. *Later.* So that you'll be editing your *finished draft* and not one sentence at a time.

- *BICHOK!* Do it. Just do it. Insert the latest internet meme here. If you're still facing writer's block or having plot flow problems, *now* is the time to apply that other awesome advice. Once you are unplugged and have your timer set, you can pour yourself into starting that story in the middle, or exploring the entire plot from your antagonist's point of view, without feeling like you're just throwing spaghetti at the wall and seeing what sticks.

- *Most importantly: Step away when you're done.* Once your allotted time is up, step back. Take a breath. Take a lap. Get a glass of whatever you feel like drinking. Get to that chore you were eyeballing before you sat down, watch another episode of something. It's not exactly giving yourself a reward but it's giving yourself a chance to breathe.

See, it's simple. BICHOK. Easy peasy. Try it. You can do this. You can do this.

Meredith is a trans, nonbinary, queer author. They like to write about spooky stuff, kissing, and sometimes spooky stuff kissing. Originally from Texas, they live elsewhere now with their family and two cats who think they are gods (in fact, they're pretty sure of it). Meredith writes queer-centered romances in various subgenres including paranormal, speculative fiction/alternate universe, contemporary, and historical. They firmly believe in happily ever afters and that there is no reason anyone should wear socks with open toe shoes.

STEALING FROM THE THIEF OF TIME
Dimitra Stathopoulos

Hello. My name is Dimi. I have a Diploma in Daydreaming, which should be good news for a writer, right? Ah, if only, dear friends, if only. Sadly, I also have a Masters of Procrastination and boy, is that qualification well-earned.

But here's the thing. The thingy thing is, I'm working on my Doctorate of Productivity. If you also have a Masters in Procrastination then you know the struggle we have when it comes to productivity. That's productivity in general but we're talking about writing right now.

Write Right Now.

Right now.

Write.

Now!

(Before I truly begin, let me acknowledge the Lords of Executive Dysfunction, of whose demesnes I have inherited a small tract of land in the mountains of the Empire of Neurodivergency. A fact which, though obvious looking back, was discovered only after the writing of this essay. While these "tips and tricks" cannot create a permanent magic cure of routine and the ability To Do, they can be helpful on those occasions when you know you gotta, you're kinda feeling it, and these are the only kicks up the bum you need to push you over the edge. They won't help every time, but the times they do can be worth it. Now back to past innocent me.)

Procrastination is nothing short of an addiction. It's an addiction to immediate gratification. Why work hard and long on your latest story when you could get immediate happy brain feels by clicking on another YouTube video of a shirtless guy in a rainforest (uh, more on that below) building a mud hut in total silence? Okay, actually that one is really cool and you should totally check it out and all the rest of his videos, but...wait...what was I talking about? No. Don't you even think about clicking that link, dammit. Come back here.

Procrastination. The thief of time, burglar of dreams, purloiner of productivity.

How do you beat it? How do you stop procrastinating and just do it, whatever *it* is?

You could listen to hours of advice on the topic instead of just doing (you're procrastinating), read a hundred books on the topic instead of just doing (you're procrastinating), but here's the crux of all the advice out there – just do it. Sure buddy. If it were that easy, quitting caffeine, nicotine, sugar, in fact quitting *any* addictive substance would be as easy as 'just do it.'

Sometimes we *can* just do it, us Masters of Procrastination. Sometimes the ability to just do it sneaks up from out of nowhere and, hell to the yeah, you've just written 10,000 words in a day. Sometimes. But let's face it, most of the time we need help and there's no shame in that.

Me? Sometimes I can just do it. But how? Thanks for asking. Let me tell you.

I started by understanding that for me, relying on willpower Does. Not. Work. And it is okay to need and to ask for help.

First, deal with the technical distractions by making use of technology. Now, I've removed most social media from my life, but that's just not realsitic for everyone. Instead, use any kind of app or program that locks you out of everything fun online or on your phone.

And I mean, Locks. You. Out. (More on that below.)

You want to check Tumblr once a writing session has started? Sorry, if you're using a lockout app, *no can do*. Delete the app, log out, try to wheedle your way around, but it knows the way our brains work and it slaps your hand and says no. This is great if you find yourself sneaking a peak at social media every five minutes or you need to immediately check who won best supporting actor in

1973 (pro-tip: you almost never *need* to do that. If you're writing, make a note on the page and do all your research later). There are some great free lockout apps – most with in-app purchases – and some pricey subscription software. The cheaper alternative is to ask a friend or family member to physically confiscate your phone and unplug the router. This is not a joke.

Then what?

"Procrastination. The thief of time, burglar of dreams, purloiner of productivity"

It's not just online distractions. Maybe you're surrounded by a to-be-read pile of books that could be used to build a life size replica of the Great Pyramid. Maybe your list of movies to watch can lasso the moon. Maybe that cross-stitch you started three years ago is staring at you accusingly – you never call, you never write – and before you know it, *you never write.*

These are vicious sirens, determined to pull you off course into a raging current of not-doing-what-you-damn-well-sat-down-to-do. Being surrounded by so much to do can end up paralyzing you into doing absolutely nothing.

So, get out, get away.

If you can, find somewhere – *anywhere* – a room at a library, a cafe down the road, a park. Go there. All you Procrastinators with a capital P, leave behind anything that can pick up a signal. If you can afford it, gift yourself a crappity laptop or tablet that has nothing on it but a word processing program. Nothing else. For me it's a pad and pencil to avoid the clutter on my digital desktop.

Lastly, find a support network. In the physical world, one person will do but they need to be a badass. They need to be able to look into your puppy-dog eyes when you're begging for your phone back and say, "Sorry, did you hear something? It sounded like someone asking for an ass whuppin." Someone who might be able to sit near you while you work – make you feel accountable. But also someone to encourage and tell you, "You're doing great, kid."

Finding a body double or an accountability buddy online (more on that below) is more possible than ever before. Team up with another Procrastinator and vow to make each other accountable. Can you find a group that schedules write-ins in person or via video call? If everyone is writing then you have to as well. Never underestimate the power of positive peer-pressure.

Sound good? Sorry, what was that? There's too much info and not enough white space? I got you buddy, I would have stopped taking anything in several pages ago too:

1. BE ACCOUNTABLE – I TELL SOMEONE
Today I'm going to write 500 words. Sometimes just pledging this and promising to report back lights a fire under my butt. Even better is writing with someone. Whether in the same room or on the opposite ends of the earth, setting a chunk of time in which I'm writing together-alone can be incredibly motivating.

2. WRITE WHENEVER I GET A CHANCE
I've got some great writing apps on my phone. Werdsmith, Pages, iA Writer, and Scrivener. These are great – especially Scrivener. You know what I use the most? Notes. Just plain Notes. I can't format, I can't play. All I can do is write wth my thumbs. Where am I drafting this right now? Notes. And of course notebooks and pencils don't have batteries. These are on me at all times too.

3. MAKE APPOINTMENTS WITH MYSELF
I'm going to write from 3pm to 6pm on Saturday. I put this in my diary and block it out in my calendar. This appointment has the same importance as going to the dentist or dinner with friends. If I can't make it, I better have a good reason. During these appointments I sometimes break down my time using the Pomodoro method (more on that below). I use a real timer that ticks and then dings loudly, and I work in 20-30 minute blocks with a 5 minute break in between to stretch or snack.

4. REMOVE THE DISTRACTIONS
I write first drafts by hand. Mostly because it means my brain can

keep ahead of my hands and let the ideas keep running. Helpful if you think slower than you type. But the best thing is that paper doesn't have wi-fi. I also have a devoted writing tablet that is relatively app (distraction) free.

5. NOISE

I can't work in silence. Music is good but if I'm trying to work with words, I prefer it without lyrics. I stick to classical music, rain or ocean sounds on the Relax Melodies app, or my latest writing song, the Jurassic Park theme slowed 1000%.

6. PODCASTS AND RESOURCES

Honestly, I don't play with this stuff anymore. Knowing resources are available is great but I've finally, *finally* learned that doing the thing is the best way to learn the thing. Writing Excuses and I Should Be Writing are great podcasts among the many.

As for books, *Story Engineering* by Larry Brooks is the best, most concise book on the mechanics of storytelling I've ever found. I also love listening to Cortex, which is great if you're interested in productivity and ways of working. If you're a YouTuber or interested in creating a podcast, do check it out. The resources and advice are endless but if you want every book, every blog, every 'Top Ten Tips' and 'How To' distilled into their basic component it's this:

Just Write.

Annoying isn't it? Turns out there's no magic turning point, no perfect advice other than what His Strangeness, Shia LaBeouf teaches us.

Just do it.

Sit down and do the thing because no one else is going to do it for you.

Now, I'm not addressing those wonderful people who *can* just do it. They're out there – hello – and all power to them. But I'm talking to you. You know who you are. You've already read all the things about procrastination, and you know as well as I they only really work for people who procrastinate and not Procrastinators. You know that each of these things work while they're shiny and fresh and very quickly lose their potency once we find our sneaky workarounds. We need to rewire our brains, and that might mean professional help to figure out if procrastination is the cause or the symptom. You've taken notes. You made a spreadsheet and spent hours on the borders and colors. You did it because you had something else you should have been doing.

So this is for you.

Now stop watching that seventeenth reaction video of Americans discovering Eurovision for the first time and write, damn you, write. Now!

Pssst, after you just do it, here's some stuff to help you keep doing it.

- Lock-out software are small apps that prevent you from checking social media for a preset time selected by you. Some I've used include: *Freedom.to, FlipdApp, Offtime Light for iOS*.

- Apps like *Focusmate* or *Supporti* can team you up with a buddy at an appointed time. If for some reason you like punishment more than reward (no judgement), things like *Stickk* might help, where you can lose your own hard earned money if you don't Do The Thing.

- *HitTheGoal* is a Discord Server community that can keep you on track, or find a group or partner to help you on *GetMotivatedBuddies* or for free in *reddit.com/r/GetMotivatedBuddies*.

- The *Pomodoro technique* helps you with time management. It's one of my main strategies, but I tailor it to my needs and my energy levels. Sometimes I have the focus to go for 60 minutes at a time. For the harder I-don't-really-want-to-do-them tasks, I stick to the traditional 20-25 minutes on, 5 minutes rest.

- Oh yeah, the Jurassic Park theme slowed down 1,000 times is great for blocking out distractions *and* silence. You can find it all over YouTube, just search for 'Jurassic park theme slowed down

1000 times.' From there you'll find several other songs slowed to glacial speed.

• Mur Lafferty's *I Should Be Writing* podcast is at murverse.com, and you can find her book of the same name wherever you like to buy books online.

• The *Writing Excuses* podcast's ridiculously wonderful tagline is "Fifteen minutes long, because you're in a hurry, and we're not that smart." Hosted by *several writers, you can find the podcast at* writingexcuses.com.

• Cortex's two hosts, Myke Hurley and CGP Grey, talk about their work as professional podcasters and professional YouTubers respectively, their lives, the technology that helps them do what they do, and how to create good behaviors that last. You can find them at relayfm.com/cortex.

So the shirtless guy in the rainforest? He creates the *Primitive Technology* videos on YouTube. "I make videos about making things entirely from scratch in the wild…then they can learn these skills too." I may have watched the one on Wattle and Daub Huts a few *mumble* times. What? It helps me think. I won't even start going on about the charcoal furnace.

Of course I won't start. Because you're in a hurry. To get writing. Because you can do it. You just have to…do it.

Dimitra Stathopoulos is a working scientist working on getting her doctorate in productivity. She hopes to help you do the same.

As a writer of fiction part of your duty and obligation is to write characters who are not you. Write them well, write them with respect and interest. And don't listen to anyone who tells you you aren't allowed to write people who aren't you. You are.

— Neil Gaiman
Hugo award-winning co-author of *Good Omens*

FLIGHTS OF FANCY:
HOW TO BUILD THE RESEARCH RUNWAY
Stacey Cunningham

Ever watched a movie or TV show and thought, this setting would make a fantastic alternative universe for my favorite characters? We've all been there, right? For me it's one of the great joys of writing fanfiction, this inspiration to learn more about a time or a place, falling down a glorious rabbit-hole of research. But what if that movie or the TV show is set in the interwar or post-war period, on the other side of the world from you, and you know virtually nothing about the lives of ordinary people in that place and time?

Research! The library and the internet are about to become the best friends you've ever had. So are museum websites, city archives, universities, fashion blogs, even passenger lists from transatlantic voyages, they're all waiting for you and your amazing story idea.

To encourage you to make use of all these wonderful resources – resources which will help you bring your story to vibrant life – I'll share the nitty gritty of my research for a series I've been writing for half a dozen years now, sharing how I've used those remarkable resources to help my imagination take joyful flight.

The series, called *Storm Passes Away,* is set in 1950s rural Ireland and is inspired by the film *Brooklyn,* and includes a character taken from *Star Wars: The Force Awakens.* My first story in the series picks up where the book and movie *Brooklyn* leave off: with Jim Farrell having been abandoned by Eilis Lacey so she can return to her life in New York. Alone and still reeling from these events, Jim meets a charming and intriguing American named Ben Organa who has just come from Dublin to assist his grandmother in executing the estate of his late grandfather. My story starts with Jim and Ben meeting, and the main story arc covers their courtship and eventual commitment to each other. The rest of the stories which make up the ongoing series are slice-of-life vignettes that I use to flesh out the world of Jim's and Ben's lives together in Enniscorthy, Ireland.

In my daily life I'm a professional historical researcher – I come by my nitpicky obsession with historical accuracy honestly. My 'leave no stone unturned' approach to my writing is the product of many long years spent shuffling through hundreds to thousands of dusty files at various archival repositories across the country. I used to think this rather clinical approach to creative writing hindered me, but now I see it as one of my strengths. I don't want my beloved characters to act upon a blank stage, and since the reader cannot possibly know what I'm imagining when I write the story, it's my job to make the world of 1950 Enniscorthy in County Wexford come to life with as much color and detail as I can possibly breathe into the words.

One would think that writing about the 1950s would be easy, right? It's a time not so far removed, not so long ago at less than a hundred years, and it seems like it should be well-documented. It's a post-war era with huge leaps forward in terms of cultural development, a time of prosperity for some and there's a lot to like about the decade: the fashions, the cars, the music, even the horrifying food has a charm all its own. The trick with researching and writing stories set in this time in Ireland is that all the trappings of culture (films, music, books, etc.) and new products that were available in Canada, America, and even England, may not have been as widely available in rural Ireland. In fact, there were parts of County Wexford that didn't even have electricity until 1957. To further complicate things, the experiences and lives of the people in County Wexford didn't necessarily line up with people in other Irish counties. The fashions and culture in Dublin aren't necessarily replicated in Enniscorthy, even though there's less than 75 miles between them.

When I began writing my Brooklyn series, I started with what

I consider my primary sources for Enniscorthy in the 1950s – the film and the book, both named *Brooklyn*. These two sources were my starting point and I still refer to them if I'm ever feeling blocked or I feel like I'm missing a key piece of information about the town and time period.

There's no real secret or magic trick to trying to evoke rural Ireland in the 1950s – or perhaps any other existing place in time – it's mainly a lot of research and constant fact-checking. One of the more exciting aspects of conducting research is falling down that rabbit-hole of information. You find one good source which leads to another, and another, and before you know it, you've gathered more information about your chosen time than you thought. Combing through bibliographies and all your gathered sources, and making notes, might seem like overkill for a fun piece of writing – then suddenly your one-shot alternative universe fic turns into a newly-minted series, and now, with all your wonderful sources, you don't have to recreate everything from scratch. A wonderful bonus is that, when someone expresses an interest in that time and place, I'm able to point them in the direction of my sources for further reading.

"Universities, museums, and city councils have a lot of extremely useful information available for free on their websites"

The book and the movie are good jumping off points for me because I can gather a lot of basic, everyday details quite easily. Things like clothing, hairstyles, makes and models of cars, and speech patterns are all right there. The speech patterns of the characters in my series, both Irish and American, are one of a couple of places where I take a lot of leeway. I am not Irish or American, and my own speech patterns are a mash-up of the various places I've lived in Canada. It sounds odd to my ear to incorporate common slang of the day into the speech patterns of Jim and Ben, so I dance around this by saying to myself, 'well they're not teenagers, they're young men, so they wouldn't necessarily still use the slang of their younger years.' So, though Ben is a young man from 1950s America, he's a teacher and I write him with slightly more adult speech. The main difference between his and Jim's speech, is that Ben is a lot more informal, he uses contractions more often, and is more forward. Jim, while I do have the dialog from the movie I can try to replicate, he's just more formal and more reserved in his speech. While research takes me far, I've learned that once I settle in to writing characters I've researched, Jim and Ben included, they find their own voices, their own speech patterns, and funny turns of phrase. They bring themselves to life in a way.

Once I feel I've gleaned all I can from a book or movie, I expand my search, casting a wider net for topics like fashion, employment, music. I have found that, frustratingly, the nitty gritty details of everyday life anywhere aren't often recorded, but I've become very good at skirting around things I can't find sources for and making educated guesses – the creative in creative writing!

Food, for example, is an area where my research has gaps. It's quite easy to determine period-typical Irish and American foods, but the gaps in my research are twofold: are those dishes ones regular people ate every day, and, as single young men, how skilled would Jim and Ben be at cooking for themselves? I try to tackle these gaps by making their meals a blend of American and Irish traditions and typically very simple. Because I didn't want a housekeeper or Jim's mother intruding on the quiet privacy of Jim and Ben's lives, I decided that both Jim and Ben would know how to cook. By virtue of being an only child, I rationalized that Jim would have spent significant time with his mother, at least while he was young, and she would have taught him how to cook, bake, and shop for himself.

I have found so many institutions – like universities, museums, and city councils – have a lot of extremely useful information available for free on their websites. In particular for me, the

National Museum of Ireland and the Dublin City Council websites provide a lot of information about daily life, and the city council website is a treasure trove of photographs. I have also begun to gather links and sources to oral histories, because this is where I'm really going to get details regarding everyday life for the average person.

My last main branch of research is going on-site. Each time I visit Ireland, I love to explore bookstores, museums, and anything that might potentially enrich my series. Of course, the highlight of my last few trips was being able to visit Enniscorthy in person. The day of the first visit my heart was beating so fast I was a bit lightheaded as I stepped off the bus, looking across the River Slaney, towards the castle and town beyond. Once on the main street and standing across from M. Kelly's store front (a set piece left in place by the movie production) I had to constantly remind myself I wouldn't actually see Jim, Ben, or Eilis around town. After spending the day walking, I was pleased to find that my extensive research on Google maps hadn't led me to flub the town's geography too badly!

For me, Enniscorthy itself is just as important as Jim or Ben to the story, so it often features prominently in any installment of the series. Fortunately, I think the organization of the town has changed little in the last sixty years and without access to town plans, I have to take it for face value that the locations of the town square, the Catholic church, and the high street are in the same places they would have been in 1951. I can walk the streets of Enniscorthy via Google maps, but it only shows me the town as it is now.

For all the research I do and the importance I place on historical accuracy, I don't want my stories to read like a textbook, so where do I begin to blur the lines between fact and fiction?

When the story really needs it.

There have been times where it's necessary to move things if I want a more romantic setting, or more privacy for Jim and Ben. Curracloe Beach is an important location in my characters' history and they visit the beach often, but in reality it's about a forty-five minute drive from the town, and too far to walk. So I moved it. I thought it sounded better if Jim only had to walk fifteen minutes though windswept pastures to get down to the beach when he needed time to grieve, rather than getting into his car and driving sadly for over a half an hour! I took a similar approach to Jim's house. Rather than have him live in apartments above his pub in town, I moved him to a nice house at the outskirts, backing on to extensive gardens, trees, and the pastures that take him down to the beach. This is purely a choice to allow Jim and Ben the privacy they need to develop their relationship at a time when that would have been difficult.

That said, I take the most leeway with the characters who fill up my meticulously-researched world of 1950s Enniscorthy and that, for me, is the only way to approach fanfiction or *any* fiction. The characters can't act upon a blank stage, so I have done my best to fill Jim's and Ben's world with reality yes, but also with color, excitement, and the romance of a story told just so.

Brooklyn, the book and movie, is Eilis's story, not Jim's, so we are told very little about his life. We know he's an only child, but not his age, that he will take over his parents' bar and house when they retire to the country, but we know almost nothing about his extended family. We know he had one previous relationship and that he's never left Ireland, but nothing about his education, where's he traveled, or his political opinions. We know he attends church, but how strong is his faith?

Because Jim is a bit of a blank slate in the book and movie, I have a lot of leeway to grow and expand him however I want, but still work within the little bit of information we have. So, in my fanfic series, he still runs his parents' pub, but he shares the workload with a school friend named Alistair, who is also a convenient stand-in when I want Jim to have several nights away from the bar. Even better, Alistair himself is saving up for his wedding so he doesn't mind working extra shifts which is extremely convenient for Jim and Ben!

Little is said about Jim's life experiences or past relationships – we know only that he's never left Ireland and he feels a bit out of place when his friends begin pairing off with girls from the town. I pounced on this section of the book and interpreted it to mean that perhaps Jim wrestled with compulsory heterosexuality. With this in mind I fleshed out his past with relationships with both men and women. He's just personally unlucky in love and that has nothing to do with his being a bisexual man. He has a lot of love to give and it's just been his misfortune to fall for people who aren't serious about him, or have misled him.

Since this series is loosely a *Star Wars/Brooklyn* crossover, Ben Organa comes with the baggage of his movie heritage and family name. He's mostly an original creation though, because Kylo Ren would be a poor match for Jim Farrell. So, while Ben has the angst and dramatic family past – with parents Leia Organa and Han Solo – rather than going berserk, killing people, and falling into madness, he recognizes that what he really needs is time and distance between himself and his family. When he takes flight to California, and then Ireland, he gets some much needed space and he's able to take the time to discover what kind of person he really is away from them. Like Kylo Ren, Ben makes a choice to become a very different kind of person from the one he was in the past but, unlike Kylo Ren, Ben chooses a much lighter path.

As Ben Organa is essentially a wholly original character, I can take so much leeway. I can give him every advantage – money, education, time to make mistakes – that Jim doesn't get to have, hemmed in by the original text as he is. Ben is from Manhattan so he has the advantage of a more worldly life than Jim was afforded, but that's part of what Jim likes so much. Ben wants nothing more than to find his place in the world, to love and be loved in return, and so how fortunate for him that he met Jim Farrell. How Jim and Ben interact with each other is one of my favorite parts of the series. They are so ready to be pleased and charmed by each other. They're each searching for a sense of belonging and home, and they finally found it in each other.

There are two major issues I rarely, if ever, touch upon in my Brooklyn series: Jim's relationship with his faith, and period-typical homophobia. Again, this is one of the benefits of fanfic. Keeping in line with the leeway I've taken with Jim's character, I can give him rather modern sensibilities towards his religion. He goes to church every week but I wouldn't say he's a fervent believer. Rather he goes because he knows it's expected of him as a local business owner from a good family. He doesn't wrestle with the fact that he's attracted to men and women, nor does he feel any shame when he thinks about his relationship with Ben. He's very much of the opinion that a relationship with so much love and mutual respect isn't wrong. Looking around for examples of happy relationships, he sees the rather strained one of his parents, Eilis's unhappy situation, and he can't help but feel like he's made the best possible choice for himself.

I don't tread lightly over such heavy and important topics, and I'm not ignoring the struggles of gay and lesbian people of this decade. I know it was an extremely dangerous time for the people who lived through it. This series is a fantasy of how it *could* quietly be, so I focus on the gentle domesticity and love these characters share. I have to believe it was possible for people to live their lives supported by sympathetic friends and family.

To my mind, it's just as important to portray happy, romantic stories where the characters live their lives softly and sweetly as it is to educate readers on the very real suffering LGTBQIA+ people faced – and still do. There's darkness enough in the world even now, it would do us all a world of good to spend some time in Jim's and Ben's Enniscorthy.

These peculiarities are how I conduct research. I've watched *Brooklyn* hundreds of times, I've had the pleasure of visiting Enniscorthy in person, and I use these gifts to evoke the time and place as best I can – you the reader can't see the Enniscorthy I see when I close my eyes, but with a mixture of research and imagination, I can take you there.

You can do this too in your own way, with your own research.

The city archives, the universities and museums, the blogs, passenger lists, old photo albums – these and so many more resources are out there waiting for you, waiting to help you build *your* runway, one which can help your marvelous stories to take flight.

Writing fic has taught me how to do that, among so many other wonderful things.

Stacey crouches like a dragon on the west coast of Canada with her large hoard of books and records. She loves Irish mythology and history and thinks she's probably smart enough not to fall for any of the Fair Folk's tricks. She writes fanfiction, mostly for the Star Wars fandom, that focus on urban fantasy and detective stories based in Ireland where all sorts of fantastical creatures cross paths with the people of Dublin. Find her on AO3 as Marlon, or Tumblr as MarlonBookcase.

Star Wars and Rocky Horror Crossover by S.L. Surovec

A LANGUAGE NOT MY OWN
Anarion

There are a couple of things I'm unable to imagine. The infinity of the universe. Living in a country where for a couple of months it's dark 24 hours a day. And writing John Watson and Sherlock Holmes in German.

I've watched *Sherlock* online and therefore in English, so it never occurred to me to write my fanfics in any other language. They automatically speak English in my head.

In the beginning, I'd constantly stop writing to search for a word I couldn't remember in English, or to check spelling. Not the best way to write. So I learned I'm more the 'word vomit first, correct later' type.

Being a non-native speaker, I had a beta reader in the beginning which helped tremendously. Then, when I started my *365 221bs in 365 days* writing challenge, posting daily for over a year improved my writing immensely, I made fewer mistakes, and I found my own style.

I've read stories from various fandoms, but I've never felt like writing much outside *Sherlock*. Maybe one day I will and maybe I will be able to do it in German. I'm not counting on it though. English is the language of my fandom tribe and the language of my heart, and to tell stories about our beloved consulting detective and his doctor…it's just the best.

Anarion writes fic mostly in the Sherlock Holmes fandom, and specializes in writing 221Bs – which the above is. A 221B is a nod to Sherlock Holmes' Baker Street address, and is a story or essay written in exactly two hundred and twenty-one words, with the final word beginning with B.

HOW TO WRITE A BOOK: DON'T FORGET THE KNEEPADS
Kameo Llyn Douglas (aka Kristine Polisciano)

First you write the book.

There's a book inside you somewhere, otherwise you wouldn't be reading this. The idea knocked on the door, you let it in, and it made itself at home.

Maybe it was after you told a story that made your friends cry laughing and one of them said, "You should write a book." Maybe it was rewriting the ending to a movie in your head on a long drive, and thinking, "I should write that down." Maybe you played back a distressing childhood memory and wondered if it would help to put it on paper.

Or maybe you're like me and it came from someplace less than kind, like after reading something really terrible and thinking, "Oh I could do so much better than that."

Fair warning before we go further: it takes a certain kind of pride to believe you can write a book, but it's the kind you have to have in order to hold your nose and jump into the pool without seeing how cold the water is. The kind that shouts "Damn the torpedoes, Sydney or the bush, full speed ahead, Cowabunga, Geronimo, what's the worst that could happen?" The brave kind. And you have it or you wouldn't be reading this, remember that.

So once you're ready, you may realize you don't know what yours is really about. This should not keep you from starting. To paraphrase John Burroughs, "Write and the book will appear." Look at that long list of ideas you've jotted down for years. Read them like you've never seen them before, or even better, read them like someone you love and admire wrote them. Why? Because you'd be all kinds of encouraging and enthusiastic if someone else wrote them, but sometimes you dismiss things because they're yours. So approach these ideas like the gems they are, then shuffle them like a deck of cards. Rattle and roll them like a pair of dice. Jumble them, mix them, tickle, and poke them until a wisp of a story rises from the ether.

You're now ready to tell the story and if you don't have a proper beginning or ending, just jump in in the middle. Tell it the way a six-year-old would talk about the game they played at lunchtime with their friend, not worried about whether they're making sense, but happily reliving it in their mind's eye. That six-year-old would not waste time thinking about the listener's perspective. They're not worried about whether you understand or not. They'll answer questions later if you have them, but if you interrupt them in the telling, they'll forget what they wanted to say and lose interest.

The same thing goes for you, for me, for most of us. So right now, just tell your story. Let it spill out of you with the excitement you felt when you first decided to tell it, when you first convinced yourself you were going to do it.

Fairly early on you might notice a nasty voice in your head doing its best to discourage you. With its sinister whispers it's the most vicious, unrelenting critic you will ever face. It will say things like:

You're not a writer.

Who are you kidding?

You have no talent.

Stop embarrassing yourself.

That voice is a bully. Like most bullies, it acts out of insecurity. You can try to be kind and give it reassurance, but if it refuses to cooperate, give it a name, and then tell it by name *to shut up*. Or drown it out. Then get back to work.

And don't hold back on the work. Don't censor yourself. Let it flow unedited. Make sure you write it all down. All of it, every single word, every irrelevant detail, every ridiculous, inelegant turn of phrase and every ramshackle sentence. Pour it out like a raging river onto the screen or paper. When you feel the urge to delete a humiliating paragraph, cut and paste it at the end of the document, because it might actually morph itself into a perfect jewel of words while you're not looking. Save your document often, every version, in multiple places. Email it to yourself at all your email addresses.

At some point, your enthusiasm will wane. Six-year-olds don't have very much stamina. But you do because you're a grown-up. So dig deep for self-discipline. It's true that a book of one hundred chapters begins with a single word, but you're going to need a lot more than that, so set yourself a daily goal. It should be ambitious enough to make you feel you're progressing, enough so you have to push yourself, enough to make you feel successful when you reach the goal, but definitely not enough to discourage you. Find your challenging yet fairly fail proof number. Consider the amount of time you have to spend writing each day. Experiment. How long does it take you to write one hundred words? Two hundred? Three hundred is what worked for me.

> ## "Don't wait on the muse! She's very busy and favors those who are ready for her to visit with no warning"

Once you decide on your own number, commit to writing that many words every day. I joined an online writers' accountability group and we all posted our daily number of words, not in a competitive way, just to have a place to keep track. You won't get a book written by waiting till you feel like it. A writer puts words on a page. So don't worry about inspiration. If you don't feel like writing, write anyway. Your goal is words and at this stage there are no quality requirements. Sometimes what you write will be pure drivel. To be honest, a lot of them will be. But I promise that some will be worth keeping. And then more. And more. Yet if you don't put any on the page, you'll have none to keep.

Many's the night I've written out of pure determination to meet my quota. This has resulted in inspiring sentences like:

Maybe I should try adding to chapter thirty-six instead.

Twenty-four more words. That's all I need.

Yesterday I had that great idea about a roulette table, but now I have no idea what I was thinking.

I'm too tired to write anything. I should just go to sleep.

Whose idea was this anyway?

(Actual quotes from early drafts)

One night I wrote three hundred and two words of what I thought was pure drivel. I may have been delirious. Luckily, I kept them all. Five of them were 'the power balance of cranberries' and somehow those five words became nuggets of gold, turning themselves into an entire chapter over the course of a week.

Some days the words flow from you like Niagara Falls. Your fingers won't be able to keep up. Some days they'll drip like honey from a hive, golden and gleaming in the sunlight. There may be three of those. Maybe four. Most days they'll only come out kicking and screaming, and it will take enormous effort, like dragging barbed wire through a sandpaper funnel. Backwards.

Don't give up!

And don't wait on the muse!

The muse, she's very busy, and she favors those who are ready for her to visit with no warning. She speaks most clearly through fingers that are already moving, so open your document and keep it open.

If you persist despite the efforts of the bully in your head (frequent shouts of "Shut up, Marvin!" led my neighbors to ask if we had gotten a new dog), you will eventually accumulate enough words to convince yourself that you might actually finish your book. Be warned though: the closer you get, the more convinced you'll be that it really sucks. You'll hate it. It's the law. You have to hate it. If Neil Gaiman feels that, you will too. You'll think the book is drek. You'll never want to look at it again and you'll want to forget you ever started it. Friends and other writers can be a big help at this point. Ask them to cheer you on. It's good if you have a couple of people along with you on your writing journey, so when your disgust with it all becomes too much, you have someone who can verify the whole thing isn't crap. Even if you have a hard time believing them, having your friends reassure you that it's really not drek will help.

If you're lucky you'll have an editor who won't let you give up. They'll remind you that they really want your book. They thought it was a great idea and they still do. They'll tell you what you're feeling is normal, that this is what happens. Trying to finish a book is like watching a baby grow into a teenager. If you don't wind up hating each other at least a little bit you'll never be able to let go of each other. Get a little distance and you'll realize the love is still there. You just need a new context.

One way to get that new context is to listen to your book. My editor suggested I read it aloud, and you should definitely give that a try. Me, I found it way too intimate and threatening. Reading, speaking, *and* hearing my words at the same time? No way. So I removed myself one step, finding a free online text-to-speech converter, and then I let Charles read it to me in his British accent. It put just enough distance between me and the work that I felt at least the illusion of objectivity, and the experience was radically different from reading it over and over obsessively. I was amazed how many times I repeated particular words and phrases, only noticing them while listening and never while writing and reading them.

It is also possible that you'll get stuck. Unless your book sprang fully formed from your skull, like Athena from Zeus' head (with the concurrent headache), you'll probably encounter A Problem. This is different from feeling uninspired or thinking the book sucks or worrying that you will never finish. A Problem is something you can't figure out how to solve. You can write around A Problem, but eventually, if you don't solve it, you'll get stuck, unable to get to the finish. The big Problem with my book, not to get too specific, was sequencing. It just didn't make sense to me and I wanted to throw the whole thing out the window. (I recommend throwing things out windows. Not your book though. Old magazines, cardboard boxes, empty plastic bottles. Things that are going out anyway. It's cathartic.)

I solved the problem and got the book into the right order by detaching from the content, figuring out the least emotional, least intimidating, least cognitively challenging task that needed to be done. For you it might be proofreading, or anything which engages a part of the brain different from the writing part. For me it was printing out all 138 chapters of my book, which immediately gave me a different relationship with it. Like that teenager who's growing up, it turns out my book had a life outside of my head! It could stand on its own. And even though I clearly remembered the animosity with which we parted, I now could see glimpses of the book I loved so much, not long ago. Now was time to stay focused on the growth and strengths and how far along we had come. This required a fairly large quantity of stationery supplies:

Binder clips

Rubber bands

Three hole punch

Loose-leaf binder

Sticky notes (assorted colors)

Highlighters (assorted colors)

Pencil (You may prefer pens.)

Also, kneepads for sliding around on the floor when all the chapters were spread out everywhere.

Essential for me was a good set of headphones and some really loud, upbeat, music compelling me to dance and sing along, making it impossible to think. Options for you might be a riveting TV show or movie, something to engage your conscious mind sufficiently to drown out the existential certainty that your book is now drek. Dead drek.

Once I had the physical pages in my hand, I spread them out on the living room floor. I sorted, arranged, rearranged, clipped, highlighted, and stuck sticky notes with wild abandon. I identified what needed additions and subtractions, recognized themes, created new outlines and lists to clarify transitions. Somehow, having the book physically, as opposed to on my computer screen, enabled me to distance my ego from the work. And the mechanical actions lifted me out of the hole in which I was stuck.

I don't write longhand anymore. I did as a child and a teenager because I never warmed up to the typewriter. Turns out the ease of the computer and word processing was liberating to me, but after thirty thousand words, the screen had trapped me. I couldn't see beyond it. It was an endless repeating mirror. My words had become senseless, like when you're a child and you say a word over and over until it loses all meaning. I stared the sense right out of the words in front of my eyes. Only by putting them into a concrete form could I make them meaningful again.

Maybe it was the stationery supplies, maybe it was the kneepads, or maybe it was the Chuck Berry, but the solution to The Problem revealed itself while I was sliding around, and I fixed it. I obsessed over word choices and punctuation for a week or so and several months over several deadlines (thank you beneficent editor), my book was finished. I handed it over to my editor and I've been letting it make its way in the world. I miss it, the love and the struggles, but I try to remember that I started the madness for a reason. I had a story to tell and it's told.

Time to find another one.

Kameo Llyn Douglas (also known as Kristine Polisciano) began writing professionally at the age of 55, thanks to Sherlock Holmes and John Watson. As a special educator and literacy coach, she spent much of her thirty-five-year career teaching teachers to teach writing to students with disabilities. Their unique characteristics inspired the version of Sherlock Holmes in her first book, Rare and Wonderfully Made, with Improbable Press. You can find Kameo on Twitter and Tumblr as KameoDouglas. She lives with her remarkable son and their three-legged dog, in Brooklyn, New York.

I have a novel due, but I definitely wrote some fan fiction the other day.

— Mary Robinette Kowal
Hugo award-winning writer of
"For Want of a Nail"

ADD GOATS:
FIC, FOOLING YOUR BRAIN, AND
THE JANET WATSON CHRONICLES
Claire O'Dell

A fanfic experiment is where Claire O'Dell's *The Janet Watson Chronicles* began.

Before that, before a friend told her he enjoyed the immersive challenge of fic, Claire had a half dozen books of fantasy and short stories and just wasn't so sure about fic's appeal.

"I'd never quite felt the pull of that before," she said in a talk with Atlin Merrick for *Spark*. Yet Claire was curious enough to commit to writing something small, something brief.

That's not what happened.

While fic may have been the starting point of Claire's experiment, the small start has since turned into a novel series with raves from Publishers Weekly, Locus, the Lesbian Review, and more.

What makes Claire's series special are Janet Watson and Sara Holmes, both Black, queer women living through a near-future American civil war, with the stories themselves focusing on Watson because, when Claire started writing, "I wanted to give Dr Watson more space and more depth."

In Arthur Conan Doyle's Holmesian canon, "Watson gets nothing. He comes home in the canon, injured, and it's never dealt with. His wound wanders, depending on the story, and I think... if you've seen battle, there's gonna be elements of PTSD, recovery, rebuilding, starting life all over again.

"So I said, 'I'll just write a short story,' which was famous last words for me. I say short story and it turns out to be a series, but as I wrote, Janet Watson would not let go of me. I built everything around her."

Everything became *A Study in Honor, The Hound of Justice,* and a third book pending, each book centering on Janet Watson, at first a surgeon home from the battlefield and learning to cope with a new mechanical arm, then joining FBI agent Sara Holmes in solving crimes across Washington DC. Claire says right from the start Janet "fell into my head like that. The war I wanted was not another Afghanistan, so it became the new civil war, which sort of reinforced everything I had come up with because who is the person with the most stakes in a world like this? It would be someone who's not white, who's not straight…and as I considered the ramifications of everything, it just kind of reinforced my first initial impression of her."

Those impressions of Watson have led reviewers to praise her Chronicles as superb, invent, intense, masterful, and riveting.

Which makes it all the more interesting that at first Claire wasn't a fan of fic.

"Well, I had never been drawn to it before then. But as I thought about it more, fic is like every type of fiction isn't it, it's a story in conversation with itself. It's just that fanfic is more deeply in conversation with the works that it's inspired by." And once that inspiration took hold, it *took hold*. "I started writing the first Janet Watson book back in 2014 and then there I was, writing it in between scenes and stories from my other series and saying, you know, I was wrong about fanfiction before."

STABBY MCSTABBERSON (OR, IT'S A MATTER OF CRAFT)

Speaking of wrong, there's a laughable phrase called 'forced diversity,' used by those who think any story featuring characters other than white, straight males, is 'forcing' unwarranted diversity. When asked about this, Claire's thoughts were delightfully clear.

"Well, once I get over feeling stabby about hearing that term, I'll say that books with a wide range of characters is not forced diversity, *it's accurate*. It's showing the world as it is. And it's a matter of craft. It's a matter of telling a story that reflects all of us, or more of us. It's not a political agenda, it's opening your eyes."

And while bringing diverse voices to publishing can be "a long, slow slog, unfortunately, believe in your writing. Write what is most important to you and it's going to come out better. And there's an audience for that, look at what happened when Wonder Woman came out, all kinds of little girls showing up, wanting to be Wonder Woman. There's an audience out there! Look at Black Panther – that was an amazing movie – and just because Hollywood or whichever publisher hasn't done it...writing just doesn't have to be the straight white male. In fact, it feels really weird when I watch something that's all about the straight white male, it just feels *fake*.

"fic is like every type of fiction isn't it, it's a story in conversation with itself"

"There's a whole world where a man might pass through, but it's not necessarily their story. There's fantastic, interesting, complex, moving fun stories, all kinds of stories that don't center around them. And they're just as worthy to be told."

IN THE BEGINNING...
Creative origin stories can inspire, giving us faith that all kinds of paths lead to all kinds of success. Claire O'Dell's author origin story began with wanting to throw a book into a fire.

"I bought a book that I wanted to be fluff, but well-written fluff is difficult, it's hard stuff to write. So we were camping in the Canadian Rockies, and I just remember reading this book by the campfire, thinking 'This is just so awful. I can't finish this. I can do better than this.'

"I couldn't, not right away, but I got addicted," says Claire, addicted to writing and to "wanting to make the story a good one." Yet good would take years. "I started writing in the late eighties and my writing was kind of spotty for the next four or five years. I got divorced, I remarried, I had a kid, and that sort of takes up time. I started getting better by the two thousands, with my first pro sale to *Strange Horizons* in 2000, and my first novel seven years later. It just took me awhile to buckle down and actually write enough that I could get better at it. I'm a slow learner."

ON BRAIN TRICKS, BETA READERS, AND *OOOOH*

On Claire's path to buckling down and getting better, she says, "I did some beta exchanges with friends, and sometimes it seems you're not ready to understand the feedback yet. Someone says, 'This isn't working because of this,' and you're looking at it and going, but I don't see that. And then a year later you'll go, *oooh.*

"As writers we have to simultaneously believe in ourselves and remain open to criticism. And that's internal criticism too, when we're writing our stuff. Not 'you suck, you're a terrible writer criticism,' but this particular scene? You can make it better. I no longer feel like 'well I can't make it better,' because I know I can. That's something you learn over time. You can learn how to be a writer and how to make it better. You learn that you can do it."

And sometimes the tricky part is finding your own tricks.

"A lot of writing is me tricking my brain, telling myself that I'm not really writing this section or rewriting it. I'm just, you know, playing with something, I'm just gonna jot some things down. And the brain says, 'oh, okay, no problem.' And then, pretty soon, I'm writing a whole bunch of and my brain's saying, 'Wait! You fooled me again!' It's kind of like when I get my cat Octavia into her carrier to take her to the vet, she's continuously astonished I've managed to fool her.

"A friend of mine, he said writing is actually harder than brain surgery and he ought to know because he's a brain surgeon. I've lost touch with him, but he was right. He wrote a really amazing near-future riff off of Hamlet, really mind-bending in a lot of ways, but I think he stopped writing because he *is* a brain surgeon and he works in the emergency room and does research. And, you know, there's only so much time in the day."

THE DARK NIGHT OF THE SOUL: IT'S A PHASE

When asked if she thinks there's a point writers reach where it's mostly gold Claire said yes, but also no.

"The truth is sometimes it does come out easily, but more often you sit down and figure out how to trick your brain into putting words on paper, and then you write and then you rewrite. It's important for each writer to understand what will get the story done," Claire says, "and to know what works best for you for a particular project. Because it my change for different projects, and you learned how to write *this* particular book that way, and that's okay. That's okay. Some people write only from beginning to end, some people skip around.

"You learn to work with your brain, which sounds weird, as if we're outside our brain, but learn your process. Learn how to recognize that maybe you've gotten into the middle of the book and it feels like a slog because it *is* a slog! Maureen McHugh had a graph of writing a novel and called the middle part the dark night of the soul but it gets better after. You have to learn to recognize that it's a phase."

The briefest search online will show you that all writers go through this dark night, from Claire O'Dell to Neil Gaiman and beyond, and when asked if it's depressing, this knowledge that no matter how many books we may have we'll always face a period of darkness, Claire said instead she finds hope.

"It's encouraging to know other people feel it, because then it's 'Oh, this is just how writers feel.' It helps us simultaneously believe in ourselves and remain open to criticism. Instead of thinking you're a terrible writer, you realize maybe it's this particular scene that might suck and you can make it better.

"That's something you learn over time. You can learn how to make it better."

Sometimes that's where goats come in.

"Yes, one time there were goats. They became the reason why a character appears."

Claire O'Dell has written the SF mystery series The Janet Watson Chronicles, and the epic fantasy series River of Souls. Her first novel, Passion Play, won the 2010 RT Reviewer's Choice Award for Best Epic Fantasy and was long-listed for the Otherwise award. Her novel A Study in Honor won the 2019 Lambda Literary Award for Best

Lesbian Mystery. Claire has an undergraduate degree in German and a thirty-plus year career in software development, with projects ranging from applied cryptography to custom web applications. She lives in Connecticut with two idiosyncratic cats.

DOWN THE RESEARCH RABBIT-HOLE…
AND BACK OUT AGAIN
Margaret Walsh

I honestly don't think I'd have found doing research quite so easy or interesting if I hadn't written fanfic that required me to do a little.

When I *first* began with fic, research wasn't really an issue. I started off writing Blake's 7. No research required, except for frequent rewatchings of the episodes. Let's be honest, there really isn't anything to research with dystopian science fiction based on fairly dodgy science principles and snarky banter.

A little more research was required when I started writing NCIS fic. Occasionally I had to turn to my forensics books to find information (at that time I really didn't think of it as research; if I thought about it at all, I called it fact checking). But the reality was that I could get most of what I needed from watching the show: team dynamics, even places and weapons could be gathered from watching. I already had an interest in forensics, so I was able to wing it with Abby, and with Ducky. Still, the internet did help a lot too, with online maps of the Washington DC area, for example.

Then along came the BBC's Sherlock. At first no research was necessary except frequent rewatchings as my Sherlock fics were all character, rather than plot, driven. However, I did get a good map of modern London to help me visualize the areas a bit better.

What came next changed everything.

I was asked to contribute to a Sherlock Holmes anthology. I was taking the first steps into pro writing. After writing what was my first Sherlock Holmes story (as opposed to BBC Sherlock), I decided I would attempt a novel. Sooner or later most of us reach this point when we write, don't we?

Now I had to plot. To have a plot I had to have an idea.

And once I had the idea I realized I really knew very little about Victorian England except what I had read in Sir Arthur Conan Doyle's stories. These turned out not to be very useful, as ACD was writing for a contemporary audience who already knew things I needed to know, so he didn't include them.

One thing I learned very quickly: *do not rely on the internet as your main research tool.*

It is incredibly easy to disappear down an internet rabbit hole. Instead of bottles with DRINK ME and food labeled EAT ME on them, you find websites tagged READ ME and WATCH ME. It is very easy to spend hours studying recipes for Tibetan cuisine and 35 minutes watching a YouTube tutorial on how to milk a yak – and still not find the information you were originally searching for, which was the governmental position on foreigners in 19th century Lhasa.

I realized I needed a solid grounding in the Victorian era. This is the first law of research: know your chosen era. If you are a member of a site like Goodreads, as I am, then a quick search of the topic 'Victorian England' and also 'Victorian London' will garner you a large number of suggestions. Almost 500 hundred of them. I made note of the ones I thought would be most useful because at this point buying the books was too expensive – I didn't know what was going to prove useful. So I checked the books against my local library's catalog and I managed to get both *How to be a Victorian,* by Ruth Goodman and *Victorian London,* by Liza Picard. Each give a solid grounding in the era.

Books need to be your first line of research. It's easier to keep track of post-it notes on book pages than it is to keep track of bookmarks on the internet. I know, because I've tried both. Unless you have multiple screens, then switching from your writing to checking research notes quickly bogs you down, making it easy to lose the thread of what you're writing.

This is where the work part of research comes in. I read both books from cover to cover, jotting down things that could prove useful. The *first* thing that proved useful was a large notebook. It's far too easy to mislay scraps of paper, so a large exercise book for information is a must.

I realized quickly I wanted at least one book I could refer to as needed. So I purchased the one by Ruth Goodman.

"I'm of the opinion that no information is ever wasted"

It is good idea to start accumulating a small reference library before you begin writing. One thing that will prove useful is a general book about the era or area you're writing about, the other thing is a map. A good large map that you can spread out over a table, like the one of London I mentioned earlier. If you're writing about Victorian London, then Charles Booth's Poverty Maps of East and West London in 1889 are an absolute boon. So much of London has changed since then that these are a must. One thing that comes to mind is a piece I read years ago set in the 19th century which mentioned the Tate Britain Gallery. At the time the story was set, Millbank Prison was still on the site!

So that's what I started with. One book and a set of maps.

Then it was time for the more specialized research. This is research, not about the time and the place, but information germane to the story. In my case, I needed to know about prostitution in London at that time. So back to Goodreads and a search for 'Victorian London,' then back to my library to see what they had and what could be sourced from other libraries by inter-library loan. A library membership is a blessing for any author.

The hard part of specialized research is working out what you can use and what can be discarded. I'm of the opinion that no information is ever wasted. If you can't use the information about male prostitutes recruited from the Telegraph Office in this story, jot down the information and save it for later.

I found the best way for me was to use two exercise books, but there is no right or wrong way to do research or organize notes. It is all about what works best for you.

Once you have your knowledge for time, place, and plot, it is time to start writing. Once you get going new research topics will pop up all the time. Some will be quickly sorted out. Other subjects will eat up your time. I once spent 30 minutes trying to find out what sort of chamber pot would be used in a flat occupied by a single, lower middle class male.

(Plain porcelain, is the answer, if you're at all interested.)

You'll notice I have refrained from mentioning Wikipedia. That is because I have only rarely used it. Where that site is useful is if you wish to add a historical figure to your work and just want a few brief facts about them, and maybe see a photo or two.

One thing you will find when you start to research is that you will accumulate a reference library by a method I call 'accidental acquisition.' This is when you buy a book to read and after reading it feel it could be useful further down the track, so you pop it on a shelf somewhere. So far I have several books tucked away for future reference, including one on hedgehogs and the memoirs of the current Ravenmaster at the Tower of London. You never know what is going to prove necessary down the track.

Good research adds depth and color to your writing. Never assume anything, especially if you are writing outside of your time and culture. One of the worst goofs I've come across in recent years was a Sherlock Holmes pastiche where the writer assumed that the British House of Lords worked the same way as the US Senate! A few moments on Google would have shown the writer they were wrong.

Don't think of research as a chore before the fun of writing begins. That will bog you down, possibly make you skimp and miss something that could prove important. Try and view research through the eyes of your characters, if you can. Is this scrap of medical knowledge something Watson should know? Would Lestrade know things London thieves don't? Do 17th century Venetian garroting methods sound like an interest for Holmes? Does my original character want or need a knowledge of single stick fighting?

One of the best things about research is the chance to read new books and learn new things, though I'm still not sure when I am ever going to actually milk a yak!

Margaret Walsh lives in Melbourne Australia. She had her first pro story included in the MX Publishing anthology "Sherlock Holmes: Tales from the Stranger's Room 3." Since then she has had three Sherlock Holmes pastiche books published by MX Publishing. Her most recent is "Sherlock Holmes and the Case of the London Dock Deaths." When not writing or reading, she can be found tweeting about writing, Sherlock Holmes, hedgehogs, and assorted other miscellanea as @EspineuxAlpha on Twitter.

5

STAYING THE COURSE
Coping with setbacks and self-doubt

THE GARBAGE WILL DO
(ON WRITING RUBBISH)
Claire O'Dell, Lyndsay Faye, George Ivanoff,
KJ Charles, Natalie Conyer

"What I try to do is write," said poet, civil rights activist, and memoirist Maya Angelou.

"I may write for two weeks 'the cat sat on the mat, that is that, not a rat.' And it might be just the most boring and awful stuff. But I try. When I'm writing, I write. And then it's as if the muse is convinced that I'm serious and says, 'Okay. Okay. I'll come.'"

With Maya Angelou's word wisdom in mind, I asked other writers for their thoughts about writing even when the writing isn't, well, good. These professionals, with two, ten, or twenty books or short stories to their names, each say essentially this: *the garbage will do.* Each author below knows that some days the words drip-drip-drip from their fingers, slow as honey but not half so sweet. And like Angelou, they say you must keep writing even when it's hard, because that's how writing goes. For all of us, no matter where we are in our writing journey.

Isn't that *fantastic?*

Because that means we share this experience, us old and new writers. Learning that successful authors find it as hard as everyone else can help us have faith that if we continue on our path, no matter how rocky, we're on the same journey as those who've gone before us.

I know that if it weren't for writing garbage I'd write nothing. Sometimes I must put every idea down on the page, a thicket of things that don't belong...and don't...and *still* don't...and then there it is, the thread tying the story together. I find the right direction by wandering my forest of ideas and words and *garbage.*

The writers below teach us to have faith that even when we're looking at a page full of *oh what the hell,* when we're sure no one else has ever found themselves buried under so much *not right,* on those days when we believe *if I was any good it wouldn't be this @*&!% hard* we can now know this: every single successful writer writes rubbish. How they differ from so many is that they don't give up. They accept that they can't edit what isn't there, that for right now the garbage will just have to do. So read on and let them give you faith. – Atlin Merrick

"I write poorly all the time and I have given myself permission to write complete crap. Because I know I can fix it. When I do write and toss something, it's because the direction or the emotional undertones are not right. So I need to get pointed in the right direction for my characters and for the story. And it doesn't have to be well-written. It just has to be somewhere it, at least in the same time zone.

"And where that is so entirely depends on the project and where I think it's going wrong. If it's just bad prose I'll wince and keep going. If there's a plot hole, I'll make a note and say, yeah, must insert something interesting here. Add goats, maybe goats. I write really rough notes, so I can kind of see where I'm going, kind of like goalposts and yes, at one point I said to myself: add more goats. I knew I needed literally to add goats."

CLAIRE O'DELL *is the author of The Janet Watson Chronicles and of the River of Souls series, along with dozens of short stories; she lives in the U.S.*

"I personally have an enormous mental hang-up over writing what I consider to be absolute trash, just throwing words at a screen till I write my way out of the pit. There has to be a certain level of coherence – I don't say good writing, but at least some progress that's real and won't trip me up later or confuse me – for the word count to go up. That's just my brain and no reflection on anyone else's whatsoever.

"This leads to another, equally maddening problem, however,

where I stare at a screen with nothing being done until I start beating my head against it. And the most important thing I can say to a rookie writer about either of these sides of the same coin, both manifestations of writing when you are uninspired, is that this too qualifies as *work*.

"Now, if you quit, then it isn't work – it was, as you suspected all along, a waste of time. On the other hand, if you don't quit? Then it was very arduous work, some of the hardest, because there's no visible reward to it. Every time you spill forth less than your best prose, you're still practicing, and you're finding out which tacks won't quite cut it. You're feeling your way through the labyrinth. And every minute you spend in mute despair without your fingers dancing across those keys like they 'should' be, you're enduring the purgatory it takes you to get to the other side and know what you need to do to reach the next chapter, or scene, or sentence. It feels like it lasts forever at times, or that you ought to be better, or that it's your fault.

"As long as you're putting the time in genuinely and not just sitting in front of your open document while Netflix plays in another window, then you're working very hard. As Churchill put it, when you're going through hell, *keep going*. Quitting will absolutely render all that effort wasted, but perseverance transforms it into the mountain you had to climb to plant your damn flag.

"That's my two cents on the subject anyway."

LYNDSAY FAYE *is the author of The Gods of Gotham, Jane Steele, and The King of Infinite Space; she lives in New York.*

"Sometimes the right words stubbornly refuse to come, no matter how much you try to coax or cajole. It's frustrating! But you know what? If the right words don't come…then just let the wrong ones flow. At least, that's what I do.

"Seriously. I just write any old garbage. Why? Well, there are a few reasons.

"It keeps me in the writing zone. And for me, this is really important. If I stop writing, I find it harder to get back into the flow. So, I just keep going. I know it's hard to keep writing if those sought-after good words aren't coming. I know it's easier to just stop and wait and hope. But the truth is, I might be waiting a looooong time. Better to bite that bullet and keep going.

"Sometimes those wrong words will eventually lead to the right ones. The trash I've been writing slowly metamorphoses into something better. So...at the end of a writing session, I might have 1,000 words of crap, followed by 500 words of not-too-bad, concluding with 200 words of pretty good. But without first having written those 1,000 words of crap, I wouldn't have got to those other usable 700 words.

"It is often easier to fix the garbage than create gold from scratch. The not-so-good words and ideas will often spark better ones when I re-write them. Then those, in turn, will spark even better ones as I rewrite again. It might take a few drafts, but I'll eventually get to where I want to go. And the fact of the matter is, I never write gold straight off. No matter how good my first draft is, I *always* have to re-write.

"And finally, sometimes the garbage isn't as trashy as I may first think. I might spend a couple of hours slogging away, thinking this is utterly unusable mega-crap as I'm writing it. But once I'm done, and I go back over it, I realize that actually, it's not as bad as I first thought. It's reasonably okay and won't take too much work to fix up.

"So there you have it. Often, the garbage will do. And sometimes, the garbage is downright necessary."

GEORGE IVANOFF *is author of The Supernatural Survival Guide, The Other Worlds series, the You Choose interactive books, and dozens of other titles; he lives in Australia.*

"There are two main thoughts I have on this topic. The first I got this from Lawrence Block, who wrote a very good book on writing, but he made the observation that one day the writing will flow from your fingers in sparkling rivers, and the next day it'll feel like you're chewing out a block of rock with your teeth.

"But six months later, when you come back to read, you won't be able to tell which was which – and that is depressingly true! Or, I suppose, it's happily true, whichever way you choose to look at it. But the other thing is a brutal reality: you can't fix a book you haven't written.

"I know it's been hard to write in the last few years. For me it's not exactly the time where I want to be writing feel-good romance, but I have finished two books recently by forcing myself to the end and then going through to edit it. Once I've got the words down on page, I've got the shape, the story, I can edit it. Editing is easy for me. But yeah, you can't fix it until you've written it. So just do it."

KJ CHARLES *is a full-time historical romance novelist whose books include* The Will Darling Adventures, A Charm of Magpies, *and dozens more; she lives in London.*

"For nearly four months now – yes, that's right, *four months* – I've wrestled with the start of a new book. Every day I write something, agonize over it, pronounce it unworthy and delete it. It's agony, and I'm getting nowhere.

"Then I realized I'm ignoring one of writing's cardinal rules. I've been trying to produce the perfect draft straight up, instead of doing what all writers need to do; that is, to start off by writing rubbish.

"Ann Lamott, in *Bird by Bird*, devotes a whole chapter to writing rubbish. It's titled *Shitty First Drafts* and in it she tells us to start a writing project by getting something – anything – down on paper. We should trust the process and write without reining ourselves in. Editing and correcting, she says, can come later.

"Lamott says that at this stage we should quiet the voices in our head, the inner critics who tell us our writing is boring, or won't sell, or is inarticulate and clumsy. This idea – that writing involves holding back the critical voice so the creative one can flourish, is also taken up by Dorothea Brande in her excellent book *Becoming a Writer*. When we write, says Dorothea, we need to suppress our rational, critical side until the flow of the story is well under way.

"So that's what I've started to do. I'm putting words down without overthinking or judgment. I've already found new ideas and pathways and things to explore, and for the moment I'll go with that. Later, I'll get out my red pen. I'll do draft after draft until the critical me is satisfied. For now, however, I'm happy writing 'rubbish.'"

NATALIE CONYER *grew up in Cape Town, South Africa, and now lives in Sydney. Her award-winning debut crime novel,* Present Tense, *is set in Cape Town.*

ACTUALLY, NO WORK IS GARBAGE
Diane Duane

One of the most liberating takes on writing that I've ever experienced, came from the very senior and much-awarded science fiction writer Larry Niven.

We were at a party somewhere, discussing writing (because no matter how assiduously writers try to stay away from the subject, it has a way of worming itself into the conversation). The subject of bad writing came up, and Larry leaned back and sighed and grinned and said: "You can always burn it."

As a new young writer, this wasn't a take I'd heard before. At that point writing seemed like the thing that was supposed to be *work,* every word hard-won and not to be lightly disposed of.

Soon enough I was going to discover what every other working writer knows: all of us have moments (or minutes, or hours, or days) when we're sure that the words coming out of us (or that have recently come out) are garbage. This value judgment tends to factor down into one or more of the following sentiments:

a) This isn't what I need to fulfill the requirements of the present work (i.e. it's good enough writing but not what I need for this)

b) This is what I need to fulfill the requirements of the present work but it feels wrong or is of low quality

c) I am so far off my normal game that I can't even tell whether this is a) or b)

After forty years' worth of doing this kind of work, I've developed a set of responses to these problems, which may or may not work for others: the normal warnings about differing mileage apply. But they might work for you.

If the issue is a), then the only sane response is to continue until that particular section of writing completes itself, and then save it somewhere. Work that is no good for one project may eventually be good for another. (Keeping the "garbage" paradigm for the moment: some garbage is perfectly good and useful as recycled material.) Then you take a break, refocus, and start over.

If the issue is b), then the thing to do is finish the short-term tranche of work, regardless of this-moment's feelings about it (which may be incorrect), and when finished put it aside for a short time. Then come back to it –after at least some hours, ideally some days – and reassess. There are tens if not hundreds of reasons why a writer's ability to correctly assess their work can temporarily go haywire. It routinely settles again in the relatively short term, at which point you pick up where you left off.

If the issue is c), then keep on writing regardless – because if your assessment abilities are temporarily that far out of kilter, the work might actually be okay, and you have no business deleting or destroying it. Put it aside and look at it again when you feel that your assessment abilities are back in something like working order.

"I hold what's probably a radical point of view: No work is garbage"

Now, the alert reader will note a similarity of result among these three approaches. All of them require you, in both the short and longer terms, to keep writing. And in all of them, the 'bad' writing gets kept.

This is because I hold what's probably a radical point of view: No work is garbage.

No work a writer produces is waste, because none of it is wasted. All the work a writer does, even if it's not saved, contributes to an ongoing process that shows no visible or otherwise easily quantifiable sign of its progress – but if you're a writer, it's unquestionably operational. The details of just how it works are obscure, and its results are stored internally, in a manner that doesn't show (which is possibly a good thing: if we added it to the outsides of us, like barnacles, it could make clothes shopping a real chore). But even when we're not sure the progress is there, it's there.

This is because the act of repeatedly writing, as with any other repetitive action, unavoidably engraves itself into our brain chemistry, making writing not necessarily easier as time goes by, but certainly less unfamiliar, and the mechanism of it more accessible.

Writing again and again, regardless of the quality of the output, carves its own habits and necessities into the architecture of the writer's mind, broadening the neural channels for the tasks that comprise the art: vocabulary and word search, the pursuit and construction of effective prose or plot structure, the analytical talents that make sense of the past and project the future: the paths of empathy and the orientation of the moral compass. Trying to catch these changes in the act of happening is a mug's game. They happen in the far periphery of the mind's eye; you'll never catch more than a flicker. But, unavoidably, they are happening.

So, going back to Larry Niven's comment, you can indeed burn your words, if you like. But it won't change the basic truth that even though they seemed not to be what you needed at the moment, having written them has made you a bit more of a writer than you were before they came out. So will the next batch of words – and next time, they might be what you need.

The whole point is not to stop…and let the garbage (if it is garbage) fall where it may. You, and the world, will inevitably be the better for it.

Diane Duane has been a science fiction and fantasy novelist and screenwriter for more than forty years. Her best known works include her long-running "Young Wizards" series (started in 1983)—parts eleven and twelve, Young Wizards: Lifeboats and Interim Errantry 2: On Ordeal, having come out in 2017—and the nine bestselling Star Trek novels for which, among many other works, she was awarded the Grand Master award of the International Association of Media Tie-In Writers. She is presently working on the completion of the LGBTQ fantasy series she began forty years ago with The Door Into Fire, and hopes to publish book 4, The Door Into Starlight, in the near future.

STOP COMPARING YOURSELF TO OTHER WRITERS
Sara Dobie Bauer

Sometimes I feel sick with it. A hollow ache starts in my stomach and rises into my chest until my heart feels like it's being squeezed in a fist. Then, the breathing starts up – panicked, rushed. My head gets fuzzy, and all I can think is:

You're not good enough. You'll never be good enough. Everyone else is better than you.

They all have new book deals. They've all signed with new agents. They're all winning awards, and the fans are talking, talking, while you watch silently from your office chair and want to give up. You'll never be them. You're just a hack, an incompetent. Your writing sucks.

How about you? Do you hear it? Do you know that harsh whisper, too? It's the whisper of comparison. It's you seeing everyone else's success as a direct attack on *you* – and it ruins everything.

Don't believe me?

Comparison causes me to freeze up. It staunches my flow of creativity. It makes whiskey sound like a good idea for dinner. Comparison makes my depression and anxiety flare. It steals my sleep. It makes me hate people I don't even know because they seem to have all the luck. Comparison makes me a delusional, self-pitying, immature little girl who can't produce a damn thing.

Except…producing usually makes me happy. *Writing* makes me happy. Comparison makes writing a punishment because every word, every sentence, is ruined by overthinking. *Will an agent like this? Will a publisher? Will this chapter put me on the map like all those other successful, smiling authors out there?*

Thinking like that makes a story disappear. Thinking like that means you're no longer writing for pleasure; you're not writing for you. You're writing for the all-powerful, invisible 'THEY,' and when you do that, your creativity and originality get sucked into a black hole of money, sales, et cetera, until you're an empty husk – a Barbie doll with no backstory.

Comparison has been a problem for me since always. Maybe it's the fragile artist's ego. Maybe it's the suspicion that I might not deserve the success I've had. Maybe it's my competitive Type A personality: I want to be the best, but the fact is, there will always be someone better than me. Someone will always be better than you, too.

So when comparison steals our joy, or even worse, our creativity, how do we fight this invisible beast? How do we claw out of the pit of despair and find a way to enjoy writing again?

TURN OFF THE DAMN SOCIAL MEDIA

Sites like Facebook, Twitter, and Instagram are Comparison City. This is where we, as authors, share our successes, joys, and accolades. I'm not saying you should keep it all inside, if you have great news, share it. Please don't spend hours of your afternoon scrolling through the feeds of 'successful' authors though, until you come to the horrible conclusion that everyone is better than you. If you have to unfollow someone because their posts make your stomach ache, unfollow them. It sounds juvenile, but if it helps your state of mind and creativity, act like a big, artistic toddler for a second and silence those destructive voices.

SHAMELESSLY ASK FRIENDS FOR SUPPORT

Last time I went through a serious creative depression (based a lot on comparison and a little on hormones), I called the troops to action. In other words, I whined to my friends and literally asked them to make me feel better. Again, I'm not calling myself the Queen of Maturity, okay? However, this is what friends are for – they lift us up and make us laugh and, in my case, send pictures of Timothée Chalamet. So ask your close friends for support. Don't feel needy or pathetic when you do it. We all need support; some people are just afraid to ask for it. Once you get much-needed texts that shout, "SHUT UP, YOU'RE AWESOME," save those messages so you can look at them the next time you fall into a funk.

READ CRAPPY FICTION

Okay, so again, I'm just a child in makeup and high heels because reading crappy fiction – whether it be a novel or a thousand words of fanfic – can really lift me up. I'm not trying to profit from other people's fudge-ups. I simply want you to understand that sometimes devouring nothing but Neil Gaiman can be really harmful because, as I've said before, someone will always be better than you. We all know this, but it sucks to be constantly reminded of it. Take a step back, read something really bad (maybe the one BDSM book that shall not be named) and dig back into your own work because honestly? You are your worst competition. The loudest doubter voice is yours.

> "You do not write for other people; you write for you. Writing is the only vocation I have ever lived for"

READ THE BEST THING YOU'VE EVER WRITTEN

I'm prouder of some of my short stories than others. When I've fallen into the comparison pit, it helps for me to revisit one of my fave stories and remember I actually can write, no matter what my busted ego is telling me. I suggest the exact same tactic for you. Dust off that ancient fanfiction you wrote years ago – the one you loved, as did everyone else – and sit there and read. Remind yourself you are a Writer, capital W, and even if you're blocked or broken right now, you wrote something brilliant before, and you will write something brilliant again. Feed that ego. Your fragile writer heart deserves a damn pat on the back.

CONGRATULATE OTHER AUTHORS ON THEIR SUCCESS

But, Sara, didn't you just talk about unfollowing successful people because (sometimes) they make you wanna throw your computer in a lake?

Yes, okay, that's why this step is further down the list. Getting to the point when you can honestly and with zero gall applaud the grand, amazing successes of other people? Welcome to writer adulthood. It takes a lot of time to get here. I realize we all want to be effortlessly supportive of our friends, but when you're in the exact same industry, it's not always easy to see them win *another* award while you applaud from the back row. You will get to the point when you'll really mean it when you say, "Congratulations!" Some days this will be easier than others, but it's an important part of adulting to understand that someone else succeeding does not mean you've lost anything. It's just a reminder that success is actually possible.

REMEMBER WHY YOU WRITE.

You don't write for the money. You don't write for the fame. You don't write to have all your books adapted into Oscar-winning screenplays. If you do write for these reasons, you will never be happy because, even if you are an amazing success, there will always be more money, more fame, and more Oscars that you need, need, need until you go crazy with needing things.

You do not write for other people; you write for you. Writing is the only vocation I have ever lived for. It's the only activity I can sit and do for hours and days and weeks and want to continue doing forever. We write because we love it. We want to create new characters and new worlds. We see a blank page and have to fill it. We write because writing makes our hearts beat. When comparison has stolen your joy and creativity, please come back to this simple question: What makes you happy? Whiskey is an acceptable answer in the short term, but in the long term, remember that writing does make you happy.

You're just having a hard time right now. You're going to have other hard times, too (mine are quarterly), but they pass.

Experiencing emotional emergencies is part of being an artist, so accept that you're allowed to be a mess.

Now, turn off Twitter, get tough, get selfish (for a second), and write your ass off.

Bestselling romance author. Bisexual witch. Feminist. Pro-choice. Anti-censorship. Timothée Chalamet freak. Horror movie aficionado. Vampire mermaid in a past life. Sara Dobie Bauer somehow survived her party-hard college years at Ohio University to earn a creative writing degree. She lives with her precious Pit Bull in Northeast Ohio, although she'd really like to live in a Tim Burton film.

Don't panic. Midway through writing a novel, I have regularly experienced moments of bowel-curdling terror, as I contemplate the drivel on the screen before me and see beyond it, in quick succession, the derisive reviews, the friends' embarrassment, the failing career, the dwindling income, the repossessed house, the divorce... Working doggedly on through crises like these, however, has always got me there in the end.

— Sarah Waters
Bestselling writer of *Tipping the Velvet* and *The Little Stranger*

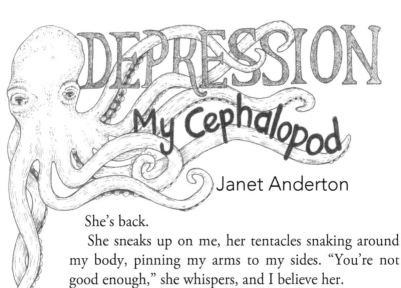

DEPRESSION
My Cephalopod

Janet Anderton

She's back.

She sneaks up on me, her tentacles snaking around my body, pinning my arms to my sides. "You're not good enough," she whispers, and I believe her.

Churchill had his black dog, mine is Stauroteuthis syrtensis, flashing her bioluminescent suckers at me. She seduces me with her pretty lights and her promises.

You see that's what gets me every time, she's familiar, I've been hanging out with her, on and off, for forty years, and familiar feels safe, so I go willingly.

And for a while, everything's quiet, there's only her voice, and she tells me tales that I recognize, as familiar to me as the Hans Christian Andersen stories from my childhood. The one about the girl no one will love unless she loses weight and attains perfection.

The one about not being good enough to show my art to people, better keep it hidden, or better still don't bother making it in the first place. The one that goes who would want you, you worthless, useless, lazy, stupid bitch.

Fully wrapped up in her arms, I hand myself over to her, she is in control, she drags me deeper, I lose track of time. Her words take root, I conceal myself from those who love me, she tells me that they don't really love me, they won't miss me, no one would. She feeds on my fears and I drown. In this place, fathoms deep, there is no light. Nothing flourishes. No ideas. Inspiration can't breathe this far down. I feel lonely. My life becomes colorless, sounds muffled, human interaction feels like it is through a smudged lens. Everyone else is moving faster than I am, I am treading water, wearing a woolen overcoat, and mittens.

And then.

Something.

It happens like this: it's a flash of yellow viewed from the very corner of my eye, but enough that I turn my head…buckets of daffodils. Or it's a familiar song, barely heard, through a passing car window, gone before the chorus. It's a scent, elderflowers, sharp enough to cut through the fog. It's a friend's persistent *are you okay's?* It's a book. A fanfic. Somehow I'm wriggling out of her grip, fighting her off and swimming up, up, breaking the surface, gasping for air, and she's gone.

Sometimes she stays away for months, years at a time. I almost forget about her, I thrive. Sure, I still hear her words, but they're so distant I can ignore them, or I drown them out singing my own song. She waves a lazy arm at me occasionally, usually when I'm about to step outside her boundaries, she reminds me that it's scary out there, but I go anyhow.

Sometimes I see her flashing her lights seductively, but other lights are brighter. My friends shout louder than she does. I keep her at bay with tiny blue pills and coaching, meditation, and mindfulness. And I read, I draw, I paint, and I write, and I figure that if I keep on creating, my fiddly fingers will be too fast for her to catch hold. She's a slippery little sucker, but then again, so am I.

Janet Anderton is an artist and writer, whose work you can find on AO3, and on Tumblr and Twitter as Allmannerofsomethings.

THE GIFT OF FAN WRITING COMMUNITIES
Diandra Hollman

For me, fanfiction has never been about practicing to become a 'real writer' one day. It's been about the simple human impulse to tell stories, to participate in a group that encourages creative thought and expression, that validates our nerdiness and our desire to have *more* of the stories and characters we love.

I stumbled into fandom when I was in high school and my voracious reading habits met my teenage hormonal surge. I devoured every romance novel that piqued my interest in my public library and then – when that well ran dry – sought out more on the internet.

I started writing for the same reason I'm sure a lot of writers write: because I had stories in my head that I needed to get out; some inspired by other stories and some by the desire to see stories nobody seemed to have written yet. My first aborted attempt at writing fanfic was a "Titanic (1997)" story from the perspective of Cal, which I began because I felt all the stories I had read in that fandom were exaggerating his role as the antagonist, to the point of painting him as little more than a two dimensional cartoon villain. I wanted more nuanced bad guys. Ones whose motives couldn't be summarized as "he is evil because he just is." It is possible that I never finished the story in part because I didn't know what I would do with it if I ever did. I didn't have anyone to send it to who would read it.

This is when I discovered *The X-Files* and joined a few Yahoo mailing groups devoted to the particular types of stories, genres, tropes or pairings I favored in my fic reading. These lists were the precursor to social media groups, where women exchanged ideas and stories and encouraged participation. Suddenly, I had a place to share the stories in my head for the consumption of an audience of like-minded people who actually wanted to read them. I was nervous, being a sheltered teenaged virgin writing mostly porn for an audience entirely made up of older women with more experience, both with sex and life in general. But I realized quickly that I was looking at the dynamics of our relationships to each other wrong. I wasn't writing for an *audience*. I was trading stories and ideas with a group of women who had found each other despite vast differences in age, experiences, social status, or geographical locations because we all shared this one thing in common: a love of the same show. The discussions and stories we shared grew out of that love.

I carried this understanding of fandom as a community to my next fandom, and the next one, each time testing and improving my writing skills even though I had no desire to make an official career out of writing. I just wanted to participate and interact with like-minded fans and satisfy the storytelling impulse.

When I came to the *Lost* fandom, the community was primarily located on LiveJournal (LJ), a place where fic and art were shared alongside ideas, prompts, theories about where the show might be headed and general talk about whatever else was going on in community members' personal lives. I was spurred to a height of creative output I haven't been able to match since, posting fics between episode analyses and theories of what, exactly, might be going on on that island and whether it could be explained using combined theories of time travel and quantum mechanics.

We kept track of every interwoven plot thread and character backstory, and talked about how they impacted each other and the whole of the series, and wrote fic about how it might all be resolved (or should have been, could have been, etc.). I didn't finish one of my works in progress until five years after the show had ended. By then, the story had a loyal readership of one as far as I could tell: a woman who made sure to comment on every chapter and told me in the end that my updates had carried her through some of the biggest changes in her life. Which I thought was fitting, since the show and its fandom had done the same for me.

By the time I came to the *Sherlock* fandom, the AO3 (Archive of Our Own) had been well established. Fan creative communities finally had a stable, multi-fandom archive where they could post fic without concerns that the platform would disappear or be bought out by a company that would casually boot them or outright ban them for sociopolitical reasons. But it felt to me like the platform was missing the social aspect of the community that had been present on LiveJournal or even in earlier message boards, mailing groups and listservs. It was great for sharing fic and I used it for whatever stories came into my head for this new canon, but I didn't feel like I was really part of the community. But I have come to discover that while fandom may have changed its outward appearance and no longer had a central location from which to conduct all activity, the community I once knew was still very much alive.

"It's the interaction with fellow fans that fuels my creativity"

In 2016, I began my longest, most complicated and, I hope, best fanfic to date. An epic romance/mystery starring Sherlock and an original male character. I started seeing some of the best and most exuberant comments I have ever received in my 15+ years of fandom writing, but I also got a lot of comments along the lines of "I really hate this original character and can't wait until you get rid of him and put Sherlock back with John where he belongs." I feared the backlash that could come once these readers realized I had no intention of taking the story in that direction and began to wonder if it was really worth my time and energy to continue writing a story for a fandom whose readers didn't want to read it. Again, it seems, I was looking at my role in fandom and my relationship to other fans all wrong.

One day, when my insecurities met a whole lot of real life problems and I felt absolutely awful, I opened my email to find an essay-long comment from one of my readers and fellow writers. Not only did she assure me she adored my original character and had no desire for me to change the course I was headed on, she noted the date stamps and praised my dedication to such a long, complicated work. By the time I finished reading the comment I was crying happy tears.

One of this reader's more recent comments compares each update to a gift, carefully wrapped just for her. And honestly? She's right. Because at this point we have entered that magical dynamic fanfiction authors dream of, where you get that one reader who is *so invested* in this story that you are practically writing each chapter with them specifically in mind and anticipating their response when you post. This sort of encouragement keeps me going, finding whatever time I can to write.

When I realized this reader was also a writer in the fandom, I started going through her stories so I could leave comments of my own. This is when I discovered she was the author of a fic that inspired one of my own stories. A lovely coincidence, but not altogether uncommon or surprising.

Most fic writers are inspired by each other, encouraged to elaborate on another's work or on ideas presented within fandom discussions or outright prompted with 'plot bunnies' for stories fans want to read. Or, as I said before was the case for me, motivated by the desire to see stories that haven't been written by anyone else. Because to paraphrase something someone once told me: chances are I'm not the only one who wants to read those stories. Even if it turns out to be only me and that one other person who wants to read them, that's okay.

The reward for writing fanfiction isn't quantifiable or even tangible. At least it isn't for me. I'm not trying to win some sort of fandom popularity contest by getting the most likes or proving that I can draw a big audience. It's the interaction with fellow fans that fuels my creativity. The knowledge that there is a *person* out there, somewhere, who is reading this ridiculous story that I write for fun and actually enjoying it. That maybe I am making somebody's day just as much as they are mine when they leave comments.

In the process of writing this essay, I found myself thinking about that one loyal reader of my *Lost* fics and regretting, not for the first time, that I hadn't kept contact with her. Since we only ever spoke on LiveJournal and I no longer have a LiveJournal account, I had accepted that I might never find her again even if she is still in fandom somewhere. Then, out of the blue, she left a comment on one of the stories I had transferred to AO3 before closing my LiveJournal account. She said she had just finished re-watching the entire series and gone in search of her favorite fics to see if they held up. "I was sad to see you'd deactivated your LJ because I loved all your fic and being able to talk with you about them and *Lost*," she said. "I am so excited with found each other again!"

This is what fanfiction is, what it does, what it has always been about. It isn't a platform to practice writing for an audience, but a place where people with common interests can meet regardless of physical geographical location and all squee over the same characters and stories. A place where we can and freely share an infinite variety of stories, especially those that would not exist in more traditional mediums. It is a community of (primarily) women where we are free to be our gloriously nerdy selves and encouraged to creatively engage with whatever media lights the creative fires within us.

Diandra is a librarian in a Twin Cities suburb and an avid devourer of all types of media. She joined fandom in the late 90s and has been writing fanfiction since the turn of the Millennium, observing the many changes fandom has gone through since the early days of the internet, both from the inside as a member and from the outside as a graduate student studying social psychology and fan culture. She is not a fan of social media, but can be found on Dreamwidth and AO3 and has a website where she keeps all her fan writings.

DEATH OF THE AUTHOR
(BABY IN THE BATHWATER)
E.C. Foxglove

In the past several years there's been an incredible push in certain areas of fandom for what essentially amounts to 'own voices' works only – i.e. that a fandom creator can only make content for characters with the same racial, ethnic, neurodivergence, disability, sexuality, gender, religious, and trauma backgrounds as themselves, and anyone who writes outside of their own lived experience is a malicious actor.

For the people who believe they're out there 'fighting the good fight' and 'trying to make fandom a better place,' I have two important questions for you:

1. Is the author dead?
2. Is your baby in the bathwater?

What do I mean by those things? Let's start with #1.

The Death of the Author is a type of literary criticism created by Roland Barthes, the extreme Cliff Notes version of which is that art exists outside of the creator's life, personal background, and even intentions. I'm using it slightly differently than Barthes intended, but that's okay, because the author is dead and I'm interpreting his work through my own lens.

In fandom, the author is dead. In fact, the author was never alive in the first place, not really. The author has only ever been the idea of a person, because unlike published fiction, the only thing we know about a fanfiction author is that which they choose to tell us about themselves.

Why is that important?

Because what an author says about themselves might not be true. Hell, that happens in real life with published authors, who have personal documents on file with their publishers, who pay taxes on the works they create and have researchable pasts. If the author of *A Million Little Pieces* could fake everything, why can't I? Why can't you? Why can't the writer of your favorite fic in the whole wide world?

Stop me if you've heard this before: "you can only write about [sensitive subject] if [sensitive subject] has happened to you personally, otherwise you're a disgusting monster that deserves to die!!" Or maybe "you can only write [x racial or ethnic group] characters if you're [x racial or ethnic group] otherwise you're racist/fetishizing/colonizing!"

You can play this game with any sensitive subject you can come up with. I've seen them all, on a sliding scale of slightly chastising to literal death threats.

Now, I could tell you that I'm a white-passing Latina whose grandmother is what racist white people call an anchor baby. I could tell you I speak only English because my family never taught me to speak Spanish, something which I've been told is common in the Cuban community, though I only know my own lived experience. I could tell you that I'm mostly neurotypical. I could tell you I'm covered in surgical scars. I could tell you lots of things.

Are any of these true? Maybe! I could tell you my brother has severe mental development problems, so uncommon they've never been properly diagnosed, and that he will live the rest of his life in a group home with 24-hour care. Is that true? In fandom am I now allowed to write about families struggling with America's piss-poor services for people with disabilities?

Am I allowed to write a character who is Cuban? After all, I did just say I'm Cuban. But is it true? Can I instead write a character that's Panamanian? Maybe I really am Panamanian, not Cuban. Maybe I'm both. Maybe I'm neither. Maybe I'm really French Canadian. Should we require people to post regular selfies? I can't count the number of times I've had someone come up to me speaking Arabic, and I've been told that I look Syrian. What's stopping me from making a blog that claims I am Syrian? Can you even really tell someone's race and ethnicity from a photo?

Am I allowed to write about being a teenager? Am I allowed to write about being a college student? Am I allowed to write about being an 'adulty' adult? Can I write a character who's 40? 50? 60? How old am I?

All of this is to say: you can't base what someone is or is not 'allowed' to write about – in fandom or anywhere else – on a background that may or may not be real and no matter how good your intentions are. And I get it – this insistence often comes from a place of well-meaning. You're trying to protect marginalized groups by stopping privileged people from trampling all over experiences they haven't suffered. I get that. It's a very noble thought. But you can't require a background check for every fanfic you don't like.

If you say "you can only write about rape if you're a rape victim," then one of three things will happen:

Real survivors will have to supply intimate details of their own violations to prevent harassment.

Real survivors will refuse to engage and will then have to deal with death threats or people telling them to kill themselves for daring to write about experiences they haven't proven they've had.

Or, people who aren't survivors will say "yeah sure this happened to me" just to get people to shut up.

Has all of that helped anyone? *Anyone?*

So now let's get to point #2: Is your baby in the bathwater?

What does that mean? The idiom 'don't throw out the baby with the bathwater' is a way of saying: make sure you're not discarding the thing you want to keep (the baby) in pursuit of throwing away the unwanted (the bathwater), because remember the baby is currently *in the bathwater.* You can't just throw the whole tub away or you'll lose the very thing you care about the most. The saying's about inadvertently discarding the precious in pursuit of zealously eliminating the unwanted.

If your intention is to protect marginalized people from being trampled upon, stop and assess if your boot is the one now stamping on their face. Find your baby! Is your baby in the bathwater? Which is to say: find the goal that you're advocating for. Now assess. Are you making the problem worse for the people you're trying to protect? Does that rape victim really feel better, now that you've harassed and stalked them in the name of making rape victims feel safe?

"The whole point of fandom is to be able to explore all kinds of ideas from the safety and comfort of a computer screen"

Let's say you read a fic that contains explicit sex between a 16 year old and a 17 year old. Is this okay? Would it be okay if the writer was 15? 16? 17? Should teenagers be barred from writing about their own lives, and should teenagers be banned from exploring sexuality in a fictional bubble, instead of hookup culture? Is it okay for a 20-year-old to write about their experiences as a teenager? Is it okay for a 20-year-old to write about being raped at a party as a teenager? Is it okay for a 30-year-old? How about a 40-year-old? Is it okay so long as it isn't titillating? Is it okay if taking control of the narrative allows the writer to re-conceptualize their trauma as something they have control over? Is it okay if their therapist told them that writing is a safe creative outlet?

Is your author dead?

Is your baby in the bathwater?

Now let's take a hardline approach: no fanfiction with characters who are under 18-years-old. None. Is the 16-year-old who really loves Harry Potter and wants to read/write about characters their own age better off? Should they be banned from writing? Should they be forced to exclusively read and write (adult) experiences they haven't lived? Will they write about teens anyway? Should they have to share it in secret? Should 16-year-olds be ashamed of themselves? Should we just throw in with the evangelicals and say that the only answer is abstinence, both real and fictional?

Let's say that no rape is allowed in fiction, at all. None. What happens to all the hurt/comfort fics where a character is raped and then receives the support and love that they deserve, slowly heal, and by the end have found themselves again? Are you helping rape victims by banning these stories? Are you helping rape victims by stripping their agency away, by telling them that their wants and their consent doesn't matter?

Is your baby in the bathwater?

Fandom is so often split in two: on one side, the people who want to make fandom a 'safer' place by any means necessary, even if that means throwing out all of the marginalized groups they say they want to protect – and on the other, people who are saying "if you throw out that bathwater, you're throwing the baby out too."

The whole point of fandom is to be able to explore all kinds of ideas from the safety and comfort of a computer screen. You can read and write things that fascinate you, disgust you, titillate you, or make your heart feel warm. This is true of all fiction. People who want to read about rape and incest and extreme violence and torture can go pick up a copy of *Game of Thrones* from the bookstore whenever they want. Sanitizing fandom just means holding a community of people who are primarily not male, not straight, not cis, or some combination of those three, to higher and stricter standards than straight white cis male authors and creators all over the world.

There is nothing you can find on the fanfiction website Archive of Our Own (AO3) that you can't find in a bookstore. Any teenager can go check out *Lolita*, or *A Song of Ice and Fire*, or *Flowers in the Attic*, or Stephen King's *It*, or *Speak*, or hundreds of other books that have adult themes or gratuitous violence or graphic sex. The difference is that AO3 has warnings and tags and allows people to interact only with the types of work that they want to, and allows people to curate their experiences.

Are all of these adult themes eligible to be explored, but only in the setting of something produced or published? Books, movies, television, studio art, music – all of these fields have huge barriers to entry, and they're largely controlled by wealthy cishet white men. Is it better to say that only those who have the right connections to 'make it' in these industries should be allowed to explore violence or sexuality or any other so-called 'adult' theme?

Does banning women from writing male/male erotica make fan culture a better place?

Does banning queer people from writing about queer experiences make fan culture a better place?

Is m/m fic okay, but only if the author is male? What if he's a trans man? What if they're non-binary? Who should get to draw those lines? Should TERFs get a vote? What if the author is a woman who feels more comfortable writing from a male character's perspective because she's grown up with male stories her whole life, or because she identifies more with male characters? What about all the trans men who discovered themselves, in part, by writing fanfiction, and realized their desires to write male characters stemmed from something they hadn't yet realized about themselves?

How can we ever be sure that the author is who they say they are?

Who is allowed to write these stories? How do we enforce it?

Is it better for none of these stories to ever exist at all?

Have you killed your author?

Have you thrown out your baby with the bathwater?

I want to make one thing extremely clear: this discussion is not about excusing racism in fandom, or saying that fanworks are above criticism. Quite the opposite, actually. If you read a fic and go "oh holy shit that was *racist*," then the work was racist. It doesn't matter who the author is. There's not much point in going to the author's page to try and figure out what their race is because it doesn't actually matter, and you can't verify it anyway.

If the author does have a post that says something along the lines of "well I am [X minority group], so there, I can't be racist," that doesn't mean anything, and it certainly doesn't excuse anything. Maybe that person is telling the truth and has unwittingly internalized some really harmful shit; maybe that person is telling the truth and is self-hating; maybe that person is lying; maybe that person is actually white and is deliberately and maliciously pretending to be a minority online to evade criticism. White people do this *all the fucking time*. I'm not going to drop a dozen examples here because there are so many to choose from.

The point is that the harm of creating a racist work isn't undone by the author's identity, so it's pointless to try and criticize a fanfic solely through that lens.

Any author writing about a sensitive topic should approach it with respect and, if writing outside their own experience, should research and make sure they're portraying the subject respectfully. I would never claim otherwise. This essay is about a very particular type of (primarily) online extremism that pushes faux-progressivism all the way back around to actual run-of-the-mill racism again. This goes hand-in-hand with people who claim that learning another language is cultural appropriation, or that eating another culture's food is racist. Obviously, this is a fringe belief, but a few years ago a surprising number of people parroted that shit uncritically.

A person's identity can be important to fandom criticism, and I won't claim that that isn't true. But disclosing any kind of minority status, either on the part of the creator or in criticism from a reader, is only one piece of an effective discussion. It should be the beginning, not the end, of a conversation. Your background can inform a discussion and lend weight to your opinion, but it doesn't make any one person the arbiter of whether or not something is appropriate.

An important thing to remember is that no minority group is a monolith. Two people with the exact same background can disagree about whether or not something is insensitive, and one person's beloved representation can be another's racist caricature. Two queer people can disagree about queer-coded villains as representation; two women can disagree over whether or not a franchise is sexist; two people of color can have totally different experiences watching the same TV show. I don't want to get lost in the weeds giving a bunch of hypothetical examples here, but you get the picture.

I do believe the trend on insisting on 'own voices' began with good intentions: trying to prevent people from trivializing what can be very loaded subjects, and trying to protect various minority groups from being unexpectedly slapped with offensive content. Unfortunately, instead of focusing on the actual works produced in fandom (be it fanfiction, art, or something else), too often the focus is on the identity of the creator, rather than the quality or intention of the work itself. And, in a de facto anonymous place like fandom, these attempts to police other people's works can get very ugly, very quickly.

Somewhat ironically, people in fandom who are members of a persecuted minority also have good reason to *not* disclose their minority status: racism, antisemitism, transphobia, and many different kinds of discrimination are alive and well in the world, and fandom is not magically exempt from these. For example, disclosing a racial identity might quiet one group of people who believes that only members of that race should be allowed to write a particular character, but might also result in racist abuse from racist fans, or 'well-meaning' but unwanted tokenism from fans who want to take that person as some kind of authority on the character or the source material.

Added into this already thorny issue is the addition of non-visible types of marginalization: sexuality, trauma, survivor status, neurodivergency, etc. While it's somewhat possible for people to 'prove' their race by posting photos of themselves, it's impossible to 'prove' any of these non-visible minority statuses to strangers on the internet (especially bad-faith actors), nor should people have to.

This ultra-strict worldview also requires everyone to live tidily in their own little box of labels, with the assumption that humans are so different from one another that it's impossible to understand or relate to someone outside our own little box. A white person is fundamentally different from a Latinx person; a neurotypical person could never have commonalities with a person with autism; a cis person could never find meaning in a trans character's narrative. This is an unhealthy and damaging way to engage with the world.

Over time, the scales have tipped from well-meaning but harmful invasions of privacy to outright malicious personal attacks, doxxing, suicide baiting, and coordinated harassment campaigns, ostensibly in the pursuit of making fandom a 'safer' place for minority groups. And while the people involved in these attacks claim they're doing so to protect people, a fair number of them are just looking for an excuse to abuse and harass strangers with impunity. Additionally, this atmosphere also invites racism and outright white supremacy to flourish, indistinguishable from the people who claim to be acting in good faith. After all, when attacking people who create fanworks of minority characters is both welcomed and encouraged, it's easy for white-supremacists and TERFs to slip in unnoticed and do incredible damage.

Fanworks should be judged on their own merit. That's what all of this comes down to, again, and again, and again. As a community we have a responsibility to make fandom spaces welcoming to people from all walks of life; demanding that minorities prove their identities in order to participate in fandom is a ridiculous barrier that non-marginalized groups are never asked to meet.

Ultimately, the most important thing is to be kind to each other. Listen when people talk about experiences you haven't lived, don't harass strangers on the internet over fictional relationships, and, as always, remember that anyone who claims that everything is black or white is probably trying to sell you something.

E.C. Foxglove is a writer, number-cruncher, and might just be three bunnies in a trenchcoat. Having spent over 20 years both participating in and observing fandom (for better or for worse), she has a bad habit of trying to understand and contextualize the more controversial bits of fandom culture. When not writing, daydreaming about writing, or reading, she can be found tending her herb garden or trying out new recipes. You can find her on Tumblr at littlesystems.tumblr.com and on Archive of Our Own as littlesystems.

You can't walk somebody else's path, and they can't walk yours. We burn the map after we use it, and we detonate the tunnels behind us. Don't worry what others are doing. Don't compare yourself. Now, hurry! Find your path! THE NIGHT BEARS AND FOREST CLOWNS ARE COMING.

— Chuck Wendig
Bestselling writer of *Wanderers*

WHY WRITER'S BLOCK IS YOUR FRIEND
Elena Piatti

I know, I know, it sounds absurd. Offensive even. And if the very idea that writer's block could actually be your friend has caused you to at throw this book across the room or to aggressively turn off the e-reader, I thank you for coming back. Because I really want to share with you how writing a fic while writing a novel taught me to trust writer's block.

It began when a friend got me deeply into the idea of writing a manga, 'one where Moriarty is madly in love with John Watson.' That idea was so good that I went off to write the story, certain it would be easy. I mean I had the characters. I had the plot. I had my friend's encouragement. It should have written itself, right?

It very much did not write itself.

After a few chapters, major writer's block hit hard. I knew what I was supposed to write. I just couldn't. It wasn't that my muse was gone and I couldn't write anything at all, because I wrote all kinds of stories in those months. Some with a fantasy angle, like werewolf Watson, the Holmes boys being able to take their hearts out of their chests, Moriarty as the reincarnation of Sherlock's childhood pet. Others were more realistic: professional dancer Sherlock, Ancient Rome AU, the boys as crushing teenagers. That isn't even a complete résumé of what I was writing at the time, and every one of those stories came easily. But the 'easy' one I'd consciously undertaken?

Not. A. Single. Word.

I was stuck.

And it was maddening.

Maybe your situation is a little different. You've done all your homework before sitting down to write. You've outlined everything scene-by-scene, diligently followed the Hero's Journey or whatever plot structure appealed to you. Every one of your beats are there.

So why is the page still blank?

It must be a curse right? You're the author! You know what's best for the story! Things have to go your way!

Consider this: things *don't* have to go your way.

Yes, you're the author of fanfics or articles or essays or novels, and yes, you absolutely should know what's best for your story, but if you are sitting for hours undisturbed, healthy and otherwise satisfied, and the words still won't come, if own brain has mutinied, ask yourself *why?*

Maybe you got it wrong. Maybe you *don't* know what's best.

Wait, let me finish!

When I was ready to throw my stuck story in the rubbish bin, I had an epiphany. My manga's Watson? My protagonist? A character famous for his iron spine…he was an absolute wimp (in his defense, he was a teenager, too).

Of course the actual John Watson wanted no part of that!

Once I adjusted the character's attitude and created behavior fitting for an army captain, the story suddenly flowed without a hitch right to its ending, and it was tremendously fun to write, just like my friend had promised.

"You know what's best for the story! Things have to go your way!

Consider this: things *don't* have to go your way."

Today I'm grateful to my subconscious for recognizing a flaw that would have destroyed my little tale, and though I'm ashamed it took me months to realize what later seemed obvious, I'm happy my brain kept the block up as long as it did, despite my utter frustration all those weeks.

Of course the blocks – and epiphanies – didn't end there, because we can get blocked for so many reasons.

Another that stopped me dead in my tracks was my own expectations.

See, I was writing multiple fanfictions at the same time I was writing a book. I had deadlines looming all the time. So I wanted to be super strict. "You can't get distracted," I told myself, "you have to write this book! And even if you ignore the book, you still have fic readers waiting! Why are *you* waiting Elena? Why? *Why?*"

Not surprisingly my high expectations created anxiety, which led to more expectations and *more* anxiety, until of course the only reasonable response was avoiding everything and playing video games or watching TV. Your preferred avoidance techniques might be different. I've heard some people wash curtains.

Clearly I had to break this block before it broke me.

So again I shelved duty and plans. I needed writing to be fun if any writing was to be had.

The answer was to give myself permission to play with words, permission to come up with random vignettes, to ignore the calendar awhile. And guess what? I wrote. And wrote. I finished fanfics, which showed me I *could* finish. And though I didn't make my novel's first deadline, I did make the second.

People say work smarter, not harder, and you and me? We're not just creative, we're smart, too. This just might be why our brains sometimes refuse to put words down, knowing we'll only erase them later. We need to learn to trust ourselves, to trust our stories.

So the next time you find yourself staring at a blank page with an apparently blank mind, please don't indulge in self-flagellation, despite how tempting it is. Your brain is not an empty chasm, it's glittering and full to the brim with ideas, but right now all that treasure is hiding a little deeper than usual. Finding it might require digging somewhere else, or using other tools, but those jewels are worth a bit of extra work, aren't they? Especially when that work is as fun as writing about supernatural twins or hellhounds or whatever gives your brain a chance to rest or to come around to an old idea in a new way.

So, breathe. Get rid of the "have to," " should," and "must" looping in your head. Write something else today and I promise, once you stop trying to push everything, the words will come.

Aplenty. The stories will bubble out of you. Instead of staring alternately at the blank page and a clock that coldly ticks away the rhythm of your disappointment in yourself, you'll be writing and wondering, "Wait, it can't be this late already…oops, apparently it is. This chapter is finished, though."

Listen to yourself, okay?

And have a good day.

Elena Piatti is an Italian woman and possibly the only person to study Ancient Greek and Latin at university out of laziness. Depression got in the way of her degree, and she survived the last decade thanks to writing and reading fanfictions. When the Muse agrees (not often lately, apologies) she writes fic on AO3. Born to a Doyle fangirl, Sherlock Holmes can't escape his fate – John Watson and dense policemen will find him anyway.

THE FINE ART OF POSITIVE FEEDBACK
May Shepard

I have a confession to make: for a long time, I thought I was a writer who could not receive feedback. In an effort to hone my craft, I attended workshops and took classes where critique circles were part of the deal, hoping that any insights my crit partners offered would help me get better and better. This, I thought, was what I needed: another cudgel, in addition to the ones I applied to my work myself.

You know the kind of attitude that flourishes at this sort of workshop. Maybe you are holding onto it yourself: the idea that good writers are forged in Hell Places, where All Mistakes Must Be Pointed Out and Eliminated, and If You Can't Take the Heat Get Out of the Kitchen. I was told that my use of commas was annoying. I was told that my choice of subgenre was untimely. I was red penned into a stupor.

I emerged from these workshop experiences both pissed off and self-flagellating. I couldn't see through the multiple and often contradictory corrections offered by my fellow critters, or the instructor, when I was taking a course.

Any piece I exposed to someone else's crit, I always trunked, totally convinced the problems with it were intractable, and there was no point in trying to fix them. Worse yet, I felt like somehow I'd failed as a writer. I couldn't take the heat. Perhaps it was time for me to exit the kitchen.

After a few failed attempts to find a crit situation that worked for me and a really long bout of writer's block, I managed to recover enough that I could write – I was able to edit myself to the point where I got a few pieces accepted for publication – but I refrained from seeking out critique again. Maybe I just wasn't a crit sort of a writer, I reasoned. I limited myself to troubleshooting my plots with my partner, who is great at that, and tends to be nice about it. As for making my craft better, I decided to go it alone.

Then I met my friend Mash – shamelessmash on AO3 – and everything changed, because she changed the way I look at the act of offering feedback, and the way I do it.

When we first got to know each other, Mash and I were both working on longish projects. In part because I had a hand in helping her develop the idea for her lovely Sherlock fic *A Case of Identity–The Musical*, we agreed to trade betaing. As much as I've loathed receiving feedback, I've always enjoyed reading other people's stuff. (I can admit now that I hoped that she would accept betaing from me and then perhaps forget she'd offered to beta my fic in return.)

Things took a turn for the surprising when Mash sent me the first chapter of *A Case of Identity*, long before I'd expected her to. She specified that she wanted squee only on this early draft, just positive feedback on what was working so far. I'd never had anyone ask that before, so I had no idea what was going to happen next.

(Spoiler: really great things.)

At first, I thought, no problem, we all want a little bit of encouragement along the way. As I read, and I noticed, *oh, there's a comma here, a verb that could verb in a verbier way over there*, I was tempted to mention it, but then I remembered her request and I refrained. I try, when I can, not to be a shitty friend. I also try not to be a shitty beta, which, hey, means respecting the writer's right to ask for the kind of feedback they want, and trying your best to offer it.

At the same time, the part of me that wants to be useful was squirming. How could 100% positive feedback possibly help someone hone their work into something better?

Boy was I about to find out.

It turns out, receiving positive feedback makes you want to keep going.

Mash, super smart awesome writer that she is, knew she wanted motivation to carry on. She was trying to get as much of the draft done as possible, before she started to post chapters online. There is nothing wrong with needing positive feedback in order to keep going. It's really clever to ask for it. Knowing that the premise was working and what she'd written so far was charming (and it was, so, so, so charming, holy crap) gave her a boost, and who the fuck doesn't need that?

Asking for positive feedback only is *a good idea.* Try it the next time you ask for help with a story's early draft.

"She changed the way I look at the act of offering feedback, and the way I do it"

The other lessons came when it was time for me to share my stuff with her. See above re: reasons why I really hesitate to let people crit my stuff, but, given who Mash is, I was pretty sure it would be okay.

It was okay. It was more than okay. It was brilliant, amazing, incredible.

If you've never had the pleasure of receiving critique from a writer who is great at knowing what works in a story, and is willing to yell at you about what's working in yours, let me tell you, it is a treat, and so helpful. As I watched Mash go through my Google doc containing the first couple of chapters of my Sherlock fic *The Burning Heart,* leaving trails of keysmash and screaming as she went, I not only felt like a goddamn writing genius, but I also was taking substantial notes about where she was doing it.

Because knowing what's working in a story is even more important for a writer than knowing what is not working.

If you know what works, you can play that up, and do more of it. That's one reason, one very good reason, why telling a writer what you like in their story is a good idea, but there's an even more important one.

Telling a writer what works helps them understand their own magic.

What makes a writer great is not whether they can follow writing rules, but whether they can bring something uniquely theirs to a story. Good craft, which you can learn, will always,

always help you make your story more clear to whoever is reading it. Good magic, the unique ineffable sense of play that makes you want to tell this story in this way at this point in time, that's what makes people think, *whoa wow whoa, this is amazing.* And that ineffable something flourishes when it's praised. When your magic is ignored, like it is when you receive crit that's 100% focused on mistakes, it lies down on the floor and refuses to get up again.

This is one major source of writer's block. Even if you think offering positive feedback is bullshit, perhaps you would agree that it's good, from a writerly karma POV, to avoid doing things that block other writers, especially the ones who've asked you for feedback.

But wait there's more!

Mash did a lot more than keysmash and scream all over my manuscript: she also asked questions when she was particularly excited.

The questions you, as a reader, are dying to have answered are invaluable writer feedback.

'Hey is x going to do y next?' (Insert inevitable joke about x being y's love interest.) Or 'Oh my god what did he mean by that?' Or 'How long is it going to be before we find out the answer to the question you laid out in chapter three?'

These questions let me know where the breadcrumb trail I was trying to leave was effective. Under some circumstances, they let me know when I was waiting too long for a reveal. This alone helped me hone my plot.

Radio silence helps you see where what you wanted to achieve isn't coming through.

We all have those places in our writing where we think we've really nailed it. As writers we understand what we're trying to achieve, and we're all attempting to bridge that gap between what's in our heads and what's on the page. When you're dealing with a beta whose primary mode is positive, and they skim right past the moment you hoped was Big and Significant and Came Off Well, you know you have more work to do. A lukewarm response to a big deal moment is a great indicator that we need to hit it harder or make it more clear.

THE ROLE OF WHAT WE USUALLY THINK OF WHEN WE THINK OF CRIT

What do I think about comments that point out errors or ask thornier questions about what isn't working? I think they have a place. I think that place is probably less important than most of us imagine.

It is still definitely helpful, and useful, to let a writer know if you think they've made a mistake, or if you think something could be clearer. If they have an excessive attachment to a particular word or sentence structure, or whatever it may be, it's fine and helpful and good to note that.

There are gentle ways of doing this.

Instead of citing a 'writing rule,' consider pointing out what the writer has done.

Instead of 'never use adverbs they are the devil' it's more useful if you stick to observing what's on the page: "you've used twelve adverbs in the last three paragraphs."

'Show don't tell' could become "instead of saying he's sad, what about one sentence describing his internal reaction to finding his former partner's scarf in the glove box?"

If you're offering critique in order to show off your knowledge of 'the rules' and to talk about how you would never break those rules, your ego has taken over and you're probably not going to be super helpful in this moment.

Teach, don't overcorrect.

When a writer makes the same grammar mistake over and over, this is not the time to judge them and point out every single instance – unless they've asked you for a spelling, punctuation, and grammar edit. It *is* the time to recognize that they probably don't understand semicolons. Link them to a post that explains them, point out one or maybe two wrong uses of semicolons as you do your crit, and leave it up to the writer to correct it themselves (or not!).

Believe it or not, people generally like it better when you leave it up to them to be responsible for their own work, and allow them to decide how much they want to take on board at any given time. If that writer doesn't want to learn about semicolons in this exact moment, then that is cool. If you're not cool with it, perhaps it's time to examine your excessive attachment to semicolon evangelism.

Consider the level of the writer and emphasize the positive anyway.

If you're dealing with a beginner writer who is just figuring shit out, for the love of all that's sweet and tender, just pick one or two mistakes to work on. Tackle verb tenses or POV this time, leave run on sentences for some future moment, and let them know, in no uncertain terms, what you like about what they've done. You could be the difference between shutting a writer down for good and ensuring that they keep going.

If you're dealing with an advanced writer, please, please don't assume they don't need positive feedback. Mighty oaks need the sun just as much as seedlings do. I by no means know everything about writing, but I'm not a beginner either, and I always, always learn so fucking much when I see what people respond to in my work, and when I understand what resonates with them.

A note on the proportion of positive to negative comments. There's an old saying I've always found to be a bit cynical, about sharing something positive before offering something negative in crit. This is a great idea, in theory. In practice, sometimes people following this rule offer comments like this:

'This paragraph has some nice description in it, but'

deep, sucking inhale

…eight sentences follow that go into intimate detail about how many times the writer has used the word *feel* and how 'that is not a great idea for these thirteen reasons' and also 'there's a mistake in the research with reference to the specific century the armor the main character is wearing was most likely to be manufactured and and and and'

I'm hoping you can see why, if this is the only form of positive feedback offered, it might come off as insincere.

On the other hand, in the context of a crit that lavishes praise on everything good, a genuine observation that a particular paragraph has issues, or a particular aspect of the timeline is self-contradictory, or the writer flips wantonly between first person and third person, is so much easier to take, and so much more likely to be received as genuinely helpful.

When I go into a crit, I usually try to get my energy up and my mindset into a positive space before I comment. I try to remember that on the other end of this work of fiction is a human person who, in the act of offering their writing up for feedback, is making themselves vulnerable. If I catch myself dryly pointing out errors without saying much that's positive, I know it's either not a good time for me to be offering crit, or I need to slow down a little and enjoy what I'm reading. (In rare cases, it means I'm not the right person to be critiquing that particular story.) I try to read like a reader, not like a writer. I try to avoid reading like I do when I'm combing my own stuff for infelicitous turns of phrase or bad logic, unless that's what the writer has requested.

If you yourself are from the Hell Place and believe You Work Best When You're Being Punched In the Face and So Should Everyone Else, first, uh, you probably need a hug, but also, try offering positive crit the next time you read for someone, and see what a difference it makes. If you've never received a crit that's largely positive, consider asking for one the next time you go to a trusted beta. Ask them to tell you what they think is working. (If they refuse, find someone who is not from the Hell Place.)

Give positive crit a try. We certainly have enough misery in this world. There are many, many reasons to spread some joy, especially where that joy is functional, helpful, and potentially life changing.

I think you'll be pleasantly surprised.

May Shepard lives in a small city on the shores of a big lake in Canada. She writes queer stories, mostly historical, sometimes fantastical, and usually romantic. Find her on Tumblr @may-shepard, and on AO3 at May_Shepard.

Quantity produces quality.

— Ray Bradbury
Hugo award-winning writer of
The Martian Chronicles

DEAR WRITING FRIENDS
Hannah S.

First: whether you write fanfiction, original fiction, or a combination, it's perfectly natural to feel disheartened when your efforts seem to go unnoticed.

It can be difficult when you put so much effort into something and yet it seems to make no traction, while you look over at someone seeming to put minimal effort in getting so much more attention than you. And it's okay. You're not less than them. You don't matter less. Your words still matter and your efforts do as well. This is why comparison is an enemy to our craft.

Second: You are not any less important than other writers no matter who or how famous they are. They may get more attention but your words still have the potential to help someone else, inspire them, motivate them, uplift them, help them heal...your words have so much power to them, even if you don't see what they're doing for others. Even if it feels and appears that all of your effort is in vain.

Third: Writing is *hard*. It takes a lot of work, a lot of patience and creativity and it does not make you any less to be exhausted by it. Take breaks when you need to. You are human, you need breaks, you need time for yourself to get your mental energy back. It is perfectly normal to get drained from using your creativity so much and you should feel *no* shame for needing to rest. Creativity is draining.

Fourth: What you do is *amazing*. Just think about it...we take thoughts in our heads and we can create entire worlds, galaxies, universes from a single thought. You can have the simplest thought that a non-creator would just let go by. But you're creating this massive project out of that single thought. That's amazing. *You* are amazing.

Fifth: To writers that have tons of works in progress (WIPs), you're awesome. It's not something to be upset over or feel bad about. If you're jumping WIP to WIP and never able to finish your WIP, that's nothing to be ashamed of. You don't need to change yourself. Your creativity is just that massive and expansive and maybe you just haven't quite gotten *the* million dollar idea yet. It's okay, keep trying, keep trekking, and keep writing.

"You're doing incredible things. Don't let the self-doubt monster scream at you"

Sixth: To writers that only write one WIP at a time, you amaze me. Your dedication to a single idea is inspiring. It really is. It may not always feel that way, but you are dedicated and passionate about your work and that's amazing. You have the ability to create something so vivid because of how much time you put into this one project, that it could feel like you're in the world. You are doing amazing things. Keep it up!

Writing is a challenge. It's not something that should be taken lightly. We shouldn't be putting ourselves down because we don't write like our more successful friends. We shouldn't be comparing ourselves to other writers because there are just *so many* ways to be a writer, so many ways to write. There are fluff writers, angst writers, horror writers, writers who work on 100 WIPs at a time, writers that work on one at a time, writers who are highly into description and those more into dialogue. No matter what kind of writer you are, you should be proud and love your work and the energy you put into your craft because it's something that is admirable. Even if you're not where you want to be as far as how good of a writer you are, you have the potential to be as good as you want.

Keep writing. Keep pushing forward and putting in the effort. Keep *trying*. Your efforts are seen and they're not in vain. You're doing incredible things. Don't let the self-doubt monster scream at you. Scream back and let it know you won't be bullied into silence.

Hannah S. is a 30 year old American writer. The last 20 years of her life have been full of many creative endeavors, such as text based game design and web design. However her greatest passion and love has always been writing. One of Hannah's greatest pastimes is blogging, and one of her favorite topics to blog about is encouraging posts geared towards writing. However, writing has always been one of Hannah's greatest passions and hobbies, so she hopes to continue to inspire other writers and aspiring authors while working on her own projects for many more years to come.

6

TAKE AWAY MESSAGES
What fandom means to us

A HIGHLY IMPROBABLE COMMUNITY
Hubblegleeflower

It started with a throwaway post one dark February.

February is kind of a lousy month. It's cold, it's dark, report cards are due, it's harder to chuck the kids outside. I'm never at my happiest in February. This particular February, I was almost a year into my writing revival; I'd started reading and writing fic the previous year, and like so many of you other writers out there, a) I loved it, and b) my real life did not allow me anywhere near enough time for it.

Which meant, of course, that when I did have some free time to spend on my laptop writing, I was instead scrolling Tumblr. If I hadn't been, I'd never have seen doctornerdington's throwaway post saying wouldn't it be nice if there was a retreat just for fic writers.

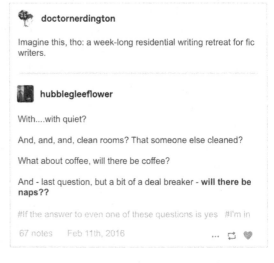

doctornerdington

Imagine this, tho: a week-long residential writing retreat for fic writers.

hubblegleeflower

With....with quiet?

And, and, and, clean rooms? That someone else cleaned?

What about coffee, will there be coffee?

And - last question, but a bit of a deal breaker - **will there be naps??**

#If the answer to even one of these questions is yes #I'm in

67 notes   Feb 11th, 2016   ... ♻ ♥

That was it, just a musing thought, no detail, no time frame, but the second I read it, I needed it like air. So I asked her, "Well, why not?"

And we were away.

ORIGINS

A retreat for fic writers. Simple enough. Book the space, arrange the food, add up the cost, set a price, and invite people to sign up.

Eighty or so people were interested in principle. I thought maybe, once there was a solid date and cost, that number would dwindle considerably. I thought maybe I'd get twenty people.

I got seven.

It made sense to me, actually. Think of the risks involved. First of all, here was some rando from Tumblr (that's me, by the way, hello), saying yeah, sure, I'll give you a writing retreat, it's all organized, trust me, just go ahead and fork over $480, and meet me in Canada in four months. Buy an air ticket, too, probably – they're usually nice and non-refundable.

There are very few people that I know of on Tumblr for whom several hundred dollars is a negligible risk. They'd need to take time off work, plan around appointments and prescription renewals, apply for passports, arrange four days of childcare...everyone has substantial responsibilities, which is why a retreat held such allure in the first place. That first year, there was no evidence that this wasn't just a huge scam that carried significant practical repercussions if it didn't work out. That in itself was an enormous risk.

Above and beyond the financial risk, it's also four days of emotional exposure. Four days at a conference center with a bunch of people you've never met, pursuing a passion you're used to keeping secret, keeping quiet. Four days, face to face with real human beings, when usually you spend the time hidden. Hidden safely behind a computer screen, where none of your awkwardnesses or anxieties, none of the hurts you usually hide, none of the parts of your identity that you don't quite understand or that you keep very quiet around the people in your family or your community... none of those things are visible. Where you are safe from discovery. Four days where you risk being seen.

For many of us, this was by far the greater risk.

Anxiety, PTSD, chronic pain, insomnia. *Will I have a panic attack? What if they hate my writing? How will they respond to my pronouns? What if I can't eat any of the food? Is my English good enough? Am I too young? Am I too old? What if they find out I don't belong here?* It's much easier to hide on the internet than in a meeting room.

Perhaps the people who came thought it might be possible to participate, and still be invisible. They soon learned that they couldn't. Talk about writing was talk about hiding, and healing, and growth. About discovery, identity, self, and self-doubt. Creating and becoming. We could not be there halfway; we couldn't hide. But we also discovered that we didn't need to.

Somewhere in that risk and visibility, something happened that made the space one of the safest I've ever encountered. "Safe and sacred," we started saying. It became a mantra. How else could we describe a space where everything about us was genuinely...fine? Our hurts and fears, our inconvenient needs, the demands of our imperfect bodies and brains, and all our quirks and weirdnesses – these were seen, protected, cherished...and very often shared. Our secret selves did not need to be secret.

It would be an understatement to say that this was novel for all of us; for many of us, it was a revelation.

By the end of the retreat, we had built something precious. We were able to carry away a renewed motivation and confidence for our writing, and a sense that writing fanfiction is a legitimate, healthy, and uplifting pursuit. More than that, though, we took away a feeling that we weren't alone. That who we are and how we are is every bit as acceptable and valuable as whatever we manage to create.

And that the people who had made us feel that way were only as far away as our wifi connection.

GROWTH

The wifi connection was key, because this entire beautiful community began on the internet. It began in the spaces that have been carved out for fandom, by queer fans, by trans fans, by women. These spaces that allow us to share our love of the stories that touch us, and also to reframe those stories, re-imagine them, in ways that let us do the same for our own lives.

It was the winter of 2015 when I first watched BBC *Sherlock*. Like many before me, I was struck by the disconnect between what was said in the show, and what was shown. I had no capacity at the time for 'reading' television, but I wasn't blind. When Sherlock watched John through the window, storming away across the street, after they'd argued, I could see the regret and longing in his face, and I *knew* what I was seeing. But then what Sherlock said ("Look at that, Mrs. Hudson. Quiet…") was about something else entirely and it was almost physically jarring. *Oh*, I thought. *I must be mistaken.* Because I thought that only what is talked about, only what is *textual*, is real.

Then I learned the word *subtext*.

"I came to understand myself through fanfiction and fandom. I saw the fluidity and complexity of sex, of love, of identity"

I remember very clearly the sensation of my mind rapidly expanding as I learned the extent of what is present but unspoken in film and television, and discovered the extent to which the spoken is privileged over the unspoken. It is privileged to the point that the overwhelming majority of viewers will only believe in what has been said out loud, and remain completely unaware of any other layers of meaning, of reality. How I felt when I realized that our own realities are also defined by what we can express in language. What, I wondered, was I failing to see in my own life due to a lack of language?

Fandom gave me the tools I needed to understand the stories I loved on a much, much deeper level. Fandom showed me what could be read in the spaces between the words. Fandom taught me that a great deal of those negative spaces are, in fact, queer spaces. Queer people have been able to imagine themselves in those spaces, because when it comes to queer realities, there *are* no words. The words are silent. My own words were also silent, when it came to my own queerness.

In fandom, people were filling in those silences with their own words.

I found that I could do that, too; write my own words and explore my own silences. Writing in the spaces left empty by the show itself was the beginning, for me, of writing in my own spaces. And the people in the fandom, with wisdom and intelligence, taught me what I needed to write there. It was me, the missing pieces of me, waiting to be written and made real.

Interacting online, reading meta, reading essays, taught me the language I needed to talk about the missing pieces of my own identity. The phrase, 'Who I am is not determined by who I'm with' was groundbreaking to me. 'Bi-erasure' is a term I learned in fandom, and its necessary corollary, Bi visibility.

What was more, everything I learned was delivered with clarity and sincerity, courage and compassion...and with humor, irreverence and a deep appreciation of the absurd. One time, thewimpytentacle answered an ask to the effect that even when John was married to Mary, it was not a straight relationship, because John is not a straight person, and that floored me. In that moment I learned a new way to see myself, to make my pieces fit. I am bisexual, so my marriage is not a straight relationship. It is not a contradiction of who I am; it is one of many possible expressions of it.

The fact that the realization came from the musings of a fictional sentient tentacle does not detract from its impact: I could be openly queer *and* have a husband. I could acknowledge all aspects of my identity without negating any of the others. They were all real, together.

The spaces in the show and the spaces in my life are closely entwined. In the person of John Watson, I discovered that it is not only possible but likely that, in 2010, a queer man in his forties, with a wife and child, might be closeted, even to himself. In the same way, it was not only possible but likely that, in 2015, a bisexual woman in her forties, with a husband and children, might be closeted. Even to herself.

I came to understand myself through fanfiction and fandom. I saw the fluidity and complexity of sex, of love, of identity. I learned that certain assumptions I had made about myself lacked nuance, at the very least, and tended to erase elements of my own identity in a way very common to queer women. For example: the phrase with which I once explained my queerness: 'I *used to* be bisexual.' That statement has been permanently removed, and I don't miss it one bit.

Visibility came next. I came out as bisexual to close family members (who were confused and irritated), and reiterated it to my husband (who was supportive but somewhat at a loss), and became more active in the Gay/Straight Alliance at my school, which I now run. I even came out to my students by the end of 2016. Can you imagine knowing, in middle school, that queer people are just... people? That you could...meet? That *gay* and *straight* are merely two ends of a wide spectrum? That queer people who could 'pass' as straight might still choose to be visible, out of *pride*? That it really is *all fine*? Perhaps you knew all of that at the age of 12. I did not; but now my students do, and I call that a result.

So there I was, busily filling in the spaces and the silences, in canon and in my own life, but there was a rigid division between my fandom life and my 'real' life. I had a multi-faceted community who knew some of the most precious secrets of my heart but whom I'd never met. No one in my real life acquaintance was learning this language or using these lenses. I wanted to talk about what I was learning, but I could only pursue these conversations with people I had never actually met.

It matters, meeting people in person.

Online friendships are so valuable, and cultivating them is profoundly worthwhile even if you never meet them in person. That being said, human beings are creatures of their bodies. It makes a difference to see and touch each other, maybe eat together. To hear each other laugh – to *make* each other laugh. We write about our characters' physical relationships because we know that bodies are important, that there are no stories without bodies. Physical presence matters to our stories too.

The person I had become in fandom, her thoughts, her flights of intuition, her fears and moments of courage, her creativity and sensuality...these remained a little blurred, a little undefined, as though behind a veil. That is, until I walked into that little cottage at that first retreat. These people suddenly had faces. Faces and fears and bodies, chronic pain and anxiety and dietary restrictions. They had smiles, and wry wit, and dirty jokes. (Housekeeping got a bit of an earful that year.) They were real people, *and* they had the same symbolic language I had, knew the same references, were steeped in the same memes.

Meeting them brought my whole fandom experience into focus and made it just as real as anything I'd ever referred to as 'real life.'

TRANSFORMATION

Every year we've had the retreat has been a little bit different. Each time a few more people take a risk and join us; each time the rest of us wonder and worry what might happen to the dynamic; each time every single new person is a miracle and an inspiration.

It's become its own entity. There is contact all year round. There's a hangout group and regular video chats and we all follow each other on Tumblr. Any one of us can get lightning-fast beta with no prior notice whatsoever, because there are twenty or thirty people who'll get the call, and a few of them will always be free. We run writing sprints together. We have drama, and argue, and grow, and discover. We miss each other's faces.

We've taught each other how to write, too. At various times, there have been workshops on writing problems, beta reading, technology and writing tools, keeping your erotica effective, fandom as therapy, fandom and trauma recovery, discipline (discipline *in writing practice*, not that other kind, although that came up too), editing, impostor syndrome, and plot. This is not an exhaustive list. And all these workshops have been expertly handled by the participants who signed up to deliver them. I'll say that again: every expert at this retreat is simply a participant sharing their own knowledge and experience. And they've always been *excellent*.

It's important to remember, though, that writing in fandom is not just about writing. It's about sex. We write about sex. Well?

Wasn't this whole journey about sex? Who's having it, or not, and why, and with whom? In our writing, sex as the physical act stands in for sex as identity, sex as relationships, sex as our messy animal nature and our fraught relationship with our bodies. As women, or queer people, or trans people, our bodies are overwritten, judged by the extent to which they resemble or deviate from the 'baseline' bodies of cis men. So when we get together in a group, and write unapologetic sex, and inhabit our own desires, it is a radical act. Writing over what has been written over us; writing over it with womanness, transness, queerness. And at a basic level, we're also writing really arousing sex to be read by others who are like us. The important part of the sex we're writing isn't so much the fictional people engaging in it, but the real people being turned on by it. It isn't just philosophy.

These are the people I am writing for; the erotica that I create is for the sake of *their* desires, and their erotica is for mine. Throughout the year, this exchange, this exploration, takes place at a distance, anonymously. In private. Even so, it is achingly intimate.

At the retreat, we share our fic in person. Out loud.

How is that for *intimate*? After the workshops, after dinner, in a common room rather than a meeting room, we snuggle into our pjs and fire up our laptops and read our erotic writing out loud. We experience, in a group, in real time, the feelings of yearning and arousal we normally only allow ourselves to feel in isolation. We listen to the little shifts and sighs around us, our breathing quickens. I gasp, and so does my neighbor, and a muffled groan might emerge from the far side of the room. We're not touching – it's not *that* kind of retreat – but we are inhabiting our erotic selves, together. Utterly without shame.

In our everyday lives, most of us don't talk about what we write and read; it is almost certain to be misunderstood. We know, in our solitude, that sex is nothing to be ashamed of, that for those who choose to have it, it can be beautiful, and that even when it is not beautiful, it is human, as are the many reasons humans engage, or don't engage, in sex. We know that denying the embodied, animal side of our nature is dishonest, and does not help us. We know this, but we still keep quiet. At the retreat, we actually live out that knowledge. We *feel* its truth, instead of just knowing it. This absence of shame, this embracing of our whole selves, is responsible for the metamorphosis we undergo in the course of this retreat. I believe we have all experienced some kind of growth, some kind of learning, some kind of...transformation.

It's more than just the fact that we all write fanfiction, or like the same shows; it's that we share the same kind of longing. For time and space to be creative, yes, but also for common ground. Corroboration, affirmation. Acceptance.

We all carry our fragility with us when we come here, the tender places in our souls where we love so deeply and feel so keenly. We cup them in our palms, so gently. We look into the faces of these strangers, look across at their cupped palms, and we decide to trust. Then we uncurl our fingers, and find that everyone around us treats our treasures as if they were precious to them as well. We utter out loud our worst fears and insecurities, and are met with compassion and recognition.

We share a language, learned in fandom, and we use it to figure out who we are, to explore the negative spaces, the silences, in our lives. At the retreat, we discover the power of taking a silent language and speaking it out loud.

Hubblegleeflower (she/her) has been present on Tumblr and AO3 since early 2015, and now has thirty-three posted works and thousands of memes, gifs, and microblog posts for your reading pleasure. After a decade-long hiatus, she came back to writing, thanks to the Sherlock fandom and gay erotica. Thinking and writing about stories, justice, identity, queerness, and erotica takes up a hefty chunk of her time. Whatever's left over is dedicated to teaching, parenting, music, and crochet. The Fic Writers' Retreat takes place in Ontario every August (global disasters and pandemics permitting); new folks are always welcome.

They looked toward Susannah, but she slept ... sturbed. Once there had b... m named Odetta Sus... ...olmes; later there had b... amed Detta Susan... r. Now there ... ... Susannah Dean ... Rola... ...e she would ... ...ive in; he feared ... h... ...ause he knew he would sacrifice her.

Susannah Dean, Gunslinger by Adalisa Zarate

WIDENING THE LENS:
WRITING BEYOND LIVED EXPERIENCE
Audra McCauley

There's an adage about writing which dictates you should 'write what you know.'

The implication is that you should not endeavor to write something you don't understand. There's sense there, in that you can't write based on guesswork alone, but it's also patronizingly limiting. It narrows the scope of what you can write to only your lived experience. If writers followed that creed, our breadth of literature would be sadly limited. We'd have no historical fiction (the author didn't live during that time), or science fiction (you don't live in the future), or even characters of another sex or gender identity than the writer's. Part of writing is challenging yourself to look beyond what's familiar and comfortable – to produce a piece of fiction that offers diverse perspectives.

With that said, you can't dive into an experience or a perspective you aren't at least somewhat familiar with and expect to do it justice. That's where research comes in. I was trained as a historian, and to produce a piece of historical writing requires a deep dive into primary sources to analyze and synthesize them into a coherent narrative. That's something that can be equally applied to fiction, and fanfiction. I've written historical fics with months of research backing them, but I've also explored characters in a modern setting whose experience is vastly different from mine.

The best example of this is a fic I wrote for the Kylux (Kylo Ren/ Armitage Hux) fandom called *Allemande*. The premise actually came from a fandom artist's concept of a high school AU where Kylo – known often in the fandom by his original name, Ben Solo – was profoundly deaf (which means a complete loss of hearing, rather than partial hearing loss). I was captivated by the idea, but had never been a part of the Deaf community or even spoken to a deaf person. My understanding of how one would navigate the world without hearing was minimal at best. I was too inspired by the idea, though, to not write something based on it. That meant exploring the Deaf experience.

My go-to resource is, as it is for most of us, the internet. I began to seek out forums and Deaf community websites that addressed the experience of deaf individuals. I knew that everyone's life experience varies, and that no matter what I wrote, the details would not line up with everyone in the community. Still, I sought out as many sources as I could that addressed those experiences.

I read about how young deaf people in the United States learn American Sign Language (ASL), and that there are many variations of the language – dialects – based on where one lives. Other countries have different signs that are not comprehensible across all borders (British Sign Language, or BSL, for example).

Hearing loss over time affects when people learn sign language and there are defined norms and expectations of behavior in the Deaf community. There are even prejudices and stratification of what it means to be 'truly' deaf. Those little nuances were not necessarily something I picked up from the forums alone, but from a deaf person with whom I struck up a relationship during the writing of the story.

One of the most fascinating parts of the fanfiction writing process is that someone can find your story within its first few chapters and engage with you in a way that will be beneficial to the overall accuracy and authenticity of the narrative. My 'source,' who is now one of my very best friends, came into my life about two chapters into *Allemande*. He left an anonymous message on Tumblr which read: "I read *Allemande* and I must say, as a deaf person, you did a great job writing Ben realistically and without any ableism. I would have loved to have had a friend like (your) Hux in high school!" I was stunned and immensely pleased to receive that kind of message, which indicated that I had done Ben Solo's experience justice and had given at least one person a character they could fundamentally relate to.

In my reply to the message, I invited the sender to direct message me to talk about their experience so that it could inform the story. He actually created a Tumblr account to do this, for which I will always be grateful – not only for the help in shaping the fic but in that he's now a cherished friend. Alex, as I found out his name was, is a profoundly deaf person who has provided insights I could not have otherwise found through internet research alone. His perspective became invaluable in crafting Ben Solo's journey, and that of his to-be boyfriend, Armitage Hux, as he began to learn ASL to communicate better with Ben.

"Part of writing is challenging yourself to look beyond what's familiar and comfortable – to produce a piece of fiction that offers diverse perspectives"

I invited Alex to read the forthcoming chapters of *Allemande* and give me feedback on how the story was shaped around Ben's experience. By design, I didn't write from Ben's point of view, but from that of hearing Hux. While I wanted to explore a deaf character, I did not feel confident in narrating the story from his perspective. That would have required even more research and interviews than I was able to conduct. It's not to say that it would be impossible for me to do so, but the construction of the story was meant to take the reader on a journey of a hearing person learning to communicate with a deaf person and the challenges and joys of falling in love when there is a language barrier.

It was important to me to emphasize that picking up American Sign Language is not something that can be done very quickly, which Alex agreed with; like any spoken language, it takes years of experience to master. I used my own history learning a second spoken language in an immersive setting to reinforce the idea that ASL is not something anyone can pick up in a couple of weeks. Hux, in the story, seeks both formal instruction and learns signs from Ben, but is by no means fluent after the few months over which the story takes place. It wasn't until I wrote a follow-up vignette, called *Scherzo,* that was set five years later, that Hux was close to fluency.

Alex's input on the story did not necessarily change it fundamentally, since I had done research beforehand, but he expressed to me later that he held back a little for fear of getting in my way as an author. I hadn't known that at the time, but learned it only later as we became better friends and I started to consider writing *Scherzo.* That had some minor effects on the first story, mainly that originally I hadn't written Ben as having an interpreter to help him through mainstream hearing high school. This is a critical accommodation that would have been in place to make sure he succeeded as a student. It would not be impossible for him to get through school without one, but such skills as lip reading are not generally developed enough – or, quite frankly, easy enough – to get a teenager through high school. I amended this in *Scherzo,* when Ben was in college. He had a dedicated interpreter, like Alex does for his classes at university.

All these things considered, I acknowledge that fanfiction writing is a hobby that yields stories that do not have to be *perfect* in their accuracy. However, I wanted to create something that was a respectful portrayal of a deaf person. I actually received a rather confrontational message before I posted the story (the artist and I had been discussing it openly on Tumblr) that warned that I should not write a story with a disabled character because I was not myself disabled.

This is, unfortunately, a common occurrence in fandom. The automatic assumption is that an author without direct experience will not portray a disabled character with respect. That was something I was adamant *not* to do, hence the deep research and the subsequent conversations with Alex. I turned on the comment moderation in AO3 because I expected to get misinformed hate for the overall concept, which is an unfortunate trend in fandom these days. It's not to say that all portrayals of disabled characters in either original fiction or fanfiction are totally respectful – according to Alex, many of the stories he's read that feature deaf characters misrepresent them, and that's why my portrayal was something he appreciated – but to have potential readers automatically assume that I would do a poor job of representation is not something with which fan writers should have to contend. Let the work speak for itself rather than condemning it before it is even published.

To my surprise (and happiness), however, the response to *Allemande* was overwhelmingly positive. Those who read it were drawn into the love story and the way I represented Ben. I put a lot of love into crafting the fic, as I hope I do all my stories, and was rewarded with kind comments and beautiful art beyond even what the original artist drew herself.

Research alone, of course, does not a well-rounded story make. Much of shaping characters who are different from you takes empathy. There are fundamental human emotions that we can all relate to, which, when channeled into one's work, can bring the characters and their relationships to life. I may not have had to go through high school as a deaf person, but I could empathize with Ben's isolation in his school and his anger at Hux when he first tried to talk to him, assuming that Hux was making fun rather than earnestly trying to communicate. The gradual lowering of Ben's emotional barriers to allow him to make a friend and then to fall in love were feelings I could comprehend and then insert into the story, even if I had not lived them in the same manner. Empathy is one of a writer's greatest tools in giving their characters nuance.

Certainly, working with Alex helped to inform my perspectives, and I was able to discuss with him the emotions he experienced growing up in a hearing world. These were feelings not at all foreign to me, even if they had been lived by someone else in a wholly different situation. Mine and Alex's communication has been exclusively over text since we met, seeing as I do not know ASL and he lives several U.S. states away from me, but his descriptions and insights gave me not only the information I needed to craft the story's accuracy, but also to feel emotionally connected to a person who shared parts of Ben's experience. That has been like nothing else I've experienced in my life before: the shaping of a story by interview and the forging of a deep friendship through fanfiction.

The writing of *Allemande* and the subsequent reception served to cement my belief that writers can absolutely write what they have never experienced. It wasn't that I wrote what I didn't *know* – because I sat down and did the research and found a source upon whose personal experience I could draw – but that I wrote beyond my experience. I'd like to say that writers should do their best to understand and know as much as they can about the material they're writing about, but that they should not be limited to lived experience. They have the ability to look beyond their own lives using empathy, and to explore others' perspectives to craft compelling stories.

Audra McCauley (Gefionne) has always had it in her mind to write fiction and has been creating fan writing since before she knew that other people wrote and shared it online. She's had a formative experience in fandom, making lifelong friends and putting enough words on the page to improve – or at least learn – with every new story. She works in an academic library, where books and research databases are always at hand. She believes that reading authors one admires and dedicated practice will shape anyone into the best writer they can be – and that's her dearest hope for herself.

I love fanfiction.

— Mary Robinette Kowal
Hugo award-winning writer of
"The Lady Astronaut of Mars"

DON'T GIVE ME HEROES THAT I'D HAPPILY SET ON FIRE
KJ Charles

Everyone deserves a happily ever after.

KJ Charles is absolutely firm on this and if anyone swoops by, insisting that gay characters, Black characters, or women need to suffer for a story to be 'historically accurate' – well the title for this essay comes from KJ's blog post "Historical Romance: Who Gets the HEA," so it's clear where she stands on the matter.

Spark talked to KJ, a prolific novelist of historical m/m romances such as *Band Sinister, The Will Darling Adventures,* and *A Charm of Magpies,* about happily ever afters (HEA), fanfic, and going pro.

HAPPILY EVER AFTERS (AND WHO'S *NOT* THE DEFAULT)

"I've been marinating on this topic for some time, distilling all my thoughts," says KJ when asked about her blog essays on HEAs and who gets them. "It just comes up *so* often that I think you have to keep on *repeating* it so often, which upsets me because people will keep coming out with this rather stupidly-thought-out idea of *misery*. As if they think they said something clever. So I've just got quite annoyed how it keeps appearing and so I ended up with quite a refined script for dealing with it.

"The important thing is to remind yourself over and over again, that the cis-white heterosexual male is not the default. They think they're the default and we are encouraged to think they're the default. And yeah, I think there was a headline going around on Twitter awhile ago that said something like 'everyone disapproves of Alexandria Ocasio-Cortez, except for young people, women, and people of color.'

"What a fascinating definition of 'everyone' there! Basically everyone was white cis men. It's always white cis men. So yeah, step one on dealing with this idea of happily ever afters is actually to say, 'they're not the norm, they're not the default.' And it's really worth training yourself to use she as a default pronoun, which is always fun, or they. But actually she, without wishing to exclude anyone, it's a thought experiment and quite fun to use she all the time and see who gets upset.

"So see how you feel, just notice what it does to you. There's a marvelous series by Melissa Scott, it's so good and one of the things she does is make it a matriarchal society. She never goes into huge detail, it just all comes in the little casual remarks, like a main character will reflect that this sum of money is a woman's daily wage…and all the references are like that, just casually women where we'd say man as meaning the default. The cumulative effect of all these tiny things is really quite big. So yeah, I would say to people that you've been trained to believe that there's one default person and this isn't true. When they say something is 'a Mary Sue' as an effort to make you keep on believing that cis men are the default person, this is a lie and you should ignore it and kill it with fire."

THE PERSONAL *IS* POLITICAL

When asked if she believe it was political to give people of color, women, and queer characters joy in a story, KJ replied that everything is political. "The personal is political, I absolutely believe that. I think asserting female agency and happiness, the right of people of color to be everywhere, including in the history *where they were,* all of those are political acts.

"I wrote a story called *Unseen Attraction* where the hero is dyspraxic. I consulted with a lot of people who have dyspraxia and that book is probably the one people write in about the most, with people just saying, 'you know, I'm dyspraxic and I haven't read a book and seen myself in it before. I felt seen.'

"I've cried at my computer, quite a lot, reading some of those emails, and this is what's really going back to the people who complain about Mary Sues. These are people who've never been short of representation in their lives, and they don't have any mental capacity to understand how much other people would like to be represented. They don't even have that empathy because they have never had the experience for five minutes of not being the center of the universe. I mean, you know, my husband is a great guy and a feminist, but we had quite a row about the *Ghostbusters* with the all-female cast, because he though…why do we need it? But when was the last time you saw a movie with an all-female cast? *That's why.*

"we have this awful cultural and literary desire to say that serious things are more important than happy things"

"I feel the trick is just simply to spell these things out, because then people come back and say 'you know, you are right. I haven't thought of it like that.' They've heard 'not historically accurate' repeated so much and we have this awful cultural and literary desire to say that serious things are more important than happy things. Tragedy is more important than comedy. Romance is silly because there's a happy ending but if, at the end, people are raped and murdered, that makes it proper art.

"I feel that that taps into this problem [of dismissing historical LGBT+ romance] because people are 'oh, it's not real representation of the gay experience.' Meaning that if they don't die it's not proper, it's a disrespecting the struggle kind of thing because, basically, we prioritize sad stories over happy ones, and I see no value in that."

ON THE TOPIC OF TRANSFORMATIVE WORKS
Speaking of happy stories, KJ Charles took Anthony Hope's 19th century work *Prisoner of Zenda*, and at the request of Riptide Publishing transformed it into her charming gay romance *Henchmen of Zenda*. We asked her why that book, and what transformative means to her.

"I think everyone knows there's not an original story out there, that with every story we're taking an existing one and twisting it – leaving the issue of copyright aside, which is a completely different thing.

"A story that only exists on its own terms is kind of dead. Inert. Or it only exists on its own terms, in a bubble. And I prefer it to have tentacles going outwards and connecting, like a ganglion, you see what I mean? And I think that's what people's desire to write transformative works does, it connects.

"I'd always felt that the *Prisoner of Zenda* tells the wrong story. I mean literally the main story is this guy comes in to put a horrible rancid drunk back on the throne, because the other guy who is his brother and older and popular with the people can't be allowed to take the throne since his mother wasn't posh enough. Everything about that stinks! And the relationship stinks, and the romance stinks because it's got a sad ending for no particularly good reason.

"I loved *Prisoner of Zenda* as the concept but hated everything about its plot." So when Riptide Publishing asked for a retelling of a story "I thought, right, I'm gonna rewrite *that*. And I actually thought I was going to make Michael the other brother, the hero at one point. And then I looked into that and I realized it absolutely wouldn't work, you had to end up with the redheaded guy Rudolph on the throne, married to Flavia.

"Then I realized you could change it from within. And then of course, *Zenda* is such a heteronormative story, patriarchal, white Christian, superior Englishman, everything that's loathsome about the British empire, and it was just really nice to put women in charge, to have women running the show, to have the men very much as their puppets, to have a relationship at the heart of it affecting the way it all played out, and to show these people running circles around the patriarchy. It was just so ripe for messing around with."

When we sang the praises of Charles' version of Flavia, she talked about how it's often quite improbable for a woman to go around beating people up, saying "there are other forms of strength. Detchard can use a sword and Rupert can use a gun and Antoinette and Flavia can use *them* and they do. They're using their weapons, they're killing and they're being strong women in exactly their ways."

ON WRITING VOICE AND WRITING FIC

"I think every writer who writes for some time develops a voice in the sense that if you keep on using the same knife, it just fits to your hand, and it doesn't feel right when anyone else picks it up. I think some people have their own voice from the off and some people very much not. But I wouldn't say that relates to how good a writer you will be in the end at all. It's just some people take longer to learn, to ride a bike.

"Do I have a voice? People seem to think so. I'm not sure. I'd like to put my finger on its constituents. I mean, it's very, very hard with voice isn't it? It's a such an intangible thing. I feel like I do. I feel like, let's put it this way, if somebody wanted to parody my writing, they could probably do it fairly easily."

KJ isn't a reader of fanfic, but when we mention her novel *Band Sinister* she says readily, "You might say that *Band Sinister* comes close to fanfic of Georgette Heyer – who invented the Regency genre – because I love Heyer's work and some have described the book as very Heyer, which just made me the happiest person in earth."

How does KJ feel when she sees fic of her own books?

"Though I don't read fic of my work – I think that way worms lie – knowing that people do it absolutely amazes me.

"I've always loved fans. And I can't tell you what it was like the first time somebody sent me fan arts of my work. I was just staring at the computer and screaming. Well, apart from the time someone unsolicitedly sent me an extremely explicit drawing, which I was not fine with because one should not send those to complete strangers! – but yeah, everything else I have ever seen is just glorious and wonderful. And I can't draw at all. I mean, I can't draw a stick man. So for people to just come out with these amazing pictures, it's glorious, absolutely wonderful.

"My feeling is that fan work is a thing that should exist, and I'm happy for it to exist in its own space as long as people respect my space."

ON DOING IT

To the people who say they tried writing but they weren't any good, Charles underscores the need for practice. "You wouldn't say 'oh, I tried to play the piano once, but I wasn't very good.' You *do* actually have to learn to write, and while it can't be taught in the same way as learning the piano, it's still something that you've got to learn and develop.

"There's this thing I read that was very telling were, you know, if you're a painter of watercolors, you can be very happy doing that, and you might hang out on your wall, you might even give a card to your friend or something, but you don't feel like failure if it hasn't got into the Royal Academy, you're just doing it for your own pleasure. The problem with writing is we feel that writing needs to be read in a way that we don't necessarily feel a painting needs to be looked at, we feel that other people have to interact with the work for it to count, but if you can just slightly decouple from that a bit and actually just enjoy writing for its own sake and reading over what you've written and being pleased with that, you're more like likely to get something that other people can look at.

"But if you imagine other people reading it right from the start, you're like the watercolor painter who puts two lines on and thinks, 'oh God, what will the Royal Academy think?' It's paralyzing."

ON NOT GOING PRO

"I don't blame people who don't want to go pro," said Charles when we talked about a poll which found half of fanfic writers have no desire to publish professionally. "If this is your hobby and your joy, well the publishing industry doesn't half suck the joy out of books.

"I worked as an editor for twenty years and I used to be the first into the office and one time I came in at eight o'clock in the morning, I looked around at the usual boxes and boxes and trolleys of books, just standing there in the middle of a famous London publisher's office saying, 'God, I hate books.' And I quit about three months after that, because publishing will do that to you.

"So I don't blame people who find their joy and don't want to monetize it and worry about sales, thinking 'that will actually kill this for me.' If they know themselves to that extent, I have nothing but the utmost respect."

"TRUST ME ON THIS"

We asked KJ for recommendations of books she loves and of course she recommended Georgette Heyer. *"Cotillion* is absolutely glorious. You think the hero will be this alpha-type hero, but he's not and it's just the most adorable thing in the world, so you should definitely read that. *These Old Shades* is the most old-school, crazy pants romance novel, absolutely outrageous. It's got cross dressing, it's got age difference, it's got a man wearing a gold suit and a fan. He's constantly fanning himself with a chicken skin fan and murdering people. It's just so good. Kidnapping and wigs and everything.

"And then there's the Astreiant series by Melissa Scott. I've reread that about three times start to finish. I love those books so much. If anyone made a movie of those I would be in seventh heaven. All my big, big loves tend to be books. So the Astreiant series of books, the first is *Point of Hopes*. Look 'em up. Honestly, trust me on this."

In the end, it's all about a four-letter word ending in E

We want to close this interview with KJ Charles as we begun: talking about happily ever afters and what a romance truly is – and what it isn't.

"The absolute defining characteristic of a romance novel isn't a false sense of historical accuracy, but a four-letter word that ends in E."

Hope.

"This is exactly why romance is the most popular genre, because romance gives you hope. I can't see what's so big and clever about hopelessness and despair.

"Grim, dark, everyone is a terrible human being, I see these stories getting the literary adulation and all I think is 'I grew out of painting my bedroom black some time ago.' I think it's a lot more grown up to find hope. I've got two children and it's not actually easy to be hopeful all the time and they do need it. You'd be surprised how quickly they start seeing the bleakness in the world and it's awful to see that hope being rubbed away.

"I feel very passionately about the importance of the happy ever after."

KJ Charles is a writer of mostly LGBT+ romance, historical or fantasy or both. She blogs about writing and editing at kjcharleswriter.com. She lives in London, UK, with her husband, two kids, and a cat of absolute night. Her many books include The Secret Lives of Country Gentlemen, Any Old Diamonds, and Henchmen of Zenda.

LET THIS DAY BE YOUR BEGINNING
Anarion

Why do we start writing fanfic? Maybe because there are so many stories yet to be told?

For me, everything started with a drawing by the amazing br0_ Harry. One look and there the story was, beginning to end, multi-chaptered, possibly beamed into my brain by aliens, and it was screaming at me to write it down.

I did and I haven't stopped writing since. Over time I discovered that my favorite things to write are 221Bs, little drabbles with 221 words, the last word starting with a 'b'. (Yes, by the way, this thing here is one, too! I absolutely love the challenge of telling a story, be it funny, scary, or sad, in just 221 words.)

I have written more than 94,000 words in 221Bs and I have learned a lot about myself and others, discovered kinks I never knew existed, and acquired a shitload of obscure knowledge.

I honed my writing skills, found my voice and – most importantly – met some of my closest friends in the comment section. Even though I don't have as much time now, I still love coming up with ideas and writing them down. I hope that never stops. So go write that thing that's been sitting in your brain, find a beta if you're unsure and have fun!

Let this day be your beginning.

Anarion writes fic mostly in the Sherlock Holmes fandom, and specializes in writing 221Bs – which the above is. A 221B is a nod to Sherlock Holmes' Baker Street address, and is a story or essay written in exactly two hundred and twenty-one words, with the final word beginning with B.

CHANGING THE SCRIPT:
FANDOM INNOVATES
Henry Jenkins

If your fandom participation has an academic tilt, you know Henry Jenkins from his over one-dozen books on participatory culture and comparative media, including *Textual Poachers: Television Fans & Participatory Culture* and *Popular Culture and the Civic Imagination: Case Studies of Creative Social Change.* Along with these scholarly writings, he's also a communication, journalism, and cinema professor at the University of Southern California, and yet still shared his time, answering in-depth my questions about fic and fandom.

You've just met someone who's created a dozen Captain Marvel drawings or a bunch of Star Wars stories, but they have no idea what fandom is or can mean. You're about to tell them; kindly wax lyrical.
Fandom, at its best, offers an incredible support system for new writers and artists to share what they create with a larger public. Part of what's wonderful about fandom is not that a small number of participants go onto become professional writers (though that's great) but that it generates so much bad writing.

When the only stories we read are polished, professional work, it can be intimidating for first time creators who wonder how they can get there from where they are starting and are often too intimidated to try.

What the world needs is a place where people can be bad writers, get critical but supportive feedback, maybe even get roughed up a bit, and gradually get better. Many of the best fan writers write within the subcultural community, responding to its genre traditions, addressing its core debates, and satisfying the needs of its readers. Going Pro is great, but many prefer to write without the commercial imperative shaping what stories they can tell. And that's what fanfiction sites like Archive of Our Own offer millions of people all over the world.

More than that, fanfiction allows for a multiplicity of voices and stories, new ways of understanding the core conflicts at the heart of our favorite stories, a chance to write beyond the ending or outside the frame created by commercial media and tell the stories we want to read. It isn't that every fan has their own version of a character, it is that most fans have multiple versions dying to get out, and that they are finding readers who are open to exploring alternative perspectives on the things they love.

Here is a workshop for new ideas about gender, race, sexuality, and disability as they might influence popular fiction (in whatever media form). These writers, mostly women, have given themselves permission to participate in response to a media industry that has historically locked so many people out.

In fandom, there is the idea that every person has a story to tell, really many stories, and that they simply have not had the support they need to be able to share it with the world. That's such a wonderful way to think about creativity.

Fandoms aren't perfect. They can be ableist, racist, ageist. Please share your experiences of how they can be the exact opposite.
In terms of the above, amen. These issues are real and I admire the courage of those who are willing to call fandom out for its failures, whether the result of intentional exclusion or simple obliviousness to systemic problems that impact fandom like every other part of our society. The push to address some of these historic blind spots in fandom and in fandom studies feels increasingly urgent. We need to continue to fight those battles.

But to me, the untold stories here are the many ways that fans have become major advocates for diversity and inclusion within the entertainment industry. When Hollywood looks across Hall H at its fans at San Diego Comic-Con, for example, they are looking at one of the most racially diverse and gender balanced fan conventions in America and in doing so, they have started to develop a more diverse conception of who consumes their films and television shows. They will see fans of color transforming their characters through their cosplay. Online, we see practices such as fan-casting that imagine alternative versions of the characters from, say, the Marvel Cinematic Universe. There are also fan writing challenges on places like Archive of Our Own where people are encouraged to reimagine existing characters as people of color.

"As a fan, I got tired of having people tell me to get a life so I wrote a book instead"

Right now, Hollywood scriptwriters are grappling with the fact that the core genres of American popular culture have their roots in an era of white supremacy, settler mythology, male superiority, and global colonialism. We literally need to change the script. Fanfiction sites have the potential to function as creative commons where amateur writers can create alternative stories and alternative versions of characters and debate what does and does not work outside of the commercial imperative. Dramatically increasing the scale of cultural production may be the only way this experimentation can take place.

As they do so, the fanfiction writing sites are needing to insure greater inclusivity. And I was impressed, overall, with the ways Archive of Our Own and fanfiction writers started during the summer of 2020 to rethink what kinds of trigger warnings were required to create a safer space for people of color to participate.

How has studying participatory cultures and fandoms changed your life (and what's the difference between these terms)?
I would start with the distinction between fans and fandom. The media industry is using the term fan, to refer to any and all consumers of its content. The key word here is consumers. Fandom understands itself as participants and creators, not simply

consumers of media content. Fandom refers to an active and creative subculture, people who are not socially isolated but feel a sense of social connection with others who share their tastes and interests. Fandom has developed a support structure for grassroots creativity that is unrivaled elsewhere in our culture.

Participatory culture is a broader concept that can be used to describe any and every place where everyday people are gaining access to the means of cultural production and circulation. It can refer to the broader push to expand creative opportunities that fuels YouTube and Twitch, for example, or blogging and podcasting. It can refer to the activities of Makers, Gamers, Crafters, and so many other communities that are organized around shared cultural practices.

So, fandom is a key driver of participatory culture but it is only one tradition from which grassroots creative expression has emerged. So I would see Archive of Our Own as one of the real landmarks to emerge from contemporary popular culture, a demonstration of what a dispersed and informal network of people can do given a chance. But I would also point to Wikipedia as another such landmark as a site which brings together people with diverse commitments and expertise and creates ethical norms that govern their behavior.

As for how this changed my life – in every way possible. Professionally, the study of fandom and participatory culture more generally has been the work that has defined my identity and built my career. I have found myself part of a global conversation that bridges across culture, learning, politics, religion, and social change more broadly. I write about many other forms of popular and participatory culture in my work but fandom is what I continue to come back to as the wellspring of my inspiration and as a space where I can relax and be myself. When I write about other media, I do so as a fan, whether that is explicit in my work or not.

What keeps you writing and writing and writing about these things?
As a fan, I got tired of having people tell me to get a life so I wrote

a book instead. That was thirty years ago. *Textual Poachers* was intended as a broad overview of fans and fandom, but ended up being a more focused study of the mostly female fanfiction writing community and other forms of expression, such as viding, that grew up around it.

Textual Poachers was one of several books that were published in 1992 which is generally understood as the year that fandom studies emerged as a distinct subfield of audience research. Over the years, I have ended up pulled back to write about fans again and again, because each new fandom seems to represent a new genre, a new form of cultural production, a new mode of participation, or a new issue I want to explore.

Through the years, I have found fanfiction writing as a point of entry into talking more broadly about how literacy practices are taking shape in the new media environment, leading me into active involvement in the media literacies and connected learning movements.

I have written about amateur Star Wars films, about the debates among fanvid producers over whether to use YouTube, about Survivor spoilers as a collective intelligence community, and so much more. Fandom constantly innovates, almost always racing ahead of other trends in our culture. My concept of participatory culture is larger than fandom, describing all forms of grassroots media production and circulation, but its roots are in fandom and I keep coming back to fandom for further inspiration.

Henry Jenkins is the author or co-author of Textual Poachers: Television Fans and Participatory Culture and Popular Culture and the Civic Imagination: Case Studies of Creative Social Change along with eighteen other books on media and popular culture. He blogs regularly about participatory culture at Confessions of an Aca-Fan, henryjenkins.org, and cohosts the How Do You Like It So Far? podcast about popular culture in a changing world.

Until extremely recently, stories were born out of shared universes all the time. It was rare for anyone to create a wholly original story when there were already so many fun and exciting characters and legends and plots available to play with. Why dream up another wise and heroic king when you could write a new King Arthur story? Why tell the tale of another endless war when you could put a new spin on the Trojan War? Historically, writers constantly borrowed characters and plots from all sorts of sources and turned them into new stories. Those stories became yet more stories; that was just how storytelling worked."

— Constance Grady
Senior correspondent for *Vox*

WHAT IF WE WERE ALWAYS THE AUTHOR-GODS?
(A VALIDATION OF OUR OWN)
Melissa A. Hofmann

"Are they doing what I *think* they're doing?"
"Wait...what? Did I *really* just see that?"
"Does this mean what I think it means?"

It's time.

Time to internalize our own validation and accept our own readings of film, television, books – then harness our authority to change or add to the greater media and societal narrative. *We* are the heroes and trailblazers we have been looking for.

This – the burning need for validation combined with a burgeoning swell of squee – is how I fell, hard, into the *Sherlock* fandom after a decade of hiatus from fandom. By the end of my virgin viewing of "A Study in Pink" in late 2014 – I was a surprisingly blank slate where Sherlock Holmes was concerned, except for its ACD roots and its BBC provenance – I had Googled my way into the prolific textual paradise known as Johnlock Hell™, created by fans for fans, for the pure delight of sense-making and out of a vital desire for validation. I came, I saw, (and desperately wondering what others thought) I Tumblred.

Consumed by my unquenchable thirst for *more*, I spent the next two years drunk on fic and meta, knowing at some point I wanted to write about the mad, rollercoaster experience of canon and the brilliance of our fan creators and analysts. The bellows of our imagination on canon's coals set me ablaze. Even though I was a few years late to the party, I gave myself a crash course in all things *Sherlock*, especially reveling in the distinct essence of each hiatus. The rapturous experience of every immersive story and meta

---

I read, of each author's unique contribution to both fanon (fan canon) and the myriad conceivable directions that canon could take, sparked a spirit of inquiry and celebration in me. But what *specifically* I wanted to say took a while to crystallize through the fog of enthusiasm, as I thought about what else beyond my love for the characters – and their love for each other – drove my need to read and my compulsion to spend hours upon hours (upon hours!) scrolling through my dash feasting on art, photo- and gifsets, or fascinated by fanvids.

What ultimately intrigued me the most was the contradiction between what we were seeing in the screen text and subtext, and the denials of The Powers That Be. It was the emotional whiplash between belief and doubt, hope and hurt. Will They or Won't They? Queer or queerbaiting? Where was this story going?

The collective teetering between authorial fascination and frustration with Steven Moffat and Mark Gatiss, or "Mofftiss," made me dizzy with intellectual delight and emotional dread. The exaltation of the Author-God can be sinisterly seductive to the postmodern-minded like me, who still hope for heroes and trailblazers to right society's wrongs through the superpower of storytelling. A conspiracy theory is really not so outrageous a response, after all, when you are repeatedly told not to trust your own eyes, ears, heart, and instinct. How disconcerting, however, to believe that this Author-God must not only gaslight but demean fans in the name of progress.

Thus, the feelings were fervent and the questions urgent as I vicariously lived previous hiatuses through reading older fics and their comments and shared in the post-season three angst all at once. A new interview with Moffat and Gatiss: how many times would they (in their own words) lie? Another press junket for one of the leads' latest projects: oh god, what cringe-worthy, wildly incongruous-with-the-text pronouncement would Benedict Cumberbatch offer about Sherlock's characterization this time, or conversely, what sly bisexual innuendo or flustered denials would Martin Freeman appear to make?

"We are the heroes and trailblazers we've been looking for!"

And then the snippets of new canon-adjacent material, such as the on-set poster from "The Abominable Bride" (TAB) that spawned a Tumblr blog name and an epic meta by heimishtheidealhusband in support of the Sherlock/John arc, and the TAB app with its animated promo pictures: are those snowflakes really in the shape of hearts? Speculation abounded, combined with close readings of the series text: creativity and analysis were intertwined, as in the best of fics, dwelling in the purposeful possibility of Johnlock. Then TAB landed, with more subtext, more queerness, and more seeming references to fandom, and confirming what many had expected: Mofftiss had lied (again) about the episode's one-off status to protect the plot reveal.

I was inundated with feels and awash in my fellow fans' responses, caught in a whirlpool of a feedback loop. Being both a fangirl and an English-major academic, I was far from immune from being in any measure (over?)invested in what felt like a sophisticated game I was qualified and willing to play. I analyze for a living; textual critique is as unbidden for me as breathing. Yet, like many others, I wondered, could I trust my own judgment? Is my idealist romanticism overriding my natural skepticism? What am I missing? Am I being played?

Enter fandom meta – O meta! – in its multimedia glory. Enlightening, assuaging, confirming meta! Was literary analysis ever so fun and were the stakes ever so high? Not only did meta make every episode more enjoyable by creating connections within the show itself and to its intertextual references, ensuring us of its (perhaps questionable) internal continuity and emotional logic, it legitimized our queer readings of *Sherlock*. I came to find that we were writing meta as much for ourselves as for the detractors and deniers of a Johnlock reading. With each blog or reblog, I realized

I turned to meta for validation and community as much as for its enriching content. Accused of fantasizing and fetishization in shipping Johnlock, meta writers turned to the text for evidence against the characterizations of fans as entitled and delusional.

With all my privilege (I am a white, American, currently upper middle class, able-bodied, tenured member of the professoriate), I know what it is like to be seen as illegitimate. I am a woman, married to another woman. I am a librarian, in a feminized profession which is misunderstood and undervalued: isn't everything on the internet? No one understands what I do ("Don't you just sit and read books all day?") and, while I have two master's degrees, I don't have a PhD, which automatically reduces my status, intelligence, and capability in many other non-library faculty members' eyes. I am also in the humanities, which is increasingly sacrificed on the altar of return-on-investment neoliberalist capitalism in favor of 'employable' disciplines, and my interdisciplinary work on narrative, gender, and sexuality is often dismissed as 'soft,' or irrelevant by those outside of the humanities or higher education. (There's a reason Moffat and Gatiss had the villain Culverton Smith mocking doctors of media studies in particular, especially with all the critical analysis *Sherlock* has received.) I am all too aware that off campus or in another bloody chamber of the Ivory Tower, I may be considered invalid and expendable. And god forbid I should, as a (queer) woman, have an expert opinion or a reasoned take on social media: I may be mansplained to, trolled, and harassed. And of course, I am a Johnlock fan, one of those whom Mofftiss belittle, dismiss, and ignore.

How many Tumblr posts have I seen where the person emotes their ecstatic feelings of affirmation because their *professor* sees or is convinced of a Johnlock reading when presented with the evidence? *I* now have the clout of one of those professors. This still feels a bit surreal to me, considering how much I have turned to fandom and other academics on my own journey of validation. When I first thought about wanting to write about Johnlock meta, I was not even aware that fan studies was an actual thing. Even though

I was in the *Lord of the Rings* slash fandom ten years prior – which was my introduction to fic, slash, and the power of fandom – I did not think to explore it academically: I was mostly a lurker, awed by the prowess of the women writers and artists of the LiveJournal community I had discovered.

As I researched, I aimed to contribute my own analysis among the aca-fans (academic fans) whose work I was eagerly hoarding and ingesting. Being accepted to publish in *Transformative Works and Cultures* was one of the biggest achievements of my academic life, as it was the second time I had written and published in a new-to-me field of study. My English department colleague (and friend!) has given me confidence and helped me articulate the value of my work, and with her encouragement I submitted to and presented at two literature conferences. I would leave my fandom books, such as Anne Jamison's *Fic: Why Fanfiction Is Taking Over the World*, out on the coffee table for months to remind me and show others that fandom writing was a legitimate source of inquiry and a perfectly valid way to spend leisure time – *and I already bought in!* How devalued we are as women or queer fans, and as women or queer writers, to need this constant shoring up of our worth.

As a practitioner of critical librarianship, which addresses power structures in the creation and dissemination of knowledge, and an intersectional feminist, I am always thinking about authority: who has it, why, and how. (This is perhaps why so many women, LGBTQIA+ people, and people of color suffer from Imposter Syndrome: the more marginalized we are the more we realize how precarious our relation to authority is.) We teach that authority is constructed and contextual, that is, it is contingent upon factors of spheres of influence, specific domains, community, and audience; personality/charisma; expertise, and personal experience.

In an era of self-publication, fake news, disinformation campaigns, and the disdain of expert knowledge, asking who the author is, and what relations to authority they have, is essential in order to evaluate what you read and hear for its relation to truth. While this is no less valid in relation to meta authors, the issue is more complicated for traditionally marginalized voices such as fans, especially the non cis-straight-white-male ones. Often who we are (or are *not*) overrides what we say, where we can say it, and who will listen. Anonymity helps us to be heard and perhaps be judged on our argument's merits, at least in certain circles.

While you may not be able to judge an individual meta on its author's unknown credentials or have the requisite knowledge or time to evaluate its evidence or reasoning on your own, the beauty of platforms like Tumblr has been the ability to allow a widespread distribution and peer-review through reblogging and replies (even if the non-linear conversations are not the easiest to follow). In this way, we fans build upon, question, and supplement another's interpretation, examining the evidence of the text and the claims made from them – which then encourages our *expansion* of them.

I am less interested in any particular meta's truth value and more in how meta functions and empowers its readers and writers, and to what uses the Johnlock fandom has put meta, such as justifying or rebutting claims of queerbaiting, or to argue for or against the validity of the surface narrative of series four, for example.

Thus, I was enthralled by the best parts of The Johnlock Conspiracy, or Johnlock-as-endgame theories: the detailed and sophisticated analysis of the text (the show itself) and its intertexts, transtexts (game apps and books), and paratexts (interviews, promo photos, panels). I loved the simultaneous breadth and depth of the analyses, and marveled at the creativity of the connections meta writers were making. Meta also works to cohere a fragmented narrative, to make sense of new canon material in the light of the whole.

What could rival the flurry of meta written the week between the airing of series four's "The Six Thatchers" and "The Lying Detective" (TLD) and between the TLD and "The Final Problem," which fans quipped surpassed the output of the previous three years of hiatus? We made charts to graph the various circulating theories and curated masterlists. How we tried to make sense of this new series, which stymied our narrative predictions and took a turn that to some of us defied analysis and rendered it all pointless. While some post-series four metas strive to save the integrity of the showrunners through the text, others more urgently work to save the integrity of the text in spite of them, hoping to salvage the show itself from Mofftiss and defend our previous readings and writings.

While fanfic frees itself from canon to a large extent, meta binds itself to it, dependent on the source text in ways that fic is not. While evidence in the show (and its surrounding paratexts) is the *only* basis for meta – where such is simply a jumping off point for fic – are the connections and ideas any less creative than fic for this boundedness? And are the divergent interpretations any less valid simply because canon predictions have not come true in any particular imagined fashion? I know some feel that meta fails if canon proves it

'wrong,' thinking that the point of meta is to be 'right.' However, we can always look at it from the other direction: in an ongoing text, perhaps it is the authors themselves that fail the story. In the future I would love to explore the similarities between fic and meta further.

What's at stake is not necessarily being right or wrong, but having the *possibility* of being right acknowledged by the powers that be and other fans, of having a seat at the table for legitimate interpretation and the creation of meaning. In the case of Johnlock, the illegitimacy is felt in the gatekeeping encountered, for example, when Martin Freeman states that Johnlock is perfectly acceptable in fanfiction but not in *their show* because it is not their intent, without ever questioning, exploring, or taking any accountability whatsoever as to why fans believe that it *is* in the show. Interviewers never challenge this viewpoint or take up the analytic cause.

I take a certain pride in the fact that fandom – fic and meta writers, artists and vidders – made Johnlock a paratext powerful enough that the creators have had to respond to it, even if it has been obliquely or negatively, playfully or exploitatively (think BBC Three and iPlayer social media accounts), depending on your view of the ambiguity and openness of the text. Whether or not one believes that Moffat and Gatiss intended a queer reading, meta exists to argue with ample evidence that a romantic reading is not only a *valid* reading but a *strong* one.

What makes me happy is the collective endeavor of fandom meta, as well as the passion behind it. Fans of all backgrounds – from English, film, and media studies majors, to those who have taken just one analytical class, to those who have no such background but are learning from others – write meta, because they want to, because they have something to say, for the sheer love of the thing they love. And their interpretations have had impact, not just on each other but on the larger world. I wonder, how can this be translated to the classroom and to lifelong confidence in one's individual voice and our collective voices? How do we cope when our voices are ignored or outright dismissed? Our voices are our strength, and thus I find it a tragic loss to a fandom when a meta writer deletes their account, making their meta – and the interaction and commentary it fostered – invisible or harder to find.

Even if the suggestion of Johnlock was all just a puzzle to make us dance, look what we have wrought. Can over 70,000 Johnlock stories (more than half of all *Sherlock* fic posted on AO3) and millions of words of meta be wrong? Of course, asking about rightness or wrongness is itself the wrong question, but the pull toward validity is strong in a world where female and queer perspectives and knowledge are discounted and devalued.

Some Sherlock Holmes/John Watson fans have always preferred fic to meta because they simply doubt that the showrunners could ever be that detailed and insightful. Even meta writers and enthusiasts themselves exhort Mofftiss to #pleasebethatclever in the tags of brilliant metas. But, *what if we ourselves were always already the Author-Gods,* with our meaning-making on par with or more important than purported creator intent?

I'll say it again: let us internalize our own validation and accept our own readings as canon, for indeed *we* are the heroes and trailblazers we've been looking for! Inspired by whatever (imperfect) canon, fandom writers create and disseminate interpretations and stories that not only feature complex and whole (non) (cis)-white-(straight) male characters, but also inspire and empower each other to live fully and thrive in all of our intersecting identities. Let us fully embrace the superpower of our analysis and storytelling, where we right society's wrongs through both critique and through representing topics and identities still too rarely seen in our entertainment and news media, such as queer love stories or authoritative women critics. May my own writing about meta take us all one step closer in this journey of collective validation.

Melissa A. Hofmann is the author of "Johnlock Meta and Authorial Intent in Sherlock Fandom: Affirmational or Transformational?" published in "The Future of Fandom," special 10th anniversary issue, Transformative Works and Cultures, no. 28 (http://dx.doi.org/10.3983/twc.2018.1465). She is a professor-librarian at Rider University in Lawrenceville, NJ, USA, where she unites work and play and helps people research, write, and live their passions.

Fanfic is where we play with [characters] because we love them, and putting more love into the world is never bad.

— Seanan McGuire
Hugo award-winning writer of
Wayward Children

FANTASTICALLY CREATIVE WAYS
Michael Bond

Michael Bond is fascinated by the why and the how.

Writing, editing, and consulting on science for 20 years, including six years as senior editor at New Scientist, Michael specializes in writing about psychology and behavior, and when we talked to him, he was busy working on a book about fandom, a celebratory look on what we get from being fans with other fans. That work resulted in his latest book, called *Fans: A Journey into the Psychology of Belonging.*

While Bond isn't a trained psychologist he *is* a fan, and has applied his passion to the psychology of fandom with "a mix of academic research from the study of groups, social identity theory, and how being part of a group changes behavior, and what people get from that."

What they get, he's found, is a lot.

When people in fandoms find their own community, Michael says, it can help them finally find the joyful language for who they are.

We talked with Michael about his deep dive into fandom and where the idea to write a book on it came from.

ON BEING A FAN AND WRITING ABOUT THEM
The idea of writing a fandom book "was more like osmosis than a sort of flash of inspiration, and because I'm interested in groups, I think it just struck me that the dynamics of fandoms was seeping into other areas of life."

That's because fandoms, Bond says, seem to be becoming more significant, prominent, and powerful in public life. "I think it was the power of fans that struck me. Changing situations, getting involved in how a television series progressed by speaking loudly on social media, those were perhaps the two things that just struck me, that there's something going on. It's probably been going on for a very long time and I only just realized it!

"I feel like I'm a real amateur at fandoms, but I've definitely been a fan. I was a huge fan of the Police, I ended up owning everything that they'd ever put out, including bootleg stuff. So I've been a fan but never really connected to a community. Having said that, the point of my book is really about the social dynamics of fandoms and the social psychology of what fans get from being part of a community.

"I'm looking at fans of popular culture, media franchises, celebrities, musicians, but also of authors like Jane Austen – who has 150 years of a fan following – as well as slightly left-field fandoms like medieval reenactors and revisionist historians. For example, there's a group in the UK called the Richard the Third Society, they're trying to sort of rewrite the history of Richard III, who was put forward as this very evil, extreme king thanks to Shakespeare, so they're trying to rewrite that."

Any surprises?

"The thing that's really surprised me is just how prominent and significant people's favorite characters or heroes are in their lives, the role those characters play, and how important they are. It's been really extraordinary observing that intensity, the way people build a relationship with their character. It's a virtual relationship, but the parallels with real relationships are there. It also explains why people mind so much when a character dies or transgresses.

"I talked with a group of women in their early twenties who are Jane Austen fans. They've had quite similar paths through their lives: at school they didn't fit in, they had trouble finding friends, being accepted. They were different. And they would read Jane Austen and find characters that represented someone who they thought they could be. Female characters, role models who play the system, or resist the patriarchy as much as they can.

"And what I found among these friends is that these fictional characters were sort of sitting on their shoulder through troubled times, giving them strength. Then they found other people who had had similar difficulties and come through them in the same way, and they built a social group, found a community that way. So it's a double win: they have a fictional role model and also end up with community.

"So even though I have been a fan myself these things surprised me."

ON KNOWING WHERE IT'S AT, AND TURNING POINTS
In talking about the mockery many girls and women like the ones above might face for their fandom loves, Bond underscores not only his respect for fans, but reflects on a memorable moment.

"I think it was when Harry Styles was still in One Direction and his young, particularly female fans were getting a lot of stick from various parts of the press for the usual stuff that always gets thrown at those fans. And he came out in an interview and said something like 'these people, they know where it's at, who are you to criticize them?'

> "For many people fandoms are places to breathe. You can be what you want to be because others are also whatever they are"

"I think he was talking to a male pop music journalist, and it really stood out for me that he was celebrating his fans, who to him were the reason he's doing what he's doing. But it's so easy for those on the other side, in the media, to criticize, to imply it's threatening, to put a shadow over it, and reading that felt like a bit of a turning point for me. That was probably a few years ago now, but these things just seemed to build for me into something to say about fandoms to a general audience who wouldn't necessarily be thinking about them, so this book's absolutely a celebration of fans.

"In fact, I remember before I'd written a word, going to the

Portsmouth *Fan Studies Network* conference, and seeing you [Atlin Merrick] speak with such a positive vibe. I was right at the beginning of my research, and it was the first time I got into the academic side of fandom studies, so I was really exploring, and you were an inspiration at that stage for me, because it was another example that this really is something to celebrate.

"From an academic perspective, there's so much research that speaks about the positives of fandoms, and the negatives seem to be sort of easy tropes that get wheeled out, but the positives seem to come from actual studies. Of course there's the stuff about the extreme behavioral obsessive side, but it's really a very small part of fandom, and the book will cover that, but the general gist is celebratory, while also sort of leading people by the hand, through the stories of fans."

ON WRITING YOURSELF IN AND THE RICHNESS OF COMMUNITY

The fan revelations continue for Michael, who says, "I knew that the LGBT side of fandom existed, but I had no idea it existed in such richness, and that there was just so much written because, clearly, people observe their favorite media franchise, strive to find representation, and when they don't, they come up with a great solution: you write yourself in. It's just extraordinary how much stuff there is. I found some thousands of versions of the Hobbit and I mean that alone was astonishing to me.

"I come from a naive position, so it was also a surprise to me to discover the majority of fans participating and creating are women. Clearly that's always been the case in all areas, except for sport, and this is something I haven't really figured out, but visible sport fandom seems to be very male and male sports fan kind of get a free pass when it comes to being a fan. They can be as extreme, as obsessive, as ridiculous as they like and generally no one's going to write anything negative about it, but for other fandoms, which seem to be predominantly female, that language of obsessiveness and threat is there. I know it's decreased over the years, but it still seems to be there.

"So I'm writing about that. And again, in a naive way, this is the first time I came across this, but I think a lot of people who are not into fandoms, and are not part of those groups will find that surprising."

FANDOM IS SO VERY HUMAN

Being part of a fandom community "seems to have a psychological effect, a measurable, psychological effect on people's behavior, state of mind, the way they think of themselves and their self-esteem," says Bond. "And it doesn't take much, you can just be accepted into a family and those benefits immediately start appearing. I find that quite remarkable."

What sort of benefits does Michael see? "I guess I mean mental health benefits, benefits to your subjective wellbeing. That sense of belonging you have affects the outlook you have on your life and the way you see yourself, so maybe you'll have fewer negative thoughts, more positive, empowering thoughts.

"Also the knock-on effect is you find fewer incidents of mental illness in groups that have that sort of cohesion. So it's like there's something protective about being part of a community, being part of a fandom. It's not exclusive to fandoms, but fandom is a great example.

"I suppose the flip side of that is if you're out on your own and you're not part of a community there are plenty of studies showing *that* has a knock on effect on everything, from the risk of developing heart disease to depression.

"So fandoms can be protective, they fulfill what seems to be an essential human need. I think the social psychologists I've talk to would agree to that.

"I have learned that for many people fandoms are places to breathe. You can be what you want to be because others are also whatever they are, and so you can call yourself weird and it can be something to celebrate rather than a criticism.

"It really struck me the number of people I've talked to who've called themselves geeky, nerdy. 'Oh, I'm just, you know, a little bit weird.' But the way they say it is like, they're very happy with that, because it's not someone else telling them, so they get to own it. And that's because they're in a community where others say the same. They get to reconfigure the language, and that's a sign of something really positive.

"Fandom brings people together who imagine they are one-of-a-kind."

In the end "it turns out it's pretty normal stuff, isn't it?" Michael says. "I mean it's human. It's humans being humans. To some it looks strange from the outside, but when you get stuck in, it's just the same old emotions playing out in fantastically creative ways."

Michael Bond's books include Fans: A Journey into the Psychology of Belonging; Wayfinding: The Art and Science of How We Find and Lose Our Way; and The Power of Others: Peer Pressure, Groupthink, and How the People Around Us Shape Everything We Do. Michael can be found online at michaelbond.co.uk.

There have been great societies that did
not use the wheel, but there have been
no societies that did not tell stories.

— Ursula K. Le Guin
Locus award-winning writer of
Tales from Earthsea

TRANSFORMATIONS
Bel Murphy

"When those who have the power to name and to socially construct reality choose not to see you or hear you...when someone with the authority of a teacher, say, describes the world and you are not in it, there is a moment of psychic disequilibrium, as if you looked in the mirror and saw nothing." Adrienne Rich

In fandom, we call what we do transformative work.

It sounds like a pretty lofty title to some people, when a lot of the content we create is not safe for work, but it *is* the most accurate description for fanfiction. Of course on the surface, we're transforming characters and sometimes their universes, or even creating crossovers and fusions between existing works. In fanfics perhaps the characters take on different professions or supernatural powers. Maybe they're envisioned as a different race, gender, or sexuality than what was presented (or assumed) in the canon source. In a broader sense, through our stories and works of art, we're able to help transform the overwhelming narrative in our society by adding underrepresented or silenced voices. Many of us have a hard time seeing ourselves in that engulfing narrative and if mainstream media isn't providing enough representation, writers and artists can and do use fanworks to fill that void.

And sometimes, transforming ourselves in the process.

In fic there are whole worlds of experience to explore that are beyond the typical stories being offered in mainstream books, television, and movies. When the field is opened and we can all share our stories, the conversation becomes so much richer, because fanfiction provides a unique medium for that. By design, no one is screening what we publish on Archive of Our Own (AO3), and therefore any story a writer can dream up can be posted, read, and reviewed. One story or piece of art might even spark ideas for others and there's a system in place to network them all together.

A fic doesn't have to be deemed 'marketable.' Even if it's only likely to have niche appeal, an author can still connect with that small audience. There are probably nearly as many reasons for a writer to tell a story as there are writers, but many of those reasons involve filling in much-needed representation. Sometimes fanfiction is solving a problem of erasure, like re-including Hawkeye's hearing impairment which was left out of the media portrayals in the Marvel Universe, Katniss' PTSD and whitewashing in the Hunger Games films, or the many characters whose sexuality is never addressed or outright erased.

Other times an author might choose to explore what could change and how much might actually stay the same if one element of a familiar character were changed. I've read fics where Sherlock Holmes is blind, or deaf, or mute, and still used his incredible powers of deduction to solve crimes. Writers explore what adaptations he would need or what skills and experiences he might have that would be advantageous.

Some people with autism or other neurodivergence see themselves reflected in Spock or Holmes and want to explore what that means from that character's perspective, or take a character perceived as neurotypical and wonder what their story might look like if the character's experience more closely matched their own.

Still others explore the *what if* of characters applying their skill set differently. What if Sherlock Holmes focused his powers of observation and deduction into planning a perfect wedding, or into creating characters as an actor, or to winning contests on reality television? What if Steve Rogers was really an Olympic athlete or Bruce Wayne was a police detective rather than a vigilante? How would your favorite characters use their gifts to make their way through the gauntlet of high school? These alternate universes (AUs), even the most unlikely of them, address something fans feel is missing from the original material.

Female characters in mainstream media are often underdeveloped or their plot is secondary to that of their male counterparts. In fiction, we can write better narratives for women who were 'fridged' to further the male protagonist's journey. We can rework the protagonist's motivation to remove misogyny or just genderswap the story, so a woman *is* the protagonist.

Of course we can also create original stories that are female-centered, but there is power in demonstrating how different an already well-loved story would feel if the genders were reversed. Others take on gender in a different way, exploring agender or genderqueer characters, or creating new gender identities and social hierarchies in the fan-created world of omegaverse. For those unfamiliar with that AU, in omegaverse a character's primary gender remains the same, but usually they are given a second gender which presents at puberty. Alpha characters of any gender can get omega characters of any gender pregnant. This allows for writing male characters dealing with pregnancy or taking on what is more typically considered a women's role in society. Often rigid social and sexual roles and hierarchies are in place and an author may play with conforming to or flouting these roles.

> "Fanfiction is powerful, seeing ourselves represented is powerful, and it is socially and personally transformative."

The genre called crack transforms things into an utterly ridiculous realm, where an author can play with the absolute essence of character. Usually humorous, it's fun to see how creative we can be as writers. How will the reader know this fic is set in Sherlock Holmes' universe even if it's written from the perspective of an umbrella, a coat, or if Holmes and Watson were a glove and mitten, for example? What clues would we need to demonstrate that this is in Harry Potter's world if a fic is from the point of view of a house scarf, a broom, a cauldron?

Fanfiction also allows us to expand an expected narrative. For a long time the most prominent representations of lesbian, gay, bisexual, transgender, queer, intersex, and similar characters were as tragic figures or villains – if they were depicted at all. Although we're seeing more media that features LGBTQIA characters, often these stories either follow these older tropes or primarily deal with struggle. Rarely are they allowed a simple love story, a happily ever after. There has been an improvement, but our representation still frequently implies that either our sexuality is the only important aspect of who we are, or that our lives are destined to be ones of desperation and pain.

This is shifting, but fanfiction has progressed much faster than mainstream media, and is done without the metaphorical back-patting. With fanworks, there's no queerbaiting (creators suggesting a character may be LGBTQIA, but never following through to make that canon). A character's gender or sexuality is there as a point of fact or a necessary component of the storytelling, not as a method to gain viewers or readers. There are millions of heterosexual romantic comedies and fanfiction gives us a way to explore those cute rom-com tropes with characters that aren't two cisgender, straight, (usually) white people. A lot of people enjoy the idea of Captain America (Steve Rogers) and the Winter Soldier (Bucky Barnes) being a couple, for example, and for many part of the draw of this pairing is the exploration of getting to have a love affair that couldn't be as easily realized in the 1940s.

Fanfiction gives us a place to envision a 'happily ever after' for characters who have been killed off or villainized by homophobic narratives. We can write modern or historical AUs where homophobia doesn't exist at all. I have read an incredible fusion between the modern Sherlock Holmes adaptation, BBC's Sherlock, and Jane Austen's stories with John Watson and Sherlock Holmes as the protagonists, and it isn't mentioned as an issue that they are both men.

We can explore any genre from science fiction to period pieces to high fantasy to action where the characters happen to be LGBTQIA and that facet of their lives gets to be included without being the source of a tragic backstory or an ongoing struggle. This is part of the broad appeal of tropes like 'Oh no! There's only one bed' or fake relationships that turn real, or even coffee shop AUs. We deserve representation where sexuality or gender identity is just one aspect of a character, as in our actual lives, rather than the driving force in the plot. People make life decisions, both good and bad, and have experiences and adventures that are not directly related to their sexuality, so we appreciate seeing our favorite characters getting to do so as well.

Of course, sometimes explorations of coming out or coming to terms with sexuality can be interesting as well. Writing fanfiction has given me opportunities to explore the complex diversity of human sexuality, especially in ways that transgress society's rules for sex, gender, or sexuality. With tens of thousands of fics on AO3 that deal with sexuality, I know I am not alone in my desire for more exploration of these topics.

Fanfics can respond to questions like 'What does a transgender or genderqueer experience look and feel like within omegaverse?', 'Can a sexual act be dominant or submissive or is the true power of their dynamic found in the attitude of the characters?', 'How does an asexual character who enjoys the sensory experiences or power dynamics of BDSM find satisfaction that stays within their comfort zone?', or 'What makes an asexual or aromantic love relationship different than friendship?' We can resolve the tension of a classic love triangle with a happy polyamorous triad, a topic of personal importance to me, as I am quietly living my life that way. I also enjoy delving into the experience many of us have had, but which seems remarkably lacking from our societal conversations on the topic: what happens when you experience revelations about your sexuality as an adult rather than as an adolescent? Sexuality and gender expression may be fluid over a lifetime. Some people take shifting perspectives and identity in stride and integrate those changes easily while others feel like their whole world has been upended.

Although I like many tropes, I am most often drawn to reading and writing power dynamics. BDSM erotica I had read before discovering fanfiction seemed to be either loosely historical fiction, including glorification of actual slavery and oppression, or written with no understanding of how the actual dynamics of a BDSM relationship worked. Some of the stories were misogynistic and rarely resonated with my lived experience of dominance and submission. Of course some people want over-the-top things that could never happen in real life when they are reading fantasies, and there is a place for that. Fiction can let us explore a myriad of things that are outside our real lives, but there is also something powerful in reading about an experience that matches your own in tone and feeling, even if the events are different.

I had been part of kink communities in some way for more than a decade and craving stories that were regular stories, including romance, adventure, but also kink, more like a mainstream movie, but actual sex scenes instead of ones that are tastefully draped or fading to black, and fanfiction offers storytelling like that. Sex is just one aspect of our real lives and it's comforting for stories to be able to reflect that.

Though there is nothing wrong with enjoying porn, my demisexual self wants connection, emotion, romance, while my kinky side wants intensity and explicit content, and fanfiction allows me to bring in all of these storytelling aspects at once without the screen media trope of a knowing smile and a closed door.

Although I found some of what I was looking for, once I spent some time reading and chatting with writers, I was drawn back to writing myself. I had a long-buried desire for storytelling beyond the widely acceptable stories that could be shared over lunch with a friend, or read without looking over my shoulder while in public, and the fandom community I'd found inspired me to take the risk of actually sharing my writing with others.

Representation matters and while we're trying to see ourselves or people we know represented in the world, we might also be transforming how others see people of different abilities, races, gender variants, and sexualities.

It is not overstating things to say fanfiction was a revelation to me, as a reader, a writer, and as a human being. My online community has given me words to fine tune my understanding of my own sexuality and gender. I now recognize that I'm genderqueer and demipansexual. Since sexual attraction doesn't occur for me without intense emotional connection, fanfiction is appealing because it allows me to tap into the feelings that the characters have built up together through canon stories and various film and movie adaptations, as well as the years I have with loving these characters, so I can thoroughly appreciate porn without plot without missing that buildup. I have shipped Sherlock Holmes and John Watson in nearly every version since I first heard their stories, so I bring 35 years of connection to the experience. It isn't the only fandom I read or write, but it is certainly the one to which I'm still most frequently drawn.

Even in my small circle of friends, there have been many life-changing revelations though fiction, whether it helped them become more comfortable in their own skin or more understanding about the world around them. One of my closest friends had a conservative religious upbringing, but through reading fanfiction, they found a broader worldview, learning that love is love regardless of gender and there was nothing wrong with being LGBTQIA.

Fanfiction allows me a place to explore the male headspace of my genderqueer identity and more than one friend of mine has discovered that the reason they were so drawn to writing m/m relationships was because they were actually trans. Writing was their only way to explore the reality of being a bisexual or gay man while everyone around them was treating them as a straight woman. They were given a safe place to discuss their true identity by using characters they admired to find their voice. Through fanfiction they had an opportunity to read and write, exploring what that meant, and ultimately found the strength to transition.

Several other friends have found healing in reading about asexual characters, discovering that they are asexual themselves rather than 'frigid' or 'broken.' In a society that frequently jumbles sex together with love and views both as inevitable aspects of adulthood, it can be comforting to find characters who are asexual and living rich lives with complex fulfilling relationships. My friends learned that they, too, were perfectly fine just as they are, and didn't have to go through the motions unless they wanted to. Being in a relationship or even being married can have unique meaning to the people in it and whatever sexual experiences that includes is not a given, but an ongoing exploration for those involved.

Fanfiction is powerful, seeing ourselves represented is powerful, and I have witnessed and experienced that it is both socially and personally transformative.

Fanfiction can and does transform its readers, its writers, and the world we all live in.

Bel Murphy (beltainefaerie) has a masters in education, a lifetime love of storytelling, and is grateful for her fandom community. She has led classes and participated in panels on kink, including the "50 Shades of A" panel on asexuality and "Freaks in Love, Kink in Fic" at 221b Con. A usually submissive switch, she's spent the past twenty years in the BDSM community and acts as dungeon monitor at a local club (like a lifeguard for kink spaces). She also never met a craft she didn't like and creates with knitting, crochet, needle-felting, beading, sculpting, and multimedia projects that combine techniques.

You sit down and you do it, and
you do it, and you do it, until
you have learned to do it.

> — Ursula K. Le Guin
> Hugo award-winning writer of
> *The Left Hand of Darkness*

COURAGE WORKS – AND YOUR JOY IS ENOUGH
Atlin Merrick

"THIS HERO IS NOT FOR THEM."

Those words were about Captain Marvel, from someone discussing how Carol Danvers and the superhero she becomes is not meant for men, it's for everyone told they can't do something, because they're a girl.

By the same token, fandom and our creations in it are not for the people who think less of them. They never were. They never *will* be. We do not have to make room for people who hate what we love.

Because fandom, fic, art, it's for *us*. The gifts they give us – the strength to believe in our own creations, the focus to sit down and damn well create even when we're tired, the passion to share our stories and podcasts and drawings with other people, to be successful at reaching our goals and reaching out to each other – that's what fandom is for and it's for *us,* no one else.

I don't understand an armchair participation in sport but I don't have to. I need only smile, nod, move on and let the people who love it *love it.* We can demand the same in return and if we don't get it we need never, not one time ever justify, excuse, or minimize what we love. We need only walk away – and right toward the people who enjoy what we do, who create the fic and art we adore, who remark on the work we relish making.

Because joy is power and, like lifting weights or running or eating healthy foods, it's a power we can control; it's a boon we can absolutely give ourselves.

In a double dozen ways, films and television are the lesser-than offspring of storytelling. They will *always* be limited because they only have an hour or two to make an impression, so they use their time in big, loud, childish ways. They will almost never be elegant or subtle or particularly deep because they don't have the *time*.

"We do not have to make room for people who hate what we love."

What we create as fans of these stories – fanfiction, meta, discourse, art, podcasts – has no such limitations because *we* have no limitations. We can take as long as we like to tell every part of a story, give every character heart and reason. Holding up a film or a three-episode TV series as the source from which we shouldn't veer is like saying the egg shouldn't be changed into a cake.

Because we can do better.

We can always do right by the characters we love. We can write a grand arc for the smallest characters or the ones painted only in black, and if those characters die we can make sure that, for them, it *means* something. That they went to their end with thought and belief enough for the reader to understand their journey.

Film producers and directors, TV show runners, they may have to answer to producers or mega-media companies, and so they may write most characters in broad strokes of black and white but we don't have to. We can do better.

Let's tell fantastic stories about the characters we love.

We have no limits.

And if you want to take the skills you've learned in fandom, do it.

You won't be the first and isn't that wonderful?

Yet if you're like me, if you're like most creators I know, know this: you're going to get rejected.

You're going to get a lot of replies that say "Sorry, we don't want this," and I'm pretty sure at no time is that going to be less than really hard.

Hollow-in-the-belly hard.

If-I-was-any-good-they-wouldn't-have-said-no hard. I-should-just-stop hard.

But don't. Don't. Absolutely do not stop.

Hurt for awhile because you *are* hurt – rejection hurts, it just does. But this is the fact you want to remember: every single writer or actor or musician you love-adore-cherish was rejected.

The person whose books line your bookshelf had rejections with which they could paper walls. No. No. Another no. No no no no no no nono.

Agatha Christie was rejected, Neil Gaiman was, Arthur Conan Doyle, too.

What they did right after the rejection I don't know. I do know they did this: they went ahead and submitted that book, story, demo tape, or show reel again. And again. And again.

And again.

They got rejected and it hurt and they just did it again because *success is doable.* Publishing happens. Signing up with an agent *happens.* Every single day a creator signs on with their first agent. First comes the rejection though – for *everyone.*

"Nobody is universally embraced," writes author Chuck Wendig, but, "I can tell you this: each rejection letter is a badge of honor. It's a battle scar, baby. Proof that you're out there in the trenches, the jungles, the muddy fields and foggy bogs, and you're kicking ass and taking names. Rejection is par for the course. Everybody gets rejected."

The only difference between us and those that just signed with the agent is this: *time.*

That's it. They got there first but we'll get there after because *like them,* like Christie and Wendig, we'll keep submitting our art, stories, books, songs…all our creations.

Rejection is a sign you're trying. Tons of people don't have the courage to try. You do.

Courage works. It moves you forward. So does knowing you're not alone. The people you admire were rejected. They got there.

You can and you will, too, if that's what you choose to do.

Fandom can help you get there because it helps you keep the faith. It keeps you writing or drawing because a comment made your blood sing and your brain fizz, or a new episode had you shouting 'oh *hell* no.'

If you're still feeling shy about being part of all of this, if you're feeling that that's not how you'll grow as a writer or artist, remember what's been mentioned throughout this book: some pretty well-known names started in fandom – and then went on to create original work, work that generated its *own* fandoms.

Hugo-award winner Lois McMaster Bujold, author of stories like *The Mountains of Mourning, Paladin of Souls,* and *Cryoburn,* wrote Star Trek fan fic as a young girl. Andy Weir, writer of *The Martian,* the book from which the movie was made, wrote *Ready Player One* fan fic.

R. J. Anderson, best-selling author of young adult fiction and writer of the novels *Knife, Arrow,* and *Swift,* started out with fanfiction and says getting online, sharing her stories with other readers, and meeting other writers, encouraged her and improved her skills.

Neil Gaiman, author of *Neverwhere, Stardust,* and *The Sandman,* used to write fic, and believes *all* writing helps you hone your writing skills. "I think you get better as a writer by writing, and whether that means that you're writing a singularly deep and moving novel about the pain or pleasure of modern existence or you're writing Smeagol-Gollum slash you're still putting one damn word after another and learning as a writer."

Then there are fans who took their geek passions and turned them in to award-winning programming. Irish filmmaker Emer Reynolds devoured sci-fi growing up, her shelves full of Philip K. Dick, Michael Moorcock and H.G. Wells. Reynolds released to world-wide and award-winning acclaim the feature length science documentary *The Farthest.*

Writer Chris Charter couldn't get enough of *The Twilight Zone,* loving it so much he kept fiddling with the format – leaving failed TV shows in his wake – until he went on to create *The X-Files,* a program so popular in the early 90s that people avoided making Friday night plans.

If you've reached this point of *Spark,* you know these examples are just the tip of the creativity iceberg and the take-home message is, was, and ever shall be simply this:

Write the stories you want to write.

Create the art you want to create.

Love the fandom you love, because it can motivate you.

That's what this book is about; it's about taking whatever your next step is, it's about writing (or drawing) a poem, a story, a book, an ode. It's about your passion and finding the words to put that passion on paper.

It's about setting yourself on fire in the very best ways.

It's letting the love and passion you have for creation take you places you want to go, bring you friendships, community, and joy.

And joy is enough.

Atlin Merrick (she/they) is commissioning editor at Improbable Press, has been in fandoms for a long time, but really *been involved for the last dozen years, writing over a million words of fanfiction. Fandom has been an endless inspiration and if you ever need inspiration, drop Atlin an email over at ImprobablePress.com and she'll shout gleeful encouragement at you. Seriously.*

FANGIRLS SAVE THE WORLD
Carman C. Curton

Maybe the whole brain-eating thing isn't about hunger, Atlin thought, when the undead rose. Maybe they just want what's in there.

"Like what?" asked everyone barricaded with her in the back of the Tesco Express.

"Stories."

"Nice knowing ya!" they whispered when she walked out to share a few stories she'd read on a Sherlock fansite, and a few more she'd written.

When her voice went shallow and scratchy, she climbed up a Trafalgar Square Lion, got 1½ bars, and called out on Tumblr. And AO3. "Bring your stories – silly, clichéd, angsty, pornariffic. Please come."

The storytellers came.

Life resumed as the undead listened. And were satisfied. And so was pretty much everyone else.

Carman C. Curton consumes caffeine while writing a series of microstories called QuickFics, which she leaves in random places for people to find.

ACKNOWLEDGEMENTS
Wendy C Fries (aka Atlin Merrick)

I am exceedingly lucky.

For a double dozen years I've had the joy of meeting fellow fans and fic writers at conventions, conferences, meet-ups, and via email, people I admire for their skills in writing, drawing, and community building. These same people, who have so many things to do, responded to me when I asked for their fandom story, gifting me again and again with their time and wonderful words.

So please visualize me double-handed gesturing with glee to each name on *Spark's* table of contents, because all of those people have children, jobs, or their own creating to attend to, and yet they pressed pause on all of it, put pen to paper, and shared how fic and fandom changed their world.

And so shared how it can change yours.

There are over four dozen writers and artists in this book, and the wonderful thing is that they represent just a *few* flames from the much bigger fandom fire, one which includes thousands of others who've also found support and strength by joining a community online or in person, one which shares their love of a book, a TV show, a film, or comic.

This book began pre-pandemic, was interrupted by an international move, an overseas master's degree, and sometimes depression, and to all those who shared their story here, I'm indebted to your patience while your sparks caught fuel and became the fire of this book.

Thank you, thank you, thank you.

Atlin Merrick was born Wendy Fries but you try putting that in a search engine and see what you get. Wendy is the author of Sherlock

Holmes and John Watson: The Day They Met, 50 re-imaginings of other ways the legendary friendship of Holmes and Watson might have begun. As Atlin she's the author of Sherlock Holmes and John Watson: The Night They Met, 19 re-imaginings of other ways Holmes and Watson could have met and then fallen in love.

ARTIST BIOGRAPHIES

ADALLISA ZARATE (Susannah Dean, Gunslinger) is a comics, manga, and anime artist from Mexico. She has been a writer and editor for magazines like Conexión Manga, Anime y Manga Colección de Luxe, and Musicanime. Along with publishing her own comic series, she's also been a featured artist for Upperdeck, and worked for their card set Thor: Ragnarok. Adalisa is also a track director for San Diego Comic Con and you can find her at work at calicochimera.com.

ANDREA L FARLEY (Where the Light Enters) is an artist, writer, and amateur musician with a license to practice pharmacy. Andrea fell into her dream job of illustrating book covers and interiors by way of creating over 100 portrait studies of her favorite actor as a way to not lose her mind during the Covid pandemic. Andrea lives in the Pacific NorthWest with her family and a rather large, very friendly, black cat. Find her at www.altocello.com, and as @ altocello on Twitter and just about everywhere else.

CAMILLE HAPPERT (Fire and Water) is a forever-young technician working in a cinem'a post production lab in Paris, and who likes to draw when they're in the mood. Cam discovered RRR last year when it came out and it was a revelation: a new hyperfixation to hyperfix about. Who know how long this one will last. A month a year, a life...

S.L. SUROVEC (Star Wars and Rocky Horror Crossover) specializes in pseudo-real comic book style drawings, and loves creating Star Wars-related art. They have been known to write and draw in other fandoms, taking part in exchanges and commissions for fantasy fandoms ElfQuest, Buffy the Vampire Slayer, Battlestar Galactica, Star Trek, Aliens, and the Expanse.

KHORAZIR a.k.a. Anke Eißmann (Plot Bunnies) is a German graphic artists, writer, and graduate of Bauhaus University and the Colchester Institute. Khorazir has illustrated for Subterranean Press, Walking Tree Publishers, Portal Editions, G&G Verlag, the German Tolkien Society, and draws across many fandoms, including those for Sherlock Holmes and J. R. R. Tolkien, as well as Doctor Strange, X-Files, and Good Omens. Find Khorazir at khorazir.tumblr.com.

LUCY W (Xena and Gabrielle) is a prolific British artist and geek who loves comics, horror, fantasy, sci-fi, the 80s, music, fashion, and films. Lucy draws across multiple fandoms, including the Star Wars sequel trilogy, Xena: Warrior Princess, as well as Stranger Things, X-men, Sherlock, Inception, Star Trek, Lord of the Rings, The Hobbit, Pacific Rim, Dragon Age, StarGate Atlantis and many more. You can find them at littleststarfighter.tumblr.com.

GLOSSARY OF FANDOM

(A few fic and fandom terms found in *Spark*)

ABO (also A/B/O) stands for alpha beta omega, and is a kink trope where some people have defined biological roles based on a hierarchical system.

ACA-FAN (also acafan) stands for academic fan and is often self-applied by those who teach about popular and/or fan culture at the college level and who also identify as part of a fandom.

AO3 (Archive of Our Own) is "a noncommercial and nonprofit central hosting place for fanworks using open-source archiving software." AO3 was established by fans in 2007 – and is still run and staffed by fan-volunteers – to serve the interests of fans. They provide access to and preserve the history of fanworks and fan culture in its myriad forms on the AO3 website. Archive of Our Own is part of the Organization for Transformative Works (OTW), a nonprofit, fan activist organization.

ARCHIVE OF OUR OWN *(see AO3)*

BETA, a person (often a friend but not always) who reads a fic writer's work before it's posted. They may offer thoughts on plot, grammar, or punctuation with the aim of helping make the story better. Not every fanfiction writer works with a beta.

BIPOC is an acronym which stands for Black, Indigenous, Person of Color.

CANON, the original source material, whether a TV show, book, or film. Many fic writers write stories which fit well into existing canon, though many veer wildly from it.

COSPLAY is a portmanteau of costume play, and refers to fans wearing costumes and accessories to represent a specific character.

CRACK FIC (also crackfic and crack!fic), refers to a story which takes an outlandish premise – casting Kylo Ren and General Hux as two different gloves found on a walk, for example – and creating a fic about them. The resulting fic might be nonsensical or it may be serious.

DREAMWIDTH is an online journal service based on the LiveJournal (LJ) codebase and, like LJ, users can journal, post stories, and create online communities.

FAIR USE is a principle in United States copyright law which is based on the idea that people are sometimes entitled to make use of copyrighted material without needing to obtain permission.

FANDOM, a community of fans interacting in some way, whether through creative works, conventions, or discussions.

FANFICTION (*alternative spelling* fan fiction), is a work of fiction written by fans for other fans, taking a source text or a famous person as their point of departure.

FANFICTION.NET (also called FF.net) is a fanfiction hosting website.

FANON, this stands for 'fan canon' and is anything agreed on by many fans – whether or not it ever appears in the original source material. For example, a large group of fans agree Sherlock Holmes must be bad at making tea, and so this 'fact' appears in many fanfics.

FAN STUDIES refers to the academic analysis of fans and fandom and how they interact with a text (film, series, book, etc).

FANVID (vid), is a video edit produced by fans. Similar to professionally produced music videos and film trailers, 'vidders' arrange short film or TV clips these over a song to make an argument or tell a story.

FANZINE (also called zine), short for 'magazine,' these often refer to amateur periodicals created by different fan communities.

F/F is used to signify a story, usually romantic or sexual, involving two women (female/female).

F/M is used to signify a story, usually romantic or sexual, involving a women and a man (female/male).

FF NET *(see Fanfiction.net)*

FIC (also fanfic) is an abbreviation of fanfiction. Fic is a work of fiction written by fans for other fans, taking a source text or a famous person as a point of departure.

FLUFF (also fluffy), refers to a fic that's light-hearted, heart-warming, or feel-good.

GENDERBENT *(see genderswapped)*

GENDERSWAPPED is a fandom trope in which one or more characters switch binary sexes, such as depicting a male character as a cis woman.

HEADCANON (also head canon or head-canon), is a fan's personal interpretation of canon, such as habits of a character, their backstory, or the nature of their relationships with other characters. The term comes from the fact that it's the canon which exists in a fan's head.

INTERSECTIONALITY, a framework to understand how people's social and political identities create different privileges and discriminations. For example, studying fandom preferences for white queerness rather than the queerness of POC, and the alienation which can come from that.

INTERTEXTUALITY is the shaping of a text's meaning by another text. In fandom it can be used to weave two unrelated texts together to demonstrate how one influences the other.

JOHNLOCK, a portmanteau of John and Sherlock, it's used as a relationship tag for those who write and post fanfiction with Dr John Watson and Sherlock Holmes, characters created by Arthur Conan Doyle.

LGBTQIA+ is an abbreviation for lesbian, gay, bisexual, transgender, queer, intersex, and asexual. The plus represents minority sexualities not addressed in the main abbreviation.

LIVEJOURNAL, often called LJ, this is a social networking service where users can keep blogs, journals, or diaries. Before Archive of Our Own, which went on to offer easier posting and searching capabilities, LJ was one of the main websites hosting fanfiction.

LJ *(see LiveJournal)*

KYLUX, a portmanteau of Kylo and Hux, it's a relationship tag for those who write and post fanfiction with Kylo Ren and General Armitage Hux, from the Star Wars sequel trilogy.

META describes fan-authored non-fiction writing which discusses fandom, fanworks, or the source text.

M/M is used to signify a story, usually romantic or sexual, involving two men (male/male).

O3P, this abbreviation plays off of OTP (one true pair), but instead refers to three favorite characters a person believes belong together, for example Leia Organa/Han Solo/Lando Calrissian.

OC stands for original character. This tag is often used to indicate that a fic includes some of a writer's own original characters.

OMEGAVERSE *(see ABO)*

OTP stands for one true pair (or pairing), and often refers to favorite characters a person believes belong together, for example Andromache of Scythia and Quynh, or Edward Teach and Stede Bonnet.

OTW (Organization for Transformative Works) is a not-for-profit fan activist organization offering fan services and platforms including: Archive of Our Own (AO3); fanlore.org; legal advocacy for and assistance to the fandom community; and *Transformative Works and Cultures,* a peer-reviewed academic journal for scholarship on fanworks and practices.

PAIRING refers to the characters who make up the romantic focus of a fanwork.

PLOT BUNNY (also plot bunnies) are fanwork ideas that seem to multiply all on their own, sometimes drowning eager authors in far too many ideas.

QUEERBAITING, a term used to describe the perceived attempt by advertisers or canon creators to draw in a queer audience and/or slash fans by hinting at a gay relationship that will never actually be depicted.

REAL PERSON FIC *(see RPF)*

RPF stands for real person fic, and it's fiction which includes real people as characters, such as stories about Chris Evans and Robert Downey Jr, or Shakespeare's plays about Richard III or Henry V.

SELF-INSERT, when a writer puts their experiences or representations of themselves into fanfiction. For example, a disabled writer may write a popular, abled character as having their same disability.

SHIP is short for relationship, and it's used as a noun and verb. A fan's favorite ship may be between Scarlet Witch and Black Widow, and it can also be said that they *ship* those two characters.

SLASH is fanwork in which two or more characters of the same sex or gender are placed in sexual or romantic situations together. On fansites such works are usually notated with a slash between the names, for example: Kirk/Spock or Tahani/Eleanor. The mark *between* the names became the name for these sorts of fics.

SQUEE, a verb and noun, the word represents an expression of enthusiasm and joy.

SUPERWHOLOCK, a portmanteau for three TV shows which shared great popularity at the same time: *Supernatural, Doctor Who, Sherlock.*

TAGS are short descriptive words, phrases, or abbreviations used to describe a fic, these include character names, character pairings, and story descriptors like 'crack!fic' or 'fluff.'

TRANSFORMATIVE WORKS are creative works about characters or settings created by fans of the original work, rather than by the original creators.

TROPE or tropes are common plot devices often found in fanfiction, including There Was Only One Bed or Aliens Made Them Do It, it also applies to popular settings for fics, such as coffeeshops, florists, or college.

TUMBLR, a popular micro-blogging and social networking platform that fans use to post images, text, and videos.

WIP, an abbreviation for work in progress.

ZINE *(see fanzine).*

Thank you to all who helped with these definitions, including fandom, the Fanlore, Wikipedia, and more.

Share your fandom story

How did fic and fandom change your life for the better?
We hope to share *more* stories of how fandom sparks us,
how it fires up our dreams and our courage.

Find Improbable Press at

Improbablepress.com
and
Twitter @so_improbable
Instagram @improbablepress

Improbable
PRESS

Printed in the USA
CPSIA information can be obtained
at www.ICGtesting.com
JSHW082029101123
51663JS00001B/5